Evaluation of R&D Processes: Effectiveness Through Measurements

The Artech House Technology Management and Professional Development Library

Bruce Elbert, *Series Editor*

Applying Total Quality Management to Systems Engineering, Joe Kasser

Engineer's and Manager's Guide to Winning Proposals, Donald V. Helgeson

Evaluation of R&D Processes: Effectiveness Through Measurements, Lynn W. Ellis

Global High-Tech Marketing: An Introduction for Technical Managers and Engineers, Jules E. Kadish

Introduction to Innovation and Technology Transfer, Ian Cooke, Paul Mayes

Managing Engineers and Technical Employees: How to Attract, Motivate, and Retain Excellent People, Douglas M. Soat

Preparing and Delivering Effective Technical Presentations, David L. Adamy

Successful Marketing Startegy for High-Tech Firms, Eric Viardot

Survival in the Software Jungle, Mark Norris

For further information on these and other Artech House titles, contact:

Artech House
685 Canton Street
Norwood, MA 02062
617-769-9750
Fax: 617-769-6334
Telex: 951-659
email: artech@artech-house.com

Artech House
Portland House, Stag Place
London SW1E 5XA England
+44 (0) 171-973-8077
Fax: +44 (0) 171-630-0166
Telex: 951-659
email: artech-uk@artech-house.com

WWW: http://www.artech-house.com/artech.html

Evaluation of R&D Processes: Effectiveness Through Measurements

Lynn Ellis

Artech House
Boston • London

658.57
E47e

Library of Congress Cataloging-in-Publication Data
Ellis, Lynn W.
    Evaluation of R&D processes: effectiveness through measurements/ Lynn W. Ellis
        p.   cm.
    Includes bibliographical references and index.
    ISBN 0-89006-791-0
    1. Product management.   2. Technological innovations—Evaluation.
    3. New products—Evaluation. I. Title.
    HF5415.15E44   1997
    658.5'7—dc21   96-37126
                                                             CIP

British Library Cataloguing in Publication Data
Ellis, Lynn W.
    Evaluation of R&D processes: effectiveness through measurements
    1. Research, Industrial—Evaluation 2. Technological innovations—Evaluation
    3. Research, Industrial—Management
I. Title
    658.5'7

    ISBN 0-89006-791-0

Cover design by Jennifer Makower

© 1997 ARTECH HOUSE, INC.
685 Canton Street
Norwood, MA 02062

International Standard Book Number: 0-89006-791-0
Library of Congress Catalog Card Number: 96-37126

10 9 8 7 6 5 4 3 2 1

Contents

Preface   xiii

Part I General Aspects of R&D Process Evaluation   1

Chapter 1 Introduction to Evaluating R&D Process Management   3
    1.1 Motivation for Evaluating Projects   5
        1.1.1 An Industrial Measurement of Effectiveness
            Initiative   5
        1.1.2 Biggest Problems for R&D Directors   7
        1.1.3 An Innovation Benchmarking Proposal   8
        1.1.4 The Malcolm Baldridge National Quality Award   9
        1.1.5 Strategy, Structure, and Uncertainty   10
        1.1.6 Using Product and Technological Life Cycles   12
        1.1.7 Entrepreneurship and Intrapreneurial Organization   12
       1.1.8 Product Development Management Research   12
    1.2 Government Policy Toward R&D   13
    1.3 Finding Funds for R&D   14
    1.4 An Approach to Metrics: A Balanced Innovation
    Scorecard   15
        1.4.1 Including R&D in a Balanced Scorecard for
            Management   16
        1.4.2 Living with Shorter Time Frames   16
        1.4.3 An Innovation Process Model   16
        1.4.4 A Note on Methodology   18
    1.5 Some Lessons Learned From Selected Metrics   18
    References   19

Chapter 2 Managing the Financial Boundary   21
    2.1 Evaluating in Economic Terms   21
    2.2 Traditional Methods of R&D Evaluation   21

	2.2.1	Traditional Project Selection	22
	2.2.2	Project Selection and Evaluation Using Option Theory	24
	2.2.3	Budget Optimization	25
	2.2.4	Financial Post-Evaluation	25
2.3	Manage Within Your Firm's Financial Culture		26
	2.3.1	The Financially Driven Culture	26
	2.3.2	The Activity-Based Management and Costing Culture	27
	2.3.3	An Intermediate Culture	28
2.4	Character of Measurements		28
	2.4.1	Certainty and Urgency	29
	2.4.2	Short-Term and Certain Projects	30
	2.4.3	Medium-Term and Risky Projects	30
	2.4.4	Uncertainty	31
	2.4.5	Financial Frameworks and Empowered Organizations	32
	2.4.6	Integration of Project Selection and Evaluation	33
	2.4.7	Optimum Budgets and Shareholder Value	38
2.5	Financial Frameworks Lessons Learned		41
References			43
Chapter 3	Evaluating the External Commercial and Technical Tasks of R&D		45
3.1	Market Share		45
	3.1.1	Firms Measuring Market Share	46
	3.1.2	How Market Share Affects Results	46
	3.1.3	Market Share Lessons Learned	47
3.2	Evaluating External Sources of Knowledge		47
3.3	Evaluating the Build-up of Commercial Knowledge		48
	3.3.1	Start with Vision	48
	3.3.2	Environmental Assessment	49
	3.3.3	Industry Scenarios	50
	3.3.4	Competitive Assessment	50
3.4	Build-up of Technological Knowledge		51
	3.4.1	Technological Self-Sufficiency	52
	3.4.2	Managing Alliances With Others	52
	3.4.3	Sources of Scientific and Technical Knowledge	53
	3.4.4	Organize and Systematize Technology Acquisition	56
3.5	Effect of Internal Organization on Boundary Spanning		57
3.6	Lessons Learned on External Boundary Spanning		57

References 59

Chapter 4 Measurements in the R&D Process 61
  4.1 An R&D Process Model 61
  4.2 Processes as Functions of Time 62
      4.2.1 Processes That Are the Same From Exploration Through Extension 64
      4.2.2 Processes Most Important in Exploration Through Development 65
      4.2.3 Other Subprocesses Need to be Added With Opportunity Creation 66
      4.2.4 New Subprocesses Begin With Core Competency/Product Development 69
      4.2.5 By Product Extension/Improvement, Some Subprocesses Decline in Importance 69
  4.3 Lessons Learned on Managing Along the Process 70
  References 71

Chapter 5 Manage the Interaction With Other Functions 73
  5.1 Managing Upstream Interfaces 73
      5.1.1 Integrating Mechanisms 73
      5.1.2 Managing the Upstream Boundary: The R&D-Marketing Interface 74
      5.1.3 Quality Function Deployment (QFD) 76
      5.1.4 Use of QFD 77
      5.1.5 Comparison of QFD With Other Metrics 78
  5.2 Downstream Output Measurements 80
      5.2.1 Direct Outputs From R&D 80
      5.2.2 Downward Transfer of Technology 83
      5.2.3 Views From the Implementation Process 85
  5.3 Lessons Learned on Managing the Interaction Process 86
  References 87

Chapter 6 Evaluating Crossfunctional Innovation Teams 89
  6.1 Why Crossfunctional Teams? 89
      6.1.1 Some Background 91
      6.1.2 How Companies Actually Manage CE 92
      6.1.3 Use of CE 94
      6.1.4 Correlation of CE and Other Factors 94
      6.1.5 CE and Throughput Maximization 97
  6.2 Lessons Learned on Team Evaluation 97
  References 98

Part II Time to Market: Measurement and Management 101

Chapter 7 Cycle Time: Outcome and Output Evaluation
        Metrics 103
    7.1   Introduction to Cycle-Time Measurement 103
        7.1.1   Cycle Time as an Outcome Measurement 104
        7.1.2   R&D Time as an Output Measurement 106
        7.1.3   Cycle Time's Relation to Costs 108
        7.1.4   Cycle Time's Relation to Financial Evaluation 109
    7.2   Expanded Dimensions of Time to Market 112
    7.3   Measuring and Recording Time 112
    7.4   Measuring Overall Time 113
        7.4.1   Idea-to-Customer Time 114
        7.4.2   R&D Cycle Time 115
        7.4.3   CE Time 117
        7.4.4   Market Development Cycle Time 117
    7.5   Measuring Time Segments 118
        7.5.1   Marketing Time 118
        7.5.2   Applied Research Time 120
        7.5.3   Design Time to Concept Finalization 120
        7.5.4   Design Time to Design Finalization 121
        7.5.5   Development Time and Process Design 121
        7.5.6   Time from Prototype to Manufacturability 121
        7.5.7   Redo Loops 122
        7.5.8   Production 122
        7.5.9   Testing 123
        7.5.10 Shipping Time 123
        7.5.11 Customer Service Time 123
        7.5.12 How Often to Measure Time? 123
        7.5.13 Key Attributes of Metrics 124
    7.6   Lessons Learned on Expanded Time Measurement 124
    References 125

Chapter 8 From Time Measurement to Time Management 127
    8.1   Time Management Practices 127
        8.1.1   Diagnosing How Time is Spent 127
        8.1.2   First, Prune Time Wasters 129
        8.1.3   Consolidate Time to Use it More Efficiently 130
        8.1.4   Concentration on First Things First 130
        8.1.5   Measure Innovation Contribution 131
        8.1.6   Build Upon Strength in Core Competencies 131
        8.1.7   Decision Making 132
    8.2   Accelerating the Innovation Process 133
        8.2.1   Improving the Upstream Process 133

8.2.2 What R&D Can Do to Reduce Manufacturing Cycle
       Time   134
8.2.3 Sources of Product Development Speed   135
8.2.4 Control of Product Development Delays   136
8.3 Time Management Lessons Learned   137
References   138

Part III R&D Process Evaluation Measurements   139

Chapter 9 Interaction and Input Metrics   141
9.1 Interactions With Other Organizational Units   141
     9.1.1 Internal Company Organization   141
     9.1.2 Less-Cited Interaction Metrics   145
     9.1.3 Interaction Measurement Lessons Learned   146
9.2 Inputs to the Innovation Process   147
     9.2.1 Input Measurements Lessons Learned   149
References   150

Chapter 10 Evaluating Internal R&D Processes   151
10.1 Management of Human Resource Issues   152
      10.1.1 Motivation and Reward Systems   152
      10.1.2 Leadership   156
      10.1.3 Managing Major Cultural Change in R&D and
              Marketing   157
      10.1.4 Internal Organization of the Innovation Effort   157
      10.1.5 Quality, Performance, Planning, and Management   158
10.2 Lessons Learned on Internal Process Metrics   158
References   159

Part IV External Evaluation of R&D   161

Chapter 11 Customer Satisfaction Evaluation and
            Measurement   163
11.1 Defining the Customer and Satisfaction   164
      11.1.1 Who is the Customer?   164
      11.1.2 The Lead User   165
      11.1.3 What is Satisfaction?   166
      11.1.4 Motorola's Satisfaction Criteria   167
      11.1.5 Crafting the Evaluation Measurement   169
11.2 The Survey Instrument   169
      11.2.1 Measuring Your Company as an Innovative
              Supplier   170
      11.2.2 Measuring Your Product or Service   171
      11.2.3 Bias and Survey Reliability   172
      11.2.4 Measuring Customer Satisfaction With Innovation   173

11.3 Lessons Learned on Measuring Customer
       Satisfaction   176
References   176

Chapter 12 Improving Strategic Intent Results Through
            Other Evaluation Measurements   177
    12.1 New Products and Services   177
           12.1.1 Lessons Learned on New Products to Sales   181
    12.2 Using Benchmarking for Innovation   181
           12.2.1 Actual Benchmarking Usage   182
           12.2.2 Impact of Benchmarking on Other Outcomes   182
           12.2.3 Benchmarking Lessons Learned   183
    12.3 Measuring Improvement and Growth   183
    12.4 A Proposed R&D Effectiveness Index   185
    12.5 Key Lessons Learned on Measuring and
           Evaluating Strategic Innovation   187
    References   189

Chapter 13 Financial Frameworks in an Innovation
            Perspective   191
    13.1 Financial Evaluation of R&D   191
           13.1.1 How Financial and Nonfinancial Innovation
                   Metrics Relate   191
           13.1.2 Financial Project Selection and Evaluation   193
           13.1.3 Management Accounting   193
    13.2 Financial Analysts' Views of R&D   194
           13.2.1 Commentary on the Financial Analysts' Views 194
    13.3 R&D Executives' Panel Discussion   195
           13.3.1 Views on Option Theory as a Financial Framework 195
           13.3.2 Views on Financial Frameworks   196
    13.4 Financial Results   197
           13.4.1 An Earnings Model   197
           13.4.2 Is Speedy Innovation Really Financially Beneficial? 198
           13.4.3 Product Extensions Versus Major New Projects 199
           13.4.4 Summary of the Earnings Regression Models   200
           13.4.5 Innovation and Shareholder Value Creation   200
           13.4.6 Company Culture and Innovation   201
    13.5 Financial Frameworks Lessons Learned   202
    References   202

Chapter 14 Methods of Quantitative Measurements   205
    14.1 Methodology   205
    14.2 How the 1990 Through 1995 Studies Were Done   207

14.3 Measuring Leading Indicators of Customer
      Satisfaction   208
      14.3.1 Satisfaction With Cost Competitiveness   211
14.4 Measuring Cycle Times   212
      14.4.1 Idea-to-Customer Time   212
      14.4.2 R&D Time   213
      14.4.3 Market Development Cycle Time   215
      14.4.4 Marketing Cycle Time   216
14.5 Measuring New Products and Services   217
      14.5.1 1995 New Products as a Percent of Sales Model   218
14.6 Measuring Market Share   219
      14.6.1 How Market Share Affects Results   219
14.7 Measuring Benchmarking   222
      14.7.1 Impact of Benchmarking on Other Outcomes   222
14.8 Measuring Financial Results   223
      14.8.1 Management Accounting   223
      14.8.2 1994 EBIT Model   224
      14.8.3 1995 EBIT Model   226
      14.8.4 Summary of the EBIT Regression Models   227
14.9 1995 Effectiveness Index Model   227
      14.10 Factor Analysis   228
      14.11 Summarizing Findings   232
      References   233

Chapter 15 What Is the Best Set of Leading Indicators?   235
15.1 Innovation Outcome Evaluation and Measurement   235
      15.1.1 Reengineering the R&D Process   236
      15.1.2 Customer Satisfaction   237
      15.1.3 Timeliness   237
      15.1.4 Nonfinancial Strategic Metrics   237
      15.1.5 Financial Metrics   238
15.2 The Best Set of Innovation Precursors   238
15.3 Afterthoughts   239
      References   240

Glossary   243

About the Author   247

Index   249

Preface

Innovation management, that is, the suprafunction bridging product development and product management, is widely being recognized as the evolutionary approach to the difficult fusion of two formerly individualistic functions. To date, companies have managed these functions primarily on an open systems basis of inputs, processes, and outputs with minimal quantitative feedback. If innovation managers are to do more with less, the two former functions must be managed jointly. Their open systems must be merged, and there must be introduced some closing of the loop through more feedback and feed-forward than previously done.

As J. M. Juran so concisely stated in introducing modern concepts of quality, "What gets measured, gets done!" To this one might add, "What you measure is what you get. So make sure what you get is what you want!"

What this book is about is linking certain R&D management practices to desired effects, outputs, and outcomes. These may include better financial performance, market share, customer satisfaction, or any other outcome desired by top management. Once the chief executive officer has identified and evaluated those relationships, the R&D manager ensures effectiveness by making certain that the chosen standard of measurements, and the control system based upon them, are geared to those practices.

Thus, innovation management needs measurements by which to control the R&D management process in an effective manner, by which we mean doing the right thing as opposed to efficiency that is the measurement of output divided by input. But how can the right management actions be taken? First, consideration of the views of top management suggests that the outcome of innovation seen at that high level cannot be measured just by the outputs of the product development and product management departments themselves. Thus, it must be measured on the results of the firm taken as a whole. These results, once seen in purely financial terms, now include a broad spectrum of nonfinancial measures as well. In addition to separating outcomes from outputs, it has also been found necessary to separate the internal processes of the departments from the interactions they have with other noninnovation subdivisions of the organization in achieving the outcomes desired by top management.

The book that results is one aimed primarily at those practitioners of innovation management from research, development, and engineering; from the marketing side; and from the integration of their efforts. As such, it is intended to help those individuals select quantitative measurements to guide their management actions rather than continuing to operate with only subjective indications of what is effective. Thus, each chapter concludes with a section showing what managers should do with the information provided in the chapter. These include lessons learned from experience, from the literature, and from survey research.

For a book written primarily for the practitioner, the reader might well ask, "Then why does it focus so much on survey research?" The answer is quite simple: The rate of change of innovation management practices in the past five years has been the highest the author has known in his career. For example, as spelled out in Chapter 7, since 1991 the percentage of survey research responders measuring the cycle time from generation of an idea to delivery of the product or service to the first customer has quadrupled. Nothing experimental can prepare any manager for such a rapid rate of change.

Survey research can measure the rate of change of the use of new management tools and systems. Clearly, these are on the rise in all metrics addressed in the book. However, use does not equate to importance, satisfaction, or effectiveness. Why would any company want to use all possible management tools? What the manager would prefer are those most important, or satisfying, or most nearly suitable for forecasting the outcomes desired by management. To establish this by trial and error in one's own firm is time consuming. Statistical analysis of surveys of multiple users is one route to selecting effective measurements early in the innovation chain.

If the practice of speed to market should improve financial performance, then tracking time through the innovation chain is the appropriate measurement practice. How really beneficial is this speed-up practice? Without research and analysis, the individual manager may take an unnecessarily long time to find out. As Chapter 13 points out there are things speedy R&D does that have positive effects on some outcomes, but the cited survey research raises questions as to whether financial performance should be the major reason for reducing R&D cycle time.

The direction taken in the book is inverse to the system organization previously outlined. Thus, it represents a view backward along potential feedback paths. The many years of R&D and technology management experience of the author have shaped the view that not only must R&D processes be evaluated by financial measurements but also metrics must be selected that are balanced in that they represent the interests of all other stakeholders in the business.

A decade ago, the author wrote his then-approach in *The Financial Side of Industrial Research Management* (Wiley, 1984). About the only nonfinancial measurement then addressed was the measurement of time. Clearly timeliness is still needed as a nonfinancial metric. But times have changed. Most companies now consider measurements of the ongoing business should also include metrics of quality, customer satisfaction, and other measurements. Thus, the focus of this book is to select what these additional and new measurements should be for the effective management of future business, which is the goal of the management of technology and innovation.

The extensive literature has been searched to identify the present level of usage of effectiveness metrics and their reported contributions to results. The author's own earlier publications of journal articles have also contributed to this work. In addition, the results included are from six different recent research studies conducted by the author's students under his guidance. By both chance and the limits of available time on the part of the author, these studies were initiated in six different years from 1990 to 1995 and are so-called in the book to avoid repetitious footnoting. The results are included in the text of the book, while the specifics of how these studies were conducted is described in detail in Chapter 14. Their interpretation, however, is the author's own.

Thus, Part I of this book, entitled General Aspects of R&D Process Evaluation, presents the author's personal evolution from the finance/time orientation of his 1984 book to understanding what might be the new measurement orientation of business. By the time the background in Part One had been absorbed and some of the ideas subjected to pilot testing, it was clear that the task was far more complex than originally imagined. The author chose to limit his work primarily to the operating levels of the organization usually called the strategic business unit and its supporting R&D department. As a consequence, much of the rest of the book presents a much more detailed study in 1994 and 1995 into the finer structure of managing R&D processes and identifying more clearly the precursor or leading indicators that drive management decisions.

The author gratefully acknowledges the continued collaboration with Dr. Carey C. Curtis on this survey research, supported in part by the Consortium for Advanced Manufacturing International and by the National Science Foundation via the Center for Innovation Management Studies. The work of the *Industrial Research Institute's Research-on-Research Committee's Subcommittee on Measuring the Effectiveness of R&D* (IRIMER) has been monitored for the last four years, and that group's and the contributions of several anonymous reviewers are also gratefully acknowledged.

Rather than just restate these surveys and the publications that have resulted from them, the author has tried to capture just what are their best practices from interviewing many working innovation managers. Some updated portions of his 1984 book have also been used in this book. To the extent that this research has paralleled the on-going work of IRIMER, the author has identified these linkages. However, there is much more that IRIMER has done that has not been included in the selected focus of this book. This is summarized in Part One with directions to published references.

An additional audience for the subject matter of this book consists of professionals in the academic field in technology and innovation management. The author's earlier book, supplemented by cases from the Harvard Business School, has been used by the author as a text in courses on technology management at the University of New Haven and as a visiting lecturer at two other technologically oriented universities. For those, like the author, who wishes to use this also as a teaching text, the cases he has used in his courses will be supplied on request. However, as new cases on innovation and technology management are published annually, a current case catalog is also recommended as a source.

There is still a third audience for the book, namely, the academic researcher in the growing field of the management of technology and innovation. Recent research publications in this field have been cited in the sections where they are relevant. Yet research in this field is still so incomplete. It is hoped that this book will illuminate pathways to follow in continuing this investigation.

Lynn W. Ellis
Westport, Connecticut
January 1997

Part I

General Aspects of R&D Process Evaluation

The first part of this book addresses the general aspects of R&D process evaluation from recent published literature, conference presentations, and studies conducted annually from 1990 through 1995. It emphasizes a quantitative approach to evaluation based on the philosophy that "what gets measured, gets done; so be sure you measure what you want!" In recent years, the metrics chosen by industrial companies have branched out from being purely economic, financial, and accounting also to include nonfinancial metrics such as measures of customer satisfaction, timeliness, and quality, to name a few. What distinguishes this thrust is that the book tries to develop plausible cause-and-effect relationships between inputs and R&D processes and outcomes of interest to general management. In so doing, the reader will learn of the contribution of many R&D management actions to the success of the firm.

Following an introductory chapter, the second chapter addresses the interaction of R&D and the financial function of the firm. The third chapter covers relations between the R&D organization and external technical and commercial areas (called boundary spanning in the organizational literature). This is followed by the fourth chapter on managing along R&D department internal processes. The fifth chapter covers managing the interaction of R&D with other functions earlier and later in the innovation cycle. Chapter 6 addresses crossfunctional teams as a principal integrating mechanism of R&D with the other company functions.

Chapter 1

Introduction to Evaluating R&D Process Management

New theories of managing change for the 1990s are rolling out with increasing frequency: empowerment; reinventing or reengineering the corporation; tearing up the floors (fewer management layers); ripping down the internal and external walls; concurrent or simultaneous engineering; integrated engineering (Deere); knocking down the silos (Goodyear and Harley Davidson); taking down the smokestacks (Chrysler); crossfunctional teams; platform teams (Ford and Chrysler); and the boundaryless organization (General Electric). While no one has yet gone fully boundaryless, the boundaries in modern organizations are becoming fewer and much more permeable than in the past.

But all of these are subjective theories put forward by management fashion setters such as management gurus, consulting firms, and business schools. How is the reader to distinguish what may count in management practices in her or his own firm? Who knows whether expenditures on innovation are beneficial or not without measuring them? The contention of this book is that this must be done objectively, not subjectively. Objectivity requires discipline, and discipline can only be enforced if there are guideline measurements against which actual results can be compared. What is to be measured? Outcomes desired by management is one answer—inputs and R&D processes that contribute to these outcomes is another. But all of these are many and varied, so the R&D manager has choices to make. How does one make these choices? In the chapters that follow, the reader will travel a path through the many available metrics and learn how to distinguish which of them are important enough to be used.

The reader will quickly notice that the descriptions that began this chapter are those of manufacturing organizations. Yet, equivalent functions exist in purely service organizations, particularly those dependent upon *information technology* (IT). These companies need measurements also. The author, as a consequence, makes no distinction in what follows between R&D in manufacturing companies and in technology dependent service companies.

In practical organizations, two main groupings of once separate functional departments are becoming apparent: the implementation or supply chain, which is the order-fulfilling process, and the innovation chain, or new product and/or service creation and introduction process. In this latter process are traditional functions such as product management in marketing, R&D, engineering, and product or service qualification testing, often the quality manager's role. Both of these larger processes not only have roles for individuals working across the organizational lines between them but also most often have specialists from each side of the boundary working together from initial concept until well after initial product or service launch. Within these two processes, boundaries are a lot fewer. Most companies in advanced economies under a free market are dismantling much of their former functional structures, and the matrix ties from each new product/service team back to functional authorities.

Deere & Co. stressed the need for a lean, flexible, and barrier-free organization based on teams, concluding creating such an organization to be more difficult and protracted than managers realize [1]. Deere began in 1984 with parallel or simultaneous engineering but found that parallel tracks rarely meet. As a consequence, two different but more advanced forms of a more reciprocal form of integrated engineering are proceeding in two different divisions. In one division, four-fifths of the engineers have been shifted out of their function into one of four self-contained businesses where they remain through early manufacture of their product. The results are lower costs and shorter cycle times. Even with this success, there are still pulls from the twin masters of the business heads and the functional boss at headquarters. The other division has gone even farther into a nonhierarchical multidisciplinary organization. There they have learned that fully integrated engineering has to go beyond concurrent engineering. Effective teamwork requires abandoning matrix structures and the multiple lines of responsibility. Teamwork does not work with too many layers of hierarchy—the division is down to three layers between the general manager and operators by combining functions and broadening scope. Neither division has abandoned functions completely, preserving some to ensure that others learn and advance in their disciplines.

In industry the theme at present is very much "doing a lot more with a lot less" [2]. Company expenditures for R&D are being questioned by managements. While very few companies are increasing their investment in R&D, managements are all requesting more out of R&D. As financial pressures have increased in these competitive times, the short-term needs for profits have been in inevitable conflict with the innovation sector's longer term perspectives. Since R&D expenditure is roughly the same amount as the dividend in many companies (5 to 10 % of sales and greater in software-oriented companies), it is a tempting target for those general and financial managers of a cost-cutting mentality. As will be seen in subsequent chapters, however, this stereotype of the financial-only management shows up as only one of several innovation outcome measures currently in use in those corporations that have been surveyed thus far. Interestingly, these other outcome measures are all nonfinancial in nature.

As an introduction to evaluating R&D process management, the motivation for such evaluation is reviewed. This is followed by government policy toward R&D and finding the funds for R&D and introduces a balanced scorecard structure for the choice of metrics.

1.1 MOTIVATION FOR EVALUATING PROJECTS

This section begins by describing an industrial initiative for measuring effectiveness and is followed by what are seen by R&D directors as their biggest problems, which provide the motivation for carefully evaluating projects. Later subsections give a review of a number of broad proposals for making this evaluation.

1.1.1 An Industrial Measurement of Effectiveness Initiative

In 1992, the *Industrial Research Institute* (IRI) named a Subcommittee on the Measurement of Effectiveness in R&D, abbreviated IRIMER, drawn from member companies and others (including the author) who are interested in tackling the very difficult area of measuring innovation effectiveness on company productivity. Besides surveying some of the recent literature, this chapter is also based on an interim report on how the committee has gone about its task and gives an early look at some of its preliminary findings [2,3]. As of this writing, however, much remains to be done by the committee to link the *lagging* or *result* indicators, so much in evidence in companies surveyed, to those indicators of a *precursor* or *leading* nature that would be of most use to innovation managers in guiding their decisions.

Some examples presented to early meetings of IRIMER help to demonstrate the nature of the measurement problem. The director of the Center for Innovation Management Studies and a professor at Lehigh University, who is also an IRIMER committee member, cited interviews carried out in 1989 with about 15 CEOs of large IRI companies [4]. Some quotes follow, showing the general frustration that CEOs have with the metrics used to assess the contribution of R&D to company performance:

- "Look at them all, but don't trust any of them."
- "I never heard of a method that makes any sense to me at all, but I look at a number. . . within the context of the market place."
- "A common thread. . . is the lack of suitable measures of current R&D productivity. . . "
- "There is a need for development of a common language with which R&D and corporate management can communicate. . . "

Although it may seem strange that many companies will spend large amounts on R&D without having a clear picture of what outcomes or results it will bring, the results of interviews by committee members support that few companies seem to have any organized system for measuring the effectiveness of this expenditure. This was borne out by the answers received from a simple questionnaire designed by the IRIMER committee with the intent of discovering (1) what companies were measuring to achieve effectiveness, (2) whether these were satisfactory, and (3) whether they were prepared to discuss their experiences, as shown in Table 1.1 [2].

While the study is still in its early days, some of the findings from companies surveyed to date include the following.

- Corporate R&D, in companies that also conduct R&D in divisions, operates almost without quantitative evaluation and relies on occasional surveys and retrospective *return on investment* (ROI) calculations.
- Centralized R&D or Divisional R&D organizations that interface more directly with marketing and/or manufacturing attempt to measure R&D's contribution, but only retrospectively by such factors as contribution to sales, profit, or ROI.
- No company responding is measuring beforehand the prospective results of R&D nor measuring for use in controlling or determining the right level of R&D investment.

The consequence of these findings is that effectiveness measurement in innovation seems to be in its early stages in those companies interviewed. However, this observation is derived from such a small sample size that a more extensive review of what companies actually do in measurements is needed before accepting these conclusions.

Other departments have evolved effective measurements to which their CEOs can relate. However, the whole innovation area—and particularly R&D—is a very significant portion of annual spending, whose contribution cannot be

Table 1.1
Use of Effectiveness Measures

Systematic measures?	Yes: 50	No: 50
How satisfactory?	Could be better: 23	
	Somewhat satisfactory: 14	
	Completely satisfactory: 1	
Willing to share?	Yes: 40	

Source: [2].

measured to the same extent, let alone be well understood, particularly by CEOs of a nontechnical bent. This book is addressed to help resolve this measurement effectiveness deficiency.

1.1.2 Biggest Problems for R&D Directors

Perhaps the best manner in which to begin is to look at the problems through the eyes of those on the firing line. From 1993 to 1995, the IRI has asked its members what were their biggest problems. This generated over 200 responses. These are rank ordered for 1995 as shown in Table 1.2 [5]. The same ranking for 1993 is also given to show which problems shifted in importance over the two-year period.

The most cited problem in both years, namely, measuring and improving R&D productivity/effectiveness, is the theme of this book. The remaining problems can be classified into their categories with problem numbers as per the 1995 year ranking. Overall cycle time is an *outcome* related to problem 3; problems 3 and 12 are *outputs* from the innovation process; problems 5, 9, 10, 13, and 14 are

Table 1.2
Ranking of 16 Biggest R&D Problems

1995	1993	R&D Problem
1	*1*	*Measuring and improving R&D productivity/effectiveness*
2	4	Balancing long-term/short-term R&D objectives
3	2	Cycle-time reduction in R&D
4	n/a	Making innovation happen
5	3	Integration of strategic technology planning with corporate strategic planning (including utilization of core technologies)
6	n/a	Managing R&D for business growth
7	n/a	Accessing external sources of technology
8	8	R&D portfolio management
9	5	Organization and role of R&D in centralized and decentralized businesses
10	11	Enterprise integration (coordinating R&D with all other corporate activities)
11	10	Globalization of R&D
12	12	Internal/external technology transfer
13	7	Selling R&D internally and externally
14	13	Leadership of R&D within the corporation
15	6	Optimization of R&D spending and employment in slow economic conditions
16	9	Benchmarking of the R&D organization

Source: [5], by rank order.
Note: n/a: Not asked in 1993.

interactions with the rest of the firm; problems 2, 4, 6, 8, 15, and 16 are *internal processes* to R&D; and problems 7 and 11 represent *inputs* to the innovation process. The general problems of outcomes of a nonfinancial nature will be covered in the following subsections of this chapter, leaving the economic, financial, and more specialized processes for later chapters.

1.1.3 An Innovation Benchmarking Proposal

Benchmarking is a term that became popular in the implementation side of business with the introduction of *total quality management* (TQM) as a management process. It is a new label for the older process of setting objectives and goals, but with the twist of learning from what has been achieved by external competitors, noncompetitors, or other units within the company's organization [6, p. 36]. Since other firms have done it, benchmarking asserts that there is no logical reason why any other strategic business unit cannot match or surpass the benchmarks of others.

Benchmarking applied to innovation thus far has been directed mainly toward cycle-time in such industries as automobile manufacturing. A recent study [7] focused on three *measures of success* in innovation, namely, technology transfer to business units, cycle-time to market, and crossfunctional participation. These would be classified by this author as an output, an outcome, and an interaction, respectively. Their thirteen *best practices* included those listed in Table 1.3 [7]. The author has added in parentheses a classification corresponding to their category.

Table 1.3
Proposed Best Practices

---

1. Strategies well defined (interaction)
2. Core-technologies defined (input)
3. Multinational R&D (process)
4. Funding of research from corporate (interaction)
5. Central facility or a small number of them (process)
6. Crossfunctional teams (interaction)
7. Formal mechanisms for interactions (interaction)
8. Analytical project selection and evaluation (selection is an internal process and valuation is an outcome)
9. Technology transfer (output)
10. Effective career development (process)
11. Outside recruiting in universities and other companies (process)
12. University and third-party relationships (process)
13. Formal monitoring of external R&D activities (process)

Source: [7].

Some of these practices can be measured objectively, such as practice 4 by the percentage of total research funding obtained from corporate sources or practice 6 by the percentage of projects being conducted by crossfunctional teams. Some may be measured by formality scales described in subsequent sections. Others are so subjective that their effective measurement may well be impractical.

While the innovation benchmarking literature is limited to this one source, it greatly extends the number of interactions, internal processes, and inputs that need to be considered as potential precursor or leading indicator metrics. Current research on benchmarking in innovation, as part of the 1994 study, is discussed further in Chapter 12. Since this list is only one of its kind and minimally objective in the nature of its metrics, other more general surveys may help in guiding the search for good measures, as outlined in subsequent sections.

1.1.4 The Malcolm Baldridge National Quality Award

The U.S. Department of Commerce annually gives the Malcolm Baldridge National Quality Award [8]. The criteria for this award are all in the form of quantitative, although subjective, measurements. These were established by an eminent group of experts and are revised periodically. The scoring is based on quantification by the awards' own formality scale, which awards 0% for anecdotal use and up to 100% for world class results. Thus, it gives one method of quantitatively analyzing R&D management practices, such as those described in the previous section.

Perhaps most significant to the measurement of innovation is the seventh category, namely, Customer Satisfaction (an outcome), which accounts for 30% of the total award rating. Included in this category are the following criteria subheadings: determining customer requirements and expectations; customer relationship management; customer service standards; commitment to customers; complaint resolution for quality improvement; determining customer satisfaction; customer satisfaction results; and customer satisfaction comparison. Since this list was put together by a distinguished panel of quality experts, it emphasizes that some customer satisfaction metrics need to be a component of the nonfinancial metrics used by R&D managers. However, as used in the Baldridge Award, they do not yet identify which metrics best fit the R&D evaluation process.

While these criteria are biased somewhat toward the quality function, the pattern of multiple measurements parallels that of other broad-based studies of the measurement process that have been noted above.

The remaining six award metrics are shown in Table 1.4, with the author's category characterizations in parentheses.

Most of these are better metrics for the implementation side of the firm than for the R&D side. They do emphasize, however, that the R&D manager must include some quality metrics in evaluating department processes as well as including customer satisfaction and financial measures.

Table 1.4
Baldridge Award's First Six Customer Satisfaction Criteria

1. Leadership: Senior executive leadership; quality values; management for quality; public responsibility (internal process).
2. Information and analysis: Scope and management of quality data and information; competitive comparisons and benchmarks; analysis of quality data and information (internal process).
3. Strategic quality planning: Strategic quality planning process; quality goals and plans (internal process).
4. Human resource utilization: Human resource management; employee involvement; quality education and training; employee recognition and performance measurement; employee well-being and morale (interaction).
5. Quality assurance of products and services: Design and introduction of quality products and services; process quality control; continuous improvement of processes; quality assessment; documentation; business process and support service quality; supplier quality (interaction).
6. Quality results: Product and service quality results; business process, operational and support service quality results; supplier quality results (outcome).

Source: [8].

1.1.5 Strategy, Structure, and Uncertainty

Implicit in the theme of this book is that the firm's strategy involves innovation in either products or services [9]. This in itself specifies that a precursor of outcomes and outputs is the prior selection of the strategic path for the company to follow. Since this is formulated internally to the firm and is by nature subjective, strategy alone is not a measurable input. What is measurable, however, is the degree of formality of coordination between strategic planning and product or service innovation planning, as mentioned in the previous section.

As an alternative to the externally focused Baldridge Award type of scale, one author has suggested that subjective practices should be measured by the degree of formality that is measured on a six-point interval scale of increasing levels of internal formality [10], particularly, issue is not recognized; initial efforts at addressing issue; right skills are in place; appropriate methods are used; responsibilities are clarified; continuous improvement is underway. Strategy metrics suggested by others include the percentage of sales from new products (outcome) and, from the 1993 study, investment in major new products versus investment in product extensions (inputs). These latter two are preferred by this author to formality scales because they are objective in nature.

Structure follows strategy [11]. Structure also changes the nature of interactions. A serial structure was used in the past by most organizations. In this structure the interactions are progressively downstream. With such an organization, coordination of R&D upstream with marketing and finance and of downstream with manufacturing, operations, divisions, or subsidiaries places a limited role on interactions. The shift to a crossfunctional team organization, or any intermediate stage, expands the number of interactions considerably [12, Chap. 8]. Quality may be addressed directly, as may be many other staff sections. The CEO may take a more direct overview as project leaders grow in status.

Uncertainty also has its role in determining structure and metrics [12, Chap. 6]. An example of the kinds of structural relationships is shown in Figure 1.1 [12]. With greater uncertainty, the external boundary spanning mechanisms or gate keepers become more important, which is to some effect seen in the previous comments about benchmarking.

The two formality scales mentioned earlier [8, 10] are similar methods of measuring the structural and uncertainty dimensions. The author prefers the Baldridge Award [8] calibration against external competitors up to "world class" over internal assessment [10]. If necessary for matching conditions internal to the firm, subjective ratings from none to low to high are a less-desirable alternative to be considered than the other formality scales but better than no measurement at all.

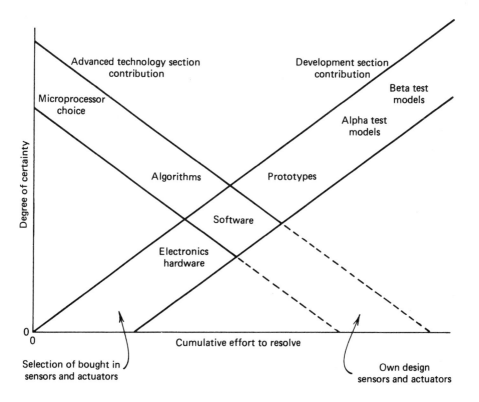

Figure 1.1. Advanced technology versus development contribution. (*Source*: [12, Figure 4.4, p. 69]. Used with permission.)

1.1.6 Using Product and Technological Life Cycles

In an innovative world, no product or service lasts forever but is replaced in time by another innovation. Usually, the time that the service or product is on the market is called the *product life cycle* [12, Chap. 4], the length of which is a potential input measurement, as used in the 1993 study. The whole technological life cycle spans individual life cycles from idea to project launch, launch to downstream transition, and the steps downstream in the implementation chain until first customer delivery [13].

For example, marketing may have an idea for a new product—a project is prepared for R&D—development takes place—a pilot is handed over to manufacturing—first serial production is done—marketing presents the product to the market—sales takes its first order—the product is delivered to the first customer.

What was clear from the 1991 and 1993 studies was that no unanimity existed on which and how much of these intermediate steps to measure. Also it was found that the idea-to-customer time was measured before 1993 by less than a quarter of the responding companies. Thus, at least two metrics arise from life cycle considerations. Specifically, idea-to-customer time is an outcome of the firm as a whole; and R&D cycle time is an output of the innovation chain at the point of downstream delivery, with only the "fuzzy front end" between R&D and marketing being an imprecise commencement point [14, Chap. 3]. A detailed explanation of these cycle-time metrics appears later in the book in Chapter 7.

1.1.7 Entrepreneurship and Intrapreneurial Organization

As mentioned above, entrepreneurship in a small company or intrapreneurial organization in a large company such as 3M brings with it problems of, for example, structure and rewards. In reviewing the entrepreneurial literature, however, no additional special metrics were identified that needed to be added to the list for consideration. This appears to be because such organizations are likely to be small. Thus they focus on just a few metrics such as a new product or service as an outcome, cycle time, and one or two others as in-process measurements. The more extended set of metrics discussed so far is likely to await entrepreneurial success in the chosen outcome and its growth into a larger business needing more sophistication in its measurements.

1.1.8 Product Development Management Research

Articles on product development management research are only rarely seen in general management publications. One recent contribution in such a journal is heavily focused on major retrospective studies [15]. As such it misses much of what is seen as important by those industrial managers closer to the market place. An expanded horizon is needed to add an industrial perspective on product development management research as a counterbalance to the academic viewpoint [16] because so much of the expansion of theories on technical and innovation management has been published in journals more attuned to industrial R&D managers, such as *Research Technology Management*, published by the Industrial Research Institute. The pace of change in this field in the past seven or eight years has been heavily driven by industrial needs to meet foreign competition. Serious investigators in this field, therefore, need to access those sources that more clearly and more timely reflect what has been happening in industry. They should acquire a close coupling to the leading companies in innovating technical management to give them an early input to this area of rapid change. The field of product development management research can benefit from a combination of academic and industrial perspectives.

1.2   GOVERNMENT POLICY TOWARD R&D

Government policy toward R&D is expressed in several ways. First, there is the direct effect of Federal spending for R&D. Historical reviews of R&D spending show much growth over the last half century [17,18]. The level of Federal funding was an obvious external force on the growth of total R&D spending. When this is done in the Federal government's own laboratories, it is accessible to industry under certain restrictions. Most of this spending, however, is done under contract with industrial firms and, therefore, is a means for them to develop core competencies.

What is less obvious are the causes of the fluctuations in R&D spending by industry, which has ranged from greater than Federal R&D expenditures 50 years ago, to less than half of Federal spending by the mid-1960s, and back to nearly twice government R&D expenditures in the mid-1990s [17–19]. Part of this comes from the indirect ways in which the government's policies affect R&D. In reaction to the decline in industrial R&D in the late 1960s and early 1970s, a positive stimulus to increased R&D return was intended by the Congress with the passage of the *Economic Recovery Act of 1981*. This Act, now several times extended in subsequent tax bills, provided a tax credit for research and experimentation at an initial rate of 25%, beginning in mid 1981 and at declining rates since 1986. After controlling for a number of other significant factors and discarding a larger number of potential causes as insignificant, it was found that each 10% increase (or decrease) in this tax credit was associated with a 4% increase (or decrease) in nongovernment R&D spending, with no time lag on an annual scale [18,19]. Since R&D spending is unlikely to be the causative factor, it may be argued persuasively that the anticipation of enactment was the cause and the increase or decrease in expenditure was the effect.

Also, government actions indirectly affect R&D by making investment in other activities more attractive than investment in R&D. In the period when industrial R&D spending was below that of the Federal government, public policy was in favor of capital investment tax credits, which were in effect from 1962 until their end in 1986 [19]. With calls occurring to the new administration to reintroduce a capital investment tax credit, an evaluation was made of its prospective effect on R&D expenditures. The conclusions were that the investment tax credit has lowered industrial R&D expenditure; while the research and experimentation credit has raised it [19]. In the present economic climate and unemployment among engineers, continuation of the research and experimentation tax credit is supported because of the aforementioned cause-and-effect relationship. Equally, support should be rejected for the investment tax credit because of its negative impact on R&D spending. Also at a time of high overall unemployment, the reintroduction of an investment tax credit should be rejected because giving industry incentives for a greater substitution of capital for labor sends the wrong message both to R&D executives and to labor in general.

In the United States, in general, the federal government has been most effective in stimulating R&D when it has supported direct procurement of high-technology products. An example is the period of World War II and a decade after when federal government spending on R&D was two-thirds of the U.S. total [17]. In subsequent years, space program spending was associated with an increase in a three-year lag in nongovernmental R&D expenditures [18]. In more recent years, neither defense nor space spending has "trickled down" to industrial R&D spending, and only the previously mentioned R&D tax credits and restoring real interest rates after the inflation of the 1970s have shown much positive effects of government policy toward R&D when measured on a macro basis [18,19]. This is not to say that more limited government initiatives have not succeeded, with a clear positive example of the National Institutes of Health.

In other parts of the world, there is often a more proactive government involvement in commercially oriented R&D. An example of this is the Ministry of International Trade and Industry in Japan. The Ministry selects areas of interest in enhancing exports and domestic well-being and leads industrial firms toward R&D in these areas. In Europe, many of these programs are multinational in nature seeking to offset the inherent diseconomies of scale of the smaller populations of the many nations of that continent. As interesting as is this topic for the future of evaluating R&D effectiveness, its complexity goes beyond the scope of this book. Thus, with limited exceptions noted in the literature, the evaluation of R&D effectiveness that follows was carried out in the context of U.S. firms dealing with the previously described nature of U.S. government involvement.

1.3 FINDING FUNDS FOR R&D

For R&D managers to interpret correctly the effects of spending on R&D over time, it is important for them to understand the external driving forces behind this expenditure, some of which may also need to be introduced into their decision chain as inputs. Finding funds for R&D begins with the choice of going after external funding or seeking funds from within the firm. As mentioned above, federal government R&D is extensively contracted out to industry. The largest share is from the Department of Defense, which can be sought by those firms with the requisite skills in technologies of interest to the military. Another substantial contract provider is NASA for those firms with space-age skills.

For companies outside the defense/space area, the *National Science Foundation* (NSF) is a source of funds, particularly for small businesses. Other government departments have contract-out programs that rise and fall with the prevailing public policy as funded by the Congress. Companies that wish to secure funds from the government need to explore continuously which programs are expanding and contracting.

Internal funding for R&D is first and foremost controlled by financial considerations. The theoretical framework used in this analysis has its roots in the concept that money is spent on industrial R&D because it is expected to earn a return [17]. This return must be better than the return that can be earned in any alternative use for the investment. Otherwise, it will not be attracted to industrial R&D. Thus, the driving forces to be examined in going after internal R&D funds are those that might be expected to change the return on R&D in economic terms, that is, those that either might have increased or decreased the benefits expected from R&D or potentially lowered the cost of R&D to the firm. One such activity is increasing market share, since this is usually correlated with increased profitability.

In the changing world since the mid 1980s, reasons for funding R&D internally have expanded with the increasing emphasis by chief executives on the use of nonfinancial measurements in guiding the destiny of the firm. Thus, industrial R&D managers need to consider which of these latter metrics best balance the financial metrics in their company. Of those metrics discussed so far in this chapter, customer satisfaction, quality, and cycle time seem most identified with effectiveness. How does a manager put these all together with R&D process metrics? The next section will outline one example.

1.4 AN APPROACH TO METRICS—A BALANCED INNOVATION SCORECARD

Under the theme of a "balanced scorecard," proposals have been made for the inclusion of nonfinancial metrics in management accounting systems [20–22]. Such a scorecard adds to financial measures by including a selection of nonfinancial metrics. This theme has been selected as the first basis for classifying metrics in this book. This section covers the concept of the scorecard and the relation of R&D to it. It continues with the need to live with shorter time frames and takes note of the innovation process model and methodology used in analysis.

1.4.1 Including R&D in a Balanced Scorecard for Management

The first "balanced scorecard" authors had their focus on the additional perspectives of the customer, internal business, and innovation and learning based on a survey of measurement practices in a limited number of companies [20–22]. Within each of these perspectives, three to five specific measurements were typically identified. These metrics naturally varied from company to company, and among authors.

Other advocates of nonfinancial metrics cite new products as a percentage of sales [23]. This metric was in use over 30 years ago in ITT Corporation during the author's experience at that company. It proved then an effective means of focusing new product selection for profitability and growth. Cost managers, on the other hand, favor quality, time, and cost [24–26]. The first two are also outcome- or impact-focused nonfinancial metrics.

General managers would wish to have hard, objective, and quantifiable measurements. While these exist for some desirable outcomes, for others measurements must deal with soft, subjective, and difficult-to-quantify factors. For example, customer satisfaction may have to be measured by independent survey or by internal reporting of customer comments [27]. While less precise than many CEOs would desire, such soft measurements are better than having no metrics at all.

1.4.2 Living With Shorter Time Frames

Company plans and strategies tend also to be focused on much shorter time frames. What is needed are measurable near-term lagging or result indicators of the outcomes to the company as a whole and their relationships to R&D outputs and long-term productivity growth and equally measurable precursor or leading indicators that can be used in a forecasting mode. Both lagging and leading indicators may vary from industry to industry and depend on whether their processes are essential to competitive advantage. What is needed by innovation managers are measures whose availability and timeliness matches the shorter time frames within which their companies now operate.

1.4.3. An Innovation Process Model

Many companies now manage their innovation activities on a classical open systems basis with minimal feedback, from inputs through processes to outputs, in the manner shown in Figure 1.2.

Depending on the degree of R&D-marketing coordination, the inputs may be jointly from these two organizational units or in serial form as marketing tosses specifications over the wall to R&D. In many companies, also the output point is where design and manufacturing information is tossed over the wall to the implementing organizations: manufacturing, divisions, or subsidiaries.

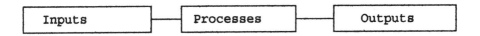

Figure 1.2 Classical open systems model.

A similar model has been proposed to the IRIMER, shown in Figure 1.3 [2,3]. In this case, processes have been incorporated into foundations and the element of technology strategy highlighted as an intervening factor.

Brown and Svenson [28] have created a partially closed systems model of R&D productivity in a serial form, incorporating feedback, from inputs through the processing system, outputs from R&D, and receiving system to outcomes of benefit to the entire company. Its significant contribution is the separation of outputs and outcomes reflecting the realities of the division between the end of the innovation chain (output) and the customer order-focused implementation chain (outcome). The last position is where the balance of a company's management operates and where the IRIMER committee had initially focused its efforts, looking at lagging indicators such as cost reduction, sales improvement, product improvements, and capital avoidance.

In reviewing the Brown and Svenson model [28], in the context of how modern companies appear to be organizing, the interaction with other organizational units in the company seems to be missing. These interactions are today not only in a serial interaction form with feedback but in various parallel or reciprocal interaction forms, often with feed-forward. A representation of this modified model is shown in Figure 1.4. The effect of modifying this model is that, while making it more complex, it allows a much greater variety of potential leading indicators to be studied.

For the purposes of this book, this expanded model of outcomes, outputs, interactions, internal processes, and inputs will be used to characterize the measurements made by others so as to bring them to a common foundation. Since the first two are after the fact, they will be classified as result or lagging indicators, and the remaining three, which should occur earlier in time, will be the base from which precursor or leading indicators are sought.

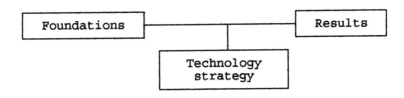

Figure 1.3 IRIMER Model (*After:* [3]).

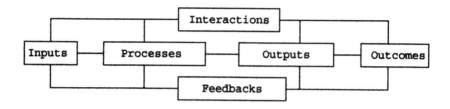

Figure 1.4   Partially closed sytems model (*After:* [28]).

1.4.4   A Note on Methodology

At this point, some methodological questions arise. What the R&D manager would like to have is a comprehensive study that shows not only the most important outcomes and outputs, but also for each potential interaction, internal process, or input how each is associated positively or negatively, and in magnitude of impact, on the individual outcome or output. It has not been within the resources of the author to approach this goal. What has been done to date is to look at many of the metrics in wider use to identify which of these are meaningful. Clearly, this required some substantial survey research, as will be seen in the studies reviewed in subsequent chapters and explained in statistical terms in Chapter 14.

1.5   SOME LESSONS LEARNED FROM SELECTED METRICS

From this overpowering array of metrics—which includes both results or lagging metrics such as outcomes and outputs and candidates for precursors of leading indicators in interactions, processes, and inputs—one could assemble a table to attempt to bring the beginnings of some order to this chapter. While this might clarify what the book is trying to do, study has found that such an attempt would be too superficial since it could not yet consider the multiple relationships that will be developed later in the book. Since more specific studies were conducted, aimed at the specific categories of Figure 1.4, it is more constructive to carry these forward into later chapters. Some clear lessons can be learned, however, from the metrics selected by the authors cited so far in this chapter.

First, there is some association between the perceived importance of metrics, satisfaction with their performance, and effectiveness, but it is not universally complete. Thus, selecting a metric that is widely used may not be the complete answer to addressing R&D effectiveness.

One such example is the array of quality metrics shown in Table 1.4 that measure the implementation of quality metrics but give little guidance for R&D process evaluation.

Another example is the increasing selection cited above of nonfinancial metrics, implying that only "bottom-line" numbers are not enough in modern business

Second, finding measures of effectiveness is a continuing high-rated effort by innovation managers as shown in the list of highest rated problems for R&D managers shown in Table 1.2.

Recognizing the inherent complexity of the task of measuring effectiveness, complex analysis may be difficult but seems the only way to sort out the few meaningful relationships found among a host of independent variables. With only a few exceptions, there is little agreement in the sources cited on which of the most logical results or lagging indicators and precursor or leading indicators to use in the more detailed study of forecasting relationships. This first chapter, however, is only a brief introduction to effectiveness through measurements. The reader will find in the chapters that follow that there is a number of these-future oriented indicators that will aid in evaluating R&D processes. The first group of these is reassessing economic, financial, and accounting indicators, which is addressed in the next chapter.

References

[1] Lorenz, C., "Team-Based Engineering at Deere," *McKinsey Quarterly*, (4), 1991, pp. 81–93.

[2] Tipping, J. W., "Doing a Lot More with a Lot Less," *Research Technology Management*, Vol. 36(5), Sept.–Oct. 1993, pp. 13–14. This article, which is based on the same source material as Chapter 1, looks at the measurement of effectiveness problem from a different perspective.

[3] Tipping, J. W., E. Zeffren, and A. R. Fusfeld, "Assessing the Value of Your Technology," *Research Technology Management*, Vol. 38(5), Sept.–Oct. 1995, pp. 22–39.

[4] Bean, A. S., "Does 'Closer to the Customer' Mean 'Further from the Truth'?" Presentation to the Conference Board, New York, 1990.

[5] Burkhart, R., "Survey Results to the *Three* 'Biggest' Problems," Washington: Industrial Research Institute, May 1, 1995.

[6] Juran, J. M., *Juran on Quality by Design: The New Steps for Planning Quality into Goods and Services*, New York: Free Press, 1992.

[7] Krause, I., and J. Liu, "Benchmarking R&D Productivity," *Planning Review*, Vol. 21(1), Jan.–Feb. 1993, pp. 16–21 and 52–53.

[8] U.S. Department of Commerce, *Application Guidelines for Malcolm Baldridge National Quality Award*, Gaithersburg, MD: National Institute of Science and Technology, 1991.

[9] Burgleman, R. A., and M. A. Madique, *Strategic Management of Technology and Innovation*, 2nd ed., Homewood, IL: Irwin, 1995.

[10] Szakonyi, R., *Measuring R&D Effectiveness: A New Approach*, IITRI Report P08530-14, Chicago, IL, IITRI Report P08530-14, Dec. 11, 1991. This document has an extensive bibliography covering measurement of R&D from 1960 to the present. A summary of this document by the same author may be found in "Measuring R&D Effectiveness—I & II,"

Research Technology Management, Vol. 37(2), Mar.–Apr. 1994, pp. 27–32, and Vol. 37(3), 1994, May–June, pp. 44–55.

[11]   Chandler, A. D., *Strategy and Structure*. Cambridge, MA: MIT Press, 1962.

[12]   Ellis, L. W., *The Financial Side of Industrial Research Management*, New York: Wiley, 1984.

[13]   Wolff, M. F., "Working Faster," *Research Technology Management*, Vol. 35(6), Nov.–Dec. 1992, pp. 10–12.

[14]   Smith, P. G., and D. G. Reinertsen, *Developing Products in Half the Time*. Florence, KY: Van Nostrand Reinhold, 1991.

[15]   Brown, S. L., and K. M. Eisenhardt, "Product Development: Past Research, Present Findings, and Future Directions," *Academy of Management Review*, Vol. 20(2), Apr. 1995, pp. 343–378.

[16]   Ellis, L. W., "Expand the Horizon of Product Development Management Research," *Academy of Management Review*, Vol. 20(4), Oct. 1995, pp. 791–793.

[17]   Ellis, L. W., "Managing Financial Resources," *Research Technology Management*, Vol. 31(4), July–Aug. 1988, pp. 21–38.

[18]   Ellis, L. W., "Some Factors Correlated with Fluctuations in Research and Development Spending," *IEEE Trans. on Engineering Management*, Vol. 36(2), Mar.–Apr. 1989, pp. 146–148.

[19]   Ellis, L. W. "The Effect of an Investment Tax Credit on R&D Spending," *IEEE Trans. on Engineering Management*, Vol. 41(2), May 1994, pp. 208–210.

[20]   Kaplan, R. S., and D. P. Norton, "The Balanced Scorecard—Measures That Drive Performance," *Harvard Business Review*, Jan.–Feb. 1992, pp. 71–79.

[21]   Kaplan, R. S., and D. P. Norton, "Putting the Balanced Scorecard to Work," *Harvard Business Review*, Sept.–Oct. 1993, pp. 134–147.

[22]   Hoffecker, J., and C. Goldenberg, "Using the Balanced Scorecard to Develop Companywide Performance Measures," *J. Cost Management*, Vol. 8(3), Fall 1994, pp. 18–27.

[23]   Gault, S., "Responding to Change," *Research Technology Management*, Vol. 37(3), May–June 1994, pp. 23–26.

[24]   Curtis, C. C., *New Product Development Cycle Time: Investigation of Cycle Time and Accounting Measures, Determinants of Cycle Time and the Impact of Cycle Time on Financial Performance*, Sc.D. diss., University of New Haven, West Haven, CT, 1993.

[25]   Curtis, C. C., "Nonfinancial Performance Measures in New Product Development," *J. Cost Management*, Vol. 8(3), Fall 1994, pp. 18–26.

[26]   Hronec, S., *Vital Signs*, New York: AMACOM, 1993.

[27]   Ellis, L. W., and C. C. Curtis, "Measuring Customer Satisfaction," *Research Technology Management*, Vol. 38(5), Sept.–Oct. 1995, pp. 45–48.

[28]   Brown, M. G., and R. A. Svenson, "Measuring R&D Productivity," *Research Technology Management*, Vol. 31(4), July–Aug. 1988, pp. 1–15.

Chapter 2

Managing the Financial Boundary

In an economic world that measures results in money, the conduct of R&D cannot be divorced from financial considerations. Of course, all R&D organizations live by expense budgets in their companies—what is meant here is the use of financial criteria beyond expense budgets in decision making.

2.1 EVALUATING IN ECONOMIC TERMS

Who knows whether expenditures on innovation are beneficial or not without measuring them? Bean [1] and coworkers have measured a number of firms using the *Total Factor Productivity* (TFP) index approach from the field of economics. This methodology measures the ratio of output (net sales) to inputs of labor, capital, and material and measures TFP growth by comparison with R&D intensity, as shown in Figure 2.1.

As can be seen, there is a correlation on a 20-year time scale between R&D intensity and productivity of companies. At this stage, most of the literature, and most industrial R&D managers, are all fairly comfortable with the relationship between industry spending on innovation, its impact on society, and long-term company performance. This metric is retrospective of the firm's entire project portfolio.

To rate projects prospectively, however, evaluate them individually, not by overall economic portfolio impact.

2.2 TRADITIONAL METHODS OF R&D EVALUATION

Much has been written in the last ten years on this subject, as will be covered below, but little survey research has been conducted as to actual practices of

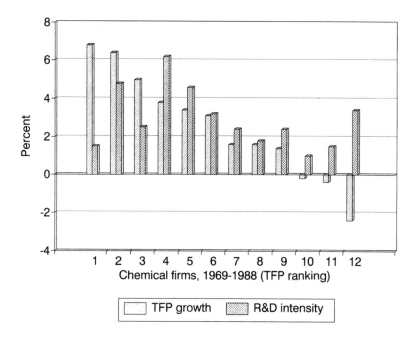

Figure 2.1 Annual R&D intensity & TFP growth. (*Source:* [1, Figure 4]. Reprinted with permission.)

profit-oriented corporations [2]. The material seems able to be grouped into three broad areas, arranged in a bottom-to-top sequence: Project selection and evaluation by (1) traditional means, (2) option theory, and (3) budget optimization.

2.2.1 Traditional Project Selection

The use of financial frameworks for R&D evaluation was thoroughly reviewed as recently as 1988, with 67 references to earlier articles [3]. That article covered contemporary and classical approaches to project selection and evaluation and optimal R&D spending. One of the key concepts is the components of improving R&D return.

2.2.1.1 Improving the Return on R&D

The principal component of *R&D return* was defined in financial terms as the "ratio of R&D rewards to R&D cost" [4,5]. By this was meant the ratio of the *net present value* (NPV) of cash flows to be received in the future to that of all costs involved in the R&D effort and its implementation. In other sources this is also called the discounted benefit-to-cost ratio.

The R&D return may be considered to be the product of two other ratios: R&D productivity (technical progress divided by R&D effort) and R&D yield (profits divided by technical progress) [4,5]. Figure 2.2 describes this graphically.

The intermediate nonfinancial factor of technical progress was broadly defined as the difference between the performance of the new product or process and that of its immediate predecessor. Its definition was conceived in terms of the customer's view of performance and as a technical measure that R&D could influence.

It was considered that R&D productivity was a metric on which the R&D manager could be judged, while R&D yield was more interrelated with other departments of the firm [4,5]. This concept introduced nonfinancial metrics such as productivity and efficiency to supplement financial metrics.

2.2.1.2 Financial Project Selection

Traditional financial development project selection has again focused largely on financial methods, such as NPV and *internal rate of return* (IRR) [3]. While these, like R&D return, incorporate the time value of money in the discounting process, more traditional processes of project selection have usually incorporated time as a nonfinancial metric in two ways, specifically, as measures of staff effort and start and

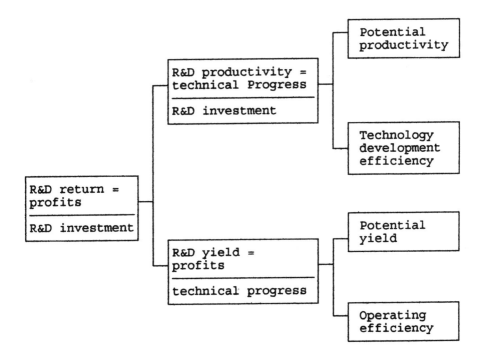

Figure 2.2. Components of R&D return. (NPV used for all financial values.) (*Source:* [5].)

complete dates. Research project selection has often had no objective measures, but only subjective ones concerning the value of the technology.

The following summarizes traditional project selection by improving R&D and financial returns:

- Improve R&D productivity principally on the R&D department's own efforts;
- Improve R&D yield in collaboration with other departments in the innovation chain;
- Use the prevailing financial metric in your firm (for example, NPV and IRR) if this communicates better than R&D return.

2.2.2 Project Selection and Evaluation Using Option Theory

The use of financial option theory in project selection and evaluation is a recent innovation [6]. An option is a contract giving the purchaser the right, but not the obligation, to purchase a financial instrument—usually common stock—at a fixed price at a future date. The parallel of R&D as an option to a common stock option is that only a small initial investment is needed to start the R&D, and this gives the firm the option to invest at a later date if the R&D is successful. For example, pioneering R&D on a new adhesive at 3M led to their ubiquitous and highly successful lightly adhering note pads. The value to the firm of the option is increased as the time horizon to future investment lengthens, as there is a greater chance that better than expected results will be obtained. Its value also increases with higher volatility (uncertainty), as there is a greater chance that the result will be better-than-expected. There is no cost besides that of the option if the results come out worse than expected, as the option will not then be exercised. The characteristics of a financial option, therefore, are a close fit to the value to a company of applied research where the potential profitability is highly uncertain.

In a 1990 discussion of R&D executives, called the 1990 study in this book and described in Chapter 14, a number of views were expressed on the validity of the option approach.

2.2.2.1 *Views on the Option Financial Framework [1990 study] [1,8]*

One point of view is that financial justification is needed for a central R&D lab. What are you going to do for the business in the future? How does the CEO know that R&D has the same view of the problem that he does? There are rapid rates of change and enormous uncertainty in some industries versus others. Option theory makes uncertainty irrelevant. We received recognition that the labs were supporting top-management objectives: "This is the right way to look at it," said our financially minded CEO (telecommunications utility).

A second viewpoint is that options are a poor model because of no branch points. CEOs and CFOs love it, and it communicates. Systems are nonlinear, while people with whom you have to communicate are linear. Options are like the ante in poker, which is liked intuitively (chemical company).

Third, the analogy to poker is good: the ante is the price of being able to play. How long should you continue alternative possibilities? What are the cancellation costs? How much hedging should you do? Benefits need to be measured as how much certainty? It is adaptive decision making, as in signal processing. Option theory only translates it into financial language (automotive company).

Others believe that options are a big trap (consumer products company).

Summarizing the use of options in evaluating R&D projects gives the following key points.

- Use option theory when a high degree of uncertainty exists but enough evidence can be found that it is worth staying in the competition long enough to find out if your firm is going to be a significant and profitable competitor;
- Move to traditional financial project selection when the uncertainty can be resolved and before shifting to higher levels of R&D investment.

2.2.3 Budget Optimization

The remaining task in financial terms is compiling the R&D budget out of the best portfolio of R&D projects [3,9]. Often the criterion of the maximum NPV for the cost outlay is used. Another criterion may be to optimize return on sales. A third method is to optimize the price of the company's common stock [9]. This is also called shareholder value creation in more recent literature. Other than the customer's view of technical performance in R&D return and the use of time as effort and dates, the traditional views of the innovation task have been completely financial. This is expanded upon in Section 2.4.7.

2.2.4 Financial Post-Evaluation

The primary purpose of financial post-evaluation is to provide feedback to project estimators to help them become better at the task. Besides which, post-evaluation takes time and effort away from the productive tasks of R&D staff. The rule to follow is to do enough post-evaluation to guide estimating and to stop the examination when the costs appear to surpass the potential benefits to be obtained from the evaluation.

Evaluation can only be effective when the firm's accounting system allows job costs to be compiled per project identification number [10]. Where standard costs or activity-based costs are used exclusively, this only allows the post-evaluation of product costs. Since staff hours and milestone progress originate in the

R&D department, they may be kept within the department and used as a substitute for the post-evaluation of estimating these two components.

This may be summarized briefly as: Look at post-evaluation as at any other R&D investment and do not continue it beyond the point where its return drops below that of other opportunities.

2.3 MANAGE WITHIN YOUR FIRM'S FINANCIAL CULTURE

While the nonfinancial measures have gained prominence in recent years, financial factors still have great weight. Financial measurements of the R&D budget and the value of individual R&D projects need to match the strategic business goals of the organization. R&D managers need agreement with top management on business priorities.

Strategic decision-making levels proceed through multiple steps. Beginning with the business vision, the company decides in which business it wants to be. From this point onward, innovation managers take decisions along a financial boundary. The firm must determine in a multifunctional manner which are the technical and commercial parameters needed to be successful and how they will be financed. The technical decision follows, within available finances, about in which areas the firm must be expert to succeed.

Working along the financial boundary, the R&D manager must establish boundary spanning mechanisms. What these are depends, first, on the firm's financial culture. The successful R&D manager learns to work within this culture and not to fight it. The empowered organization has its own needs for financial boundary spanning. This spanning must include some linkage to finance on project selection and evaluation. Finally, the boundary with finance comes to setting the R&D budget that is needed for the effective management of innovation.

Companies have strong variations in their driving cultures. Three of which—namely, the financially driven culture, the activity-based management/costing culture, and a more pliable culture in the financial sense—are discussed next.

2.3.1 The Financially Driven Culture

By financial in this context is meant a view of R&D as an investment as opposed to merely adding up costs as the accounting profession practices. All financial methods recognize the time value of money, which is the essential element separating finance from accounting.

In a decade of writing about the financial boundary, the author has clearly reflected his industrial experience with financially driven cultures.

The author's publications on R&D and finance focus on:

- Fifty years of management in an investment context [3];
- Objective R&D project selection [10,11];
- Budget optimization and rationing [10,12];
- Trends in nongovernment R&D spending [13];
- The effect of an investment tax credit in lowering R&D spending [14];
- The weak financial impact of speedy R&D [15];
- Reforming management accounting for more accurate product costing [16].

Themes that can be summarized as suggested actions for R&D managers include:

- Reach across the financial boundary, and comprehend the investment focus of financial managers.
- Learn what top management has as expectations for returns versus risks.
- Put forth requests for project approvals in financially justified form, using the selection method most acceptable to those executives across the financial boundary.

2.3.2 The Activity-Based Management and Costing Culture

Management accounting, which has strong ties to financial accounting, operates in a framework of the current income and assets statements. Thus, it does not factor in the time value of money as does the investment approach. In recent years, management accounting has received strong criticism and multiple calls for reform [16–22].

One reform movement favors a move into *activity-based management* (ABM) and *activity-based costing* (ABC) [20]. In this modernized form of cost accounting, product manufacturing is broken down into multiple tasks, each of which is further broken down into many repetitive activities for costing. ABM/ABC has accepted nonfinancial measures such as quality and timeliness in addition to costs [20]. Recently, customer satisfaction has entered the thinking of cost management [20,21].

Tasks that are not repetitive run the risk of being called time wasters. However, R&D is often not repetitive. Yet, the author has heard one ABC practitioner call a design review, which is one of the clear quality management tools of R&D, to be a time waster, "because they are not repetitive." A communications gap exists between the cost accountants and R&D people. With this communications gap, few ABM/ABC practitioners tie in R&D and capital investment.

Basically, the ABM/ABC culture is bogged down in the supply (implementation) or order processing chain. There is a lack of R&D interest in costs, while many higher managements are very cost-accounting oriented. R&D managers have been advised by ABM/ABC practitioners to create a catalog exercise of innovation activities for ABM/ABC, but few companies are anywhere near as far along in establishing such a catalog as the author has attempted in this book.

What concerns the author even more with the ABM/ABC approach is that it still does not seem to have heeded the issues in writings critical of present management accounting or in presenting suggestions for reform [16–19]. For example, product, manufacturing, and market development costs are not properly incorporated in ABC since they are expended against current production rather than against the future production that they are intended to benefit. At a recent meeting, these new approaches were sloughed off as "They have their approach, I have mine" [20].

What should the innovation manager do if ABM/ABC is the firm's culture? Again, fighting the culture is not a good solution, although educating those across the financial boundary is a needed activity. Following the ABC ideas of activity-based analysis of repetitive tasks, the first areas to join should be those of a more repetitive nature. These would include naturally support activities, such as laboratory analysis. Customer order specials, contract engineering, and qualification testing are also tasks that naturally fall into a more repetitive analysis mode. It is not clear, however, that research and much of product development can be easily adapted to ABC.

2.3.3 An Intermediate Culture

Ideally, innovation should be allowed to take place in most firms in an intermediate and more pliable culture that recognizes the need for a financial and accounting boundary but is not a slave to it. The R&D manager in such a company should tend this boundary carefully. First, using a financial project method selected with the financial manager as one criterion for project selection is recommended. Other arguments for selection or not should be raised as appropriate to the occasion. Second, along the part of the boundary facing the supply or implementation part of the organization, matching the use of costing methods used on the other side of the boundary is appropriate. Nonetheless, as expressed by the author a decade ago, the innovation manager "must consider financial methods as only tools with which to defend research expenditures in a financial and political environment rather than as a complete means to fulfillment of the overall research management task [10, p. 185]."

The suggested action for R&D managers is briefly stated as: Understand what type of financial culture you face and adapt to it as best you can without being overwhelmed by the mechanics of accounting.

2.4 CHARACTER OF MEASUREMENTS

Different parts of the R&D process, along the duration of the product or service life cycle, need to be evaluated by different financial analyses. The issue is how good your technology is perceived to be by the customer. There is usually no problem in selling advanced activity in the face of competitive threats to the business. Applied research or discovery is hard to quantify and may need a specialized interaction with the financial department. Services that evolve with time, such as those based on computer software, can follow much of the same life cycle as do products, as in the following example.

Chi Data Services Bureau was a service industry with a strong software R&D department. Its new services were focused on user industry segments. Thus, its R&D programs included credit-checking data base administration for credit bureaus, electronic funds transfers packages for banking, and multiple airline reservation systems access packages for travel agents. As the computers on which these programs ran evolved, and as competition brought out new attractive versions of software, pressure came from the users of the services bureau to modernize each of the earlier software systems.

Each of these went through R&D and service life cycles, just as did products, and required similar considerations for service life extensions. Each software development project was evaluated based on its prospective life cycle using a cash-flow payback approach. Typically, extensions were at about at one-year intervals, while new minor projects had about three-year cycles. Approval targets were for payback in two-thirds of these cycle times. The company evolved profitably for several years but found its growth was limited by larger competitors such as Service Bureau Corporation. After reviewing its prospects, its corporate owners sold the company at a profit to a larger competitor.

The segments of the R&D life cycle are shown graphically in Figure 2.3.

2.4.1 Certainty and Urgency

However, by the time a product is in development, the cash outlays required are expected to be expressed in more traditional financial terms, such as NPV. Much of the choice of financial tools depends upon the precision and urgency of the tasks involved. Table 2.1 depicts the three levels of precision and urgency often found in the company, and the financial tools most clearly matching them.

Table 2.1
Urgency versus Metrics

How Precise?	Certainty	Risk	Uncertainty
How Soon?	Short term	Mid term	Long term
How Accounted?	Expense	Investment	Options for future development

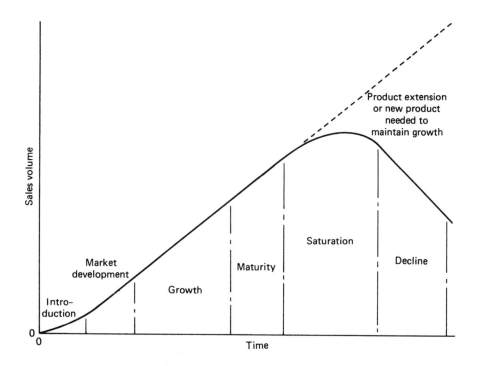

Figure 2.3   Product life cycle. (*Source:* [10, p. 61]. Reprinted with permission.)

2.4.2 Short-Term and Certain Projects

When the task is very certain, the timing is usually short term and expense methods of accounting, such as ABC, are appropriate. These are generally those tasks that interface with the downstream implementation chain or are otherwise frequent during the year.

To summarize briefly, adjust your project selection and evaluation technique based on the degrees of certainty and immediacy of the task.

2.4.3 Medium-Term and Risky Projects

The principal medium-term innovation task is product or service development. Risk is used as a measure where uncertainty that is not large with respect to the project estimate and is presumed to be approximately randomly and normally distributed around the estimate. Often this work is done in one year, but for benefits in subsequent years. Financial accounting standards require this effort to be expended for accounting purposes, with the narrow exception of software for sale. For decision purposes, however, this expenditure should be treated as the company would any other investment. In reality, at this point the R&D project is in competition for money with all other capital and market development requests in the company. Thus, financial selection methods, such as R&D return [4,5], NPV, and IRR are the most appropriate. One caution needs to be raised with NPV because it is an absolute amount, not a ratio to resources. Ranking by amount tends to favor large projects, while ranking as a ratio, such as IRR, allows proper prioritization of projects of varying sizes. Most often, NPV divided by project costs is used. In one company where skills were critical, the author has seen ranking of projects by NPV per engineer.

In the 1970s the general manager of the Tau Controls Company reasoned that the principal risk to the benefits side of the decision equation was the lack of certainty of product cost. He tended, therefore, to wait until the end of the feasibility study to begin hard questioning of business feasibility. At that point, he required a 25% adder to product costs in volume production as part of the business analysis. According to the sales-to-cost ratios and investment-to-sales ratios of Tau Controls, the general manager's requirement was the equivalent of a 15% premium on the pretax hurdle rate. When development had produced a working model that could be reviewed by the shop superintendent for reasonability of estimates of time and materials, the general manager lowered the required adder to 15%. Only when development had completed production drawings and these had been costed by accounting with the help of industrial engineering did he consider development had ended—a 5% premium was kept, however, to account for manufacturing risks. This conservatism left a number of potentially profitable projects not selected and lowered potential business growth. However, Tau Controls ran profitably for many years with these risk allowances as they certainly covered most of the project overruns [10, p. 110].

2.4.4 Uncertainty

Uncertainty denotes a lack of precision beyond the applicable range of statistical treatment. For this the author has used three standard deviations as a rough upper limit for treating risk, before moving to uncertainty. Uncertain projects tend to be longer in term such as applied research. As mentioned earlier, mathematically these may be treated by the methods of stock options as the equivalent of options for future product development [6]. The skepticism on option methods, however, has scarcely dissipated since the 1990 study. If the R&D manager's company's financial culture accepts option theory, and the manager is comfortable with it, go ahead and use it as one means of bridging the financial boundary. If not, a strategic presentation of a proposed project in terms of opportunities that might be lost and threats that may have to be faced may seem a better tactic than struggling with classic financial selection approaches that are meaningless in view of the uncertainty involved. Some crude improvisations may help span the financial boundary, such as in the following example.

One central laboratory research director, known to the author, some years ago used the sales-to-development ratio as a rough uncertainty screen [10, p. 21]. Estimating research at about 10% of R&D, which was in turn some 3% of sales, his screen was to accept only research projects that were aimed at new product sales over 300 times estimated research costs. His approach was able to communicate more clearly with the financially minded general managers than before. The technique was effective in evaluation since no good project ended up being rejected in the following three years. The rejected projects were mostly thought out again by their originators and either dropped with a better understanding of the reasons why or recast into better projects and resubmitted for evaluation. The parent company prospered and was finally acquired for a premium price by an overseas company in the same field.

2.4.5   Financial Frameworks and Empowered Organizations

Empowerment means giving the power of decision to those at the working level with the most knowledge of the task. This brings out problems with the financial boundary in both directions. First, while many at the managerial level have learned enough about dealing with their financial counterparts, it is usually a whole different story for those down at the team level who are technical specialists in their working tasks and have little knowledge about financial methods. This often justifies inclusion on the team of a finance person. The same problem occurs in empowered teams with managing interpersonal relations and conflict, where the recent literature suggests the solution is providing teams with psychologically trained mentors and facilitators. If the team has no person knowledgeable in handling the financial boundary, it may be necessary to have a pool of such people available as mentors.

In the opposite direction, few organizations are equipped to handle feeding teams with the financial and cost information they need for decision making. Cost accounting based on standard costs or ABC does not provide total project cost information easily. Yet, total project costs are needed by team leaders, just as they are by R&D managers. This is an old problem, addressed a decade ago by the author, where a solution was found through interaction with the controller to have project costs (or job costs in financial idiom) accumulated as a supplement to the regular financial accounting [10, Chap. 3]. What is new is that the division of the organization into crossfunctional empowered teams brings the necessary flow of financial and cost information to more lower level people. There is no easy answer, but the team leaders should not have to work it out alone with the financial and accounting departments.

The R&D managers have to step in to act as interpersonal facilitators for their team and negotiate free financial information flow down to the team level.

2.4.6 Integration of Project Selection and Evaluation

The contention of this book is that R&D managers need to be integrated with their financial counterparts along the entire innovation/financial boundary. This does not mean slavishly following the financial lead throughout. A view at Table 2.1 shows three broad areas from one end of the boundary to the other. At the certainty end of the boundary, whatever form of expense accounting the company adopts, the innovation manager should naturally follow. It already has been noted that along the vision (uncertainty) end of the boundary, strategic opportunities and threats govern more than finance, but even there it is important to honor the interface. Thus, the middle of Table 2.1 is the area where give-and-take with financial counterparts becomes most necessary. This is the natural scope for investment decision making along the lines of capital budgeting, even though the accounting standards of the two are very different. Both call for accounting by projects, not by activities nor cost centers. In practice, Table 2.1 is oversimplified, and this area is broken down into many more activities.

The *product life cycle* is the first of these, as shown in Figure 2.3 [10, p. 61]. Certainty increases with time along this cycle. Thus, tasks are more repetitive and more amenable to traditional management accounting or activity-based costing.

Omicron ElectroMechanical Corporation's product line had long product life cycles, a high degree of vertical integration, and good profitability. Nearly 30 years ago the company realized that the semiconductor revolution was going to change the present product line to an electronic one in time, and an appropriate R&D program was started. The R&D director, however, failed to perceive the shorter life cycle of electronic products, and so planned on continual vertical integration. By the time the first product was ready, it was later than competitors' and nearing obsolescence. His response was to request an increased R&D budget to meet the shorter life cycle, while maintaining the traditional approach of a complete product line as requested by marketing and vertical integration as requested by manufacturing, neither of which wanted to change. Several general managers have since followed each other after continued unprofitable years caused by excessive R&D-to-sales ratios. Finally, the company was sold to a competitor who had introduced their first electronic products ahead of Omicron and had learned to deal with change.

The *R&D time cycle* precedes the product life cycle, as shown in Figure 2.4 [10, p. 71]. At each phase of the R&D time cycle, cumulative project staff hours and costs increase. Exploration and pioneering are highly uncertain and, thus, difficult to justify financially. Beginning with feasibility studies, however, the project investment needs to be justified in investment terms. Near the end of the R&D time cycle, testing and commercialization for some products may become sufficiently routine for more traditional expense accounting techniques. For example, preparation of an instruction book could possibly be handled as a standard cost per page. What this chart outlines are the fine gradations that affect decision

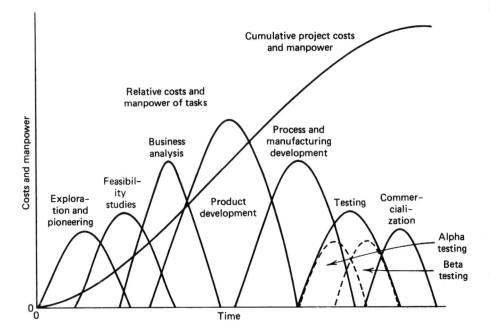

Figure 2.4 Distribution of the R&D time cycle. (*Source:* [10, p. 71]. Reprinted with permission.)

making and the need to establish costs on a project basis, even if expended for financial accounting.

Psi Radio Limited, a subsidiary of a multinational company, had a labor- and material-intensive product line. Its product development cycle was typically three years, with each year accounting for about 25, 50, and 25% of the total project cost, respectively. Its product sales life cycle of about five years gave each year, respectively, about 7, 27, 32, 27, and 7% of the cumulative net income for the five years [10, p. 22].

Psi Radio used the IRR yardstick for local project approval, based on the full five-year product life cycle. The parent company, however, used only the ratio of three years net income to projects' costs. One division manager produced the graph shown as Figure 2.5 as an aid in translation between these two methods of evaluation measurement. Figure 2.5 shows the IRR calculated from the start of R&D to the start of net income plotted against the ratio of five- (three-) year net income to total project costs. At a five-year net income equal to 2.25 times costs, the effect of going from a four to one-year delay would be to raise the IRR from 16 to 54%.

Speedy R&D may not improve financial results as demonstrated in the 1993 through 1995 surveys. All other things being equal, speedy R&D lowers costs

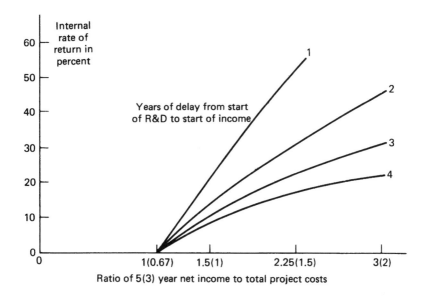

Figure 2.5 Internal rate of return versus project costs and delay. (*Source:* [10, p. 23]. Reprinted with permission.)

because of the time value of money, as may be seen from Figure 2.5. Shorter cycle time should thus raise the project return at a fixed benefit (net income) to project cost ratio, along a vertical line, as shown in the Psi Radio example above. However, the findings of the 1993 to 1995 studies reported upon in this book are more nearly represented by horizontal lines on this chart. This demonstrates that the benefit-to-cost ratio must decline with shorter cycle time for reasons described later in this book as the *acceleration trap*, after Von Braun [23].

Project selection should have a financial interface that matches whatever job cost accumulation method the company uses and, at the same time, have an investment decision-making financial tool that also fits the company's financial practices. Most often, this will be the tool used by the firm for capital investment approvals, such as NPV and IRR. These tools are all mathematically related to each other, so it matters less which is used than that there is one used for investment analysis [10, Chap. 5]. Following these rules allows for a natural flow into post-evaluation of projects.

Risk is the measure of the area between certainty and uncertainty where most product and service development projects fall [10, Chap. 6]. The use of the term "risk" implies that statistical measures may be used and that the coefficient of variation (standard deviation divided by the mean) may be used as a measure of risk. Electrical engineers will quickly recognize the analogy to the noise-to-signal ratio.

In practice, the distributions of outcomes of costs and times in a typical company are skewed or distributed with the adverse tail of the distribution longer than the favorable one.

Consider the experience of Upsilon Radio Company as an example. In 1952 Upsilon Radio Company introduced a common cost system for development and customer application engineering projects. The latter tended to have higher certainty than the former, so overall results were better than for the development sections alone. After running the costing system for a year to get section heads and managers fully familiar with it, a second year's results showed about 70% of the projects below estimate (the lowest 12% below) and about 30% above estimate (the worst 55% over). The mean was 4% over estimate, and the standard deviation 21%. Thus, the worst project was within three standard deviations, but the standard deviation was not a valid measure for projects below estimate [10, p. 105].

A second example supports the first. A series of projects were studied at a medium-sized manufacturing company overseas [24]. One abnormality in historic results was the reaction of estimators to an approval level above which all development project costs were explicitly controlled. For the controlled group, the median overrun in cost was 14% with a *standard deviation* (s.d.) of 28%. For projects below the approval limit, however, the mean overrun in cost was 93% (s.d. = 58%). Time and cost overruns were closely correlated ($r = 0.75$) [10, p. 130]. This is graphically represented (not to scale) in Figure 2.6 [10, p. 105].

Risks in innovation are higher than in the typical capital investment and thus may be expected to require higher estimated profitability at project selection time. The R&D manager should not fight this risk premium at the start of a new major project but rather aim high in anticipated project results. As the project nears completion, however, it nears certainty also, and not only should no risk premium be used, but decisions to go on should weigh the expected benefits against the cost remaining to complete. This will favor finishing satisfactory older projects over launching new ones in order to finally obtain the results of the R&D effort.

Financial project control follows naturally from the same pattern used for capital projects. Project development costs must be tracked against estimates. Since most of the costs are in R&D staff hours, this means tracking hours as well. The R&D oversees record keeping of hours worked, and it is a simple clerical task to accumulate them before sending them on to accounting. This can give the manager in most firms time results against which to control projects several weeks before the project costs rise up from the accounting department.

The R&D manager is also responsible for contributing to the project's benefits control. In a manufacturing company, this means control of product cost estimates and results. A similar responsibility exists for service development projects—for example, the needed software should not prompt the purchase of extra computing power or memory. To the extent that marketing is part of the R&D manager's team, the anticipated sales must result. Often this is tied to the timeli-

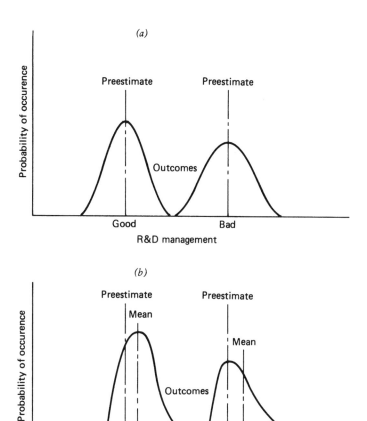

Figure 2.6. Probability distribution of outcomes: (a) idealized case and (b) realistic case. (*Source:* [10, p. 105]. Reprinted with permission.)

ness of the R&D effort, emphasizing that metrics must not only be financial metrics.

Financial post-evaluation, some time after project completion, comes logically from having had the financial boundary spanned from start to finish. How much post-evaluation should be done? Here again is an investment decision that requires interaction by the R&D and financial managers. Since resources are usually finite, post-evaluation detracts from additional innovation. Is the benefit to be gained from post-evaluation in greater understanding worth the cost not only in staff hours but also in opportunity cost of innovative work not done? In this author's experience, the principal benefit of post-evaluation is in its feedback to the original estimator to help refine future estimates. Thus, brief and to-the-point post-evaluations produce better results from feedback than do elaborate comprehensive investigations that, while intellectually stimulating to financial managers, do little to provide continuous improvement of estimating.

The lessons learned on integrating project selection and evaluation are as follows.

- Make selection decisions on an investment basis like capital budgeting;
- Negotiate accounting by projects, not departments;
- Strive to keep accounting as expenses to the certainty end of the time spectrum;
- Use speedy R&D for strategic reasons rather than as a profit enhancing technique;
- Use selection criteria that match dominant usage for capital budgeting in the company;
- Accept a risk premium at the start of a major project, but ensure it declines as certainty increases;
- Accept both financial control during the project and financial post evaluation, while keeping the latter to a level that does not impact more profitable development.

2.4.7   Optimum Budgets and Shareholder Value

The sum of approved R&D projects becomes the R&D budget. Thus, the issues along the financial boundary center on how large of a budget gets approved. Four views need to be mentioned, namely, the traditional R&D expense budget, the economic budget, the optimum budget for shareholder value, and the rationed budget [10].

The traditional R&D expense budget is the sum of all salary costs, associated labor benefits (fringes), departmental overheads, and allocations from central cost centers [10, Chap. 3]. This budget needs to be drawn according to accounting rules, which is necessary for financial accounting requirements and is the basis for allocating costs to projects by the process of determining loaded (inclusive) labor rates. So that these rates are realistic, managers need to maximize the direct application of costs by staff while minimizing the indirect costs of supervision and other unapplied time. The problem with R&D being treated as an expense rather than as an investment is that a strong culture exists in many companies to minimize expenses to aid current profit. The effect of this tactic is to mortgage future growth.

Economics provides one answer, based on the argument that there are diminishing returns to increased activity [10, Chap. 2], because companies do first what has the highest return, and then the next highest, and so on. Costs increase with activity, but returns do not, so the firm reaches a point where additional returns match the cost of additional activity. It is at this point that the budget should be set for economic reasons, as shown in Figure 2.7 [10, p. 161].

This figure is ranked from the highest return project downward. For most firms this point is where the return of the lowest accepted project matches the marginal cost of capital, which must be obtained from the financial side of the boundary. This is an approach that meets the need to fund innovative projects on an investment basis, parallels the usual company basis for capital investment projects, but falls short of matching shareholder value expectations or dealing with lower available funds than shown in Figure 2.7.

An *optimum budget* may be found in two ways [10, Chap. 8, p. 23]. First, following the economic argument, it may be optimized around a level that maximizes the firm's earnings. Since the general manager, to whom the R&D manager reports, is usually rated on earnings performance, this may be to him or her a popular approach since not spending anything on R&D is optimum if the

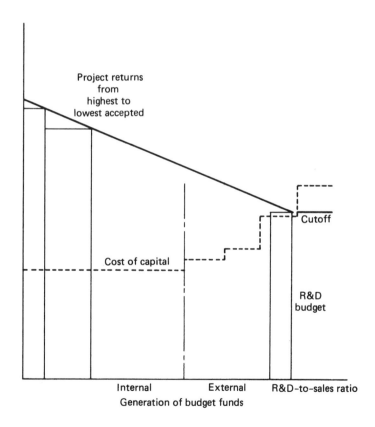

Figure 2.7 Project selection versus marginal cost of capital. (*Source:* [10, p. 161]. Reprinted with permission.)

company is selling products right now. However, too much of a focus on current earnings may miss the investment nature of innovation, which provides for future sales of the firm. The maximum return on sales is quite flat and holds over a broad range of R&D-to-sales ratios. Thus, the R&D manager can claim a wide discretion in selecting an R&D budget to propose to management.

However, the price-to-earnings ratio of the shares of companies in an industry rises with an increase in the ratio of R&D to sales [9]. Thus, optimizing for maximum share price or shareholder value yields a higher ratio of R&D to sales than optimizing for earnings. The rationale for this difference is more complicated to calculate mathematically or to explain than that for maximizing earnings [10, Chap. 8]. Thus, it may best be shown graphically, as in Figure 2.8 [10, p. 152].

This optimum also has a broad flat area allowing discretion in setting budget requests. What is important to note is that too much spending on innovation projects can be as bad for shareholder value as too little, as we now illustrate.

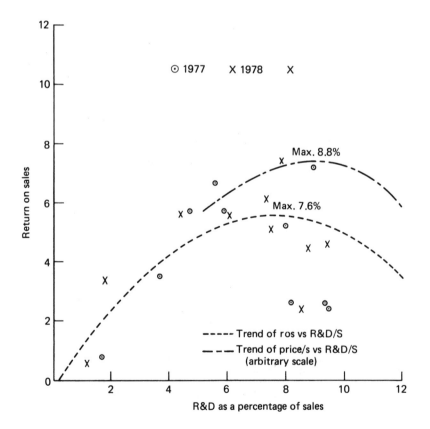

Figure 2.8 Return on sales versus R&D/sales for semiconductor industry (1977/1978). (*Source:* [10, p. 152; 25]. Reprinted with permission.)

The Pi Chart Instrument Division attempted to use the stock-price answer to establish the level of R&D spending [9]. It was dissatisfied with the results, but found the approach was modifiable to earnings optimization. Their R&D director realized that *return on sales* (ROS) treated in a linear regression with R&D spending for his industry would give him an intercept (ROS at zero R&D) and a slope defining two terms of a Taylor series approximation. A third term could be derived from internal accounting data, showing that an expenditure of 10% of sales for R&D would wipe out pretax earnings. An optimum was then calculated for 1977 from applying the calculus on a quadratic equation, giving an R&D-to-sales target of 3.5% of sales. After consultation with the division manager R&D was held to 4% of sales in 1978. A recalculation for 1978 gave a new optimum of 3.3% of sales, and a lower target was established for 1979 of 3.8% R&D-to-sales. The division continued using this approach profitably for several years, until a major recession caused emergency restructuring when profits became deficits.

Budget rationing occurs whenever the budget level is fixed by higher management at a lower level than shown in Figure 2.7 [10, Chap. 9]. This may be because external money is difficult or expensive to obtain or because management has internal reasons for keeping its budget down. In any case, some projects at the margin must be postponed or not undertaken. Good projects sell themselves and almost always get approved. Marginal projects are where budget negotiations become tense between project advocates and financial managers. The R&D manager will need a strategy for handling budget negotiations. Rather than just cut the lowest return projects, it may be preferable to assess which can be postponed and which (if cut) will be totally scrapped because the window of opportunity will close if they are not begun in the next budget period. In any case, the R&D manager must work to keep those projects in the rationed period that best maximizes the sum of the NPV of the project portfolio and that of the option value of uncertain projects so valued.

2.5 FINANCIAL FRAMEWORKS LESSONS LEARNED

The R&D manager must span the financial boundary and manage within the firm's financial culture. This means accepting accounting discipline on the most certain portion of the project portfolio and investment discipline analogous to capital budgeting on the risky middle of the group of proposed projects. Then, the R&D manager is in a better position to use nonfinancial arguments to the uncertain longer range projects. The portfolio budget should be optimized with the highest possible NPV so as to maximize shareholder value and stock price.

The message from looking at the financial scene may be summarized by recapitulating the sections of this chapter as follows.

- Financial frameworks are not enough to satisfy R&D managers, nor the more astute financial managers and analysts.

- A broader selection of nonfinancial measurements is required to adequately judge innovation effectiveness.
- To rate projects prospectively, evaluate them individually, not by overall economic portfolio impact.
- Improve R&D productivity principally on the R&D department's own efforts.
- Improve R&D yield in collaboration with other departments in the innovation chain.
- Use the prevailing financial metric in your firm (for example, NPV and IRR) if this communicates better than R&D return.
- Use option theory when a high degree of uncertainty exists but enough evidence can be found that it is worth staying in the competition long enough to find out if your firm is going to be a significant and profitable competitor.
- Move to traditional financial project selection when the uncertainty can be resolved and before shifting to higher levels of R&D investment.
- Look at post-evaluation as at any other R&D investment, and do not continue it beyond the point where its return drops below that of other opportunities.
- Reach across the financial boundary and comprehend the investment focus of financial managers.
- Make selection decisions on an investment basis like capital budgeting.
- Learn what top management has as expectations for returns versus risks.
- Put forth requests for project approvals in financially justified form, using the selection method most acceptable to those executives across the financial boundary.
- Understand what type of financial culture you face and adapt to it as best you can without being overwhelmed by the mechanics of accounting.
- Adjust your project selection and evaluation technique based on the degrees of certainty and immediacy of the task.
- Act as interpersonal facilitator for R&D team leaders.
- Negotiate free financial information flow down to the team level.
- Negotiate accounting by projects, not departments.
- Strive to keep accounting as expenses to the certainty end of the time spectrum.
- Use speedy R&D for strategic reasons rather than as a profit-enhancing technique.
- Use selection criteria that match dominant usage for capital budgeting in the company.
- Accept a risk premium at the start of a major project, but ensure it declines as certainty increases.
- Accept both financial control during the project and financial post evaluation, while keeping the latter to a level that does not impact more profitable development.

References

[1] Bean, A. S., "CIMS Productivity Studies," Bethlehem, PA: Lehigh University, 1991. Published subsequently in *Innovation Management Research Progress and Prospects: A Review of the CIMS Reunion Meeting, June 9–11, 1992*, Bethlehem, PA: Lehigh University Center for Innovation Management Studies, 1994, pp. 39–44, and in "Why Some R&D Organizations Are More Productive Than Others," *Research Technology Management*, Vol. 38(1), Jan.–Feb. 1995, pp. 25–29.

[2] Duerr, M. G., *The Commercial Development of New Products*, Report No. 890, New York: The Conference Board, 1986.

[3] Ellis, L. W., "What We've Learned: Managing Financial Resources," *Research Technology Management*, Vol. 31(4), July–Aug. 1988, pp. 21–38.

[4] Foster, R. N., "Improving the Return on R&D," *McKinsey Quarterly*, Spring 1981.

[5] Foster, R. N., L. H. Linden, R. I. Whitely, and A. Kantrow, *Improving the Return on Research and Development*, New York: Industrial Research Institute, 1984; summarized with the same title in *Research Management*, Vol. 28(1), 1985, pp. 12–17, and Vol. 28(2), 1985, pp. 13–22.

[6] Mitchell, G. R., and W. F. Hamilton, "Managing R & D as a Strategic Option," *Research Technology Management*, Vol. 31(3), May–June 1988, pp. 15–22.

[7] Industrial Research Institute, *Minutes of ROR and SIS Meetings*, and tapes of the SIS meeting, Phoenix: Tape Productions, 1990.

[8] Ellis, L. W., "Financial Frameworks for Research and Development," West Haven, CT: University of New Haven, Faculty Working Paper, May 1991.

[9] Gilman, J. J., "Stock Price and Optimum Research Spending," *Research Management*, Vol. XXI(1), Jan.–Feb. 1978, pp. 34–36.

[10] Ellis, L. W., *The Financial Side of Industrial Research Management*, New York: Wiley, 1984.

[11] Ellis, L. W., "Viewing R and D Projects Financially," *Research Management*, Vol. XXVII(2), Mar.–Apr. 1984, pp. 29–34.

[12] Ellis, L. W., "Viewing R and D Budgets Financially," *Research Management*, Vol. XXVII(3), May–June 1984, pp. 35–40.

[13] Ellis, L. W., "Some Factors Correlated with Fluctuations in Research and Development Spending," *IEEE Trans. on Engineering Management*, Vol. 36(2), May 1989, pp. 146–148.

[14] Ellis, L. W., "The Effect of an Investment Tax Credit on R&D Spending," *IEEE Trans. on Engineering Management*, Vol. 41(2), May 1994, pp. 208–210.

[15] Ellis, L. W., and C. C. Curtis, "Speedy R&D: How Beneficial?," *Research Technology Management*, Vol. 38(4), July–Aug. 1995, pp. 42–51.

[16] Ellis, L. W., and R. G. McDonald, "Reforming Management Accounting to Support Today's Technology," *Research Technology Management*, Vol. 33(2), Mar.–Apr. 1990, pp. 30–34.

[17] Johnson, H. T., and R. S. Kaplan, "The Rise and Fall of Management Accounting," *Management Accounting*, Jan. 1987; reprinted in *IEEE Engineering Management Review*, Vol. 15(3), Autumn 1987, pp. 36–44.

[18] Kaplan, R. S., "One Cost System Isn't Enough," *Harvard Business Review*, Vol. 66(1), Jan.–Feb. 1988, pp. 61–66.

[19] Kaplan, R. S., and D. P. Norton, "Putting the Balanced Scorecard to Work," *Harvard Business Review*, Vol. 71(5), Sept.–Oct. 1993, pp. 134–147.

[20] Hronec, S., *Vital Signs*, New York: AMACOM, 1993.

[21]   Curtis, C. C., and L. W. Ellis, "A Balanced Scorecard for New Product Development," *J. Cost Management*, Spring 1997, forthcoming.

[22]   Curtis, C. C., "Nonfinancial Performance Measures in New Product Development," *J. Cost Management*, Vol. 8(3), Fall 1994, pp. 18–26.

[23]   Von Braun, C.-F., "The Acceleration Trap," *Sloan Management Review*, Vol. 32 (1), 1990, pp. 49–58.

[24]   Brockhoff, K., "A Heuristic Procedure for Project Inspection to Curb Overruns," *IEEE Trans. on Engineering Management*, Vol. EM-24(4), Sept. 1982, pp. 122–128.

[25]   Ellis, L. W., "Optimum Research Spending," *Research Management*, Vol. 23(3), May–June 1980, pp. 22–24.

Chapter 3

Evaluating the External Commercial and Technical Tasks of R&D

Besides spanning the boundary to the financial world, as covered in the previous chapter, the R&D manager must span the boundaries from inside the company to other parts of the outside world. These boundaries are, in practical terms, very different from each other. The first is the boundary to the business and customer environment, which is essentially commercial in nature; and the other is to the sources of technical knowledge. Both must be spanned equally effectively if the company is to prosper. Both must also be evaluated in terms of the external commercial and technical value produced by R&D's actions and the value to R&D of the input of knowledge from these sectors.

This assertion is based more on the author's experience than on the slim record to date of solid research. In the limited 1992 study, two views across this boundary received high ratings for importance, namely, knowledge of customer needs and generation of new ideas. Knowledge of customer needs was most strongly correlated positively with the use of crossfunctional teams and had low positive and negative correlations with a number of other factors. Generation of new ideas had a strong negative correlation with output from R&D and had a minor positive correlation with new products/services as a percent of sales. The high ratings of importance, however, indicate that there is a management task to be done, and further research is needed to quantify this relationship. In the absence of this extended research base, let us look first at the commercial boundary. The effectiveness of R&D is widely evaluated by market share.

3.1 MARKET SHARE

Market share is a traditional outcome measurement in the marketing departments of companies. A foundation of strategic management theory is that increased market share leads to lower costs and, thus, higher profits [1]. In Chapter 11, it is also noted that some authors report the use of market share as an indirect measure of customer satisfaction [2]. This has been well confirmed by the 1994 and 1995 studies summarized in the following section, which also addresses how market share is associated with other measurements for some typical groups of industries.

3.1.1 Firms Measuring Market Share

The 1994 and 1995 studies found 57 and 63% of responses, respectively, measured the extent of customer satisfaction using market share as a metric. For those companies measuring market share in 1994, their responses correlated positively with a number of other factors, such as customer satisfaction with cost effectiveness, use of milestones, and longer product life.

   The cause or effect of these actions was not determined in those surveys. Based on occurrence-time relationships, it may be logically argued that customer satisfaction with cost and the use of milestones are precursor or leading indicators of whether market share will be used to measure customer satisfaction. Most likely, however, all these correlations are simply indirect measures of a disciplined strategic management of innovation.

3.1.2 How Market Share Affects Results

Market share's positive affect on financial results has a background in economic theory and strategic management literature [1]. Research surveys, however, have shown rather mixed results that vary by industry. Strategic management precepts argue that increased market share leads to higher profits, all other things being equal [1]. However, since all other things are not equal, in 1993, Ford had higher earnings than General Motors on lower sales volume. The theorists argue that, on an average basis in most industries, there are economies of scale. Thus, higher market share equates to higher sales and, consequently, lower costs and higher profits.

   Telecommunications was one of two industries with sufficient responses to the 1994 survey for such a detailed analysis. This is a competitive industry with high technology and more deliberate product development times than many other industries. It also fits economic theory well, as greater market share was correlated positively with higher earnings before interest and taxes as a percent of sales in addition to longer product life, major new products projects as a share of the R&D budget, and patents per million dollars of sales.

   Computer hardware was the second industry with enough responses for analysis. The computer hardware industry is a competitive, high-technology industry used to competing on time and performance rather than cost. In this industry, however, no relationship was found between market share and profitability. The other factors correlated with market share were increased interface with marketing, shorter time through R&D, decreasing the share of the R&D budget devoted to major new projects, and fewer patents per million dollars of sales volume. As a less deliberate industry than telecommunications, the factors cited reflect the timeliness strategic characteristic of the computer hardware industry. The remaining industries in this survey had too few responses to obtain a reasonable base for analysis.

3.1.3 Market Share Lessons Learned

The lessons learned from market share analysis are as follows.

- The single-minded pursuit of increased market share is not the panacea presented by strategic management theory because all other things are definitely not equal in different types of industries.
- Market share is best measured by key accounts or served markets as a percent share measurement by the input money value of tangible benefits resulting from all other metrics.
- Customer satisfaction with cost effectiveness, use of milestones, and longer product life are all positively associated with market share.
- Many factors other than market share, however, are part of the interface of R&D with inputs from the commercial and technical worlds, which managers must also evaluate.

3.2 EVALUATING EXTERNAL SOURCES OF KNOWLEDGE

External commercial and technical sources of knowledge are the main inputs to R&D, just as market share is a principal outcome. They are, however, far less precise to evaluate than counting up market share. Thus, they will be expanded upon in separate subsequent sections.

By what yardstick should acquiring external knowledge be judged? The thought process is a type of benefit-to-cost analysis. While the costs of acquisition of knowledge are real in dollars, the benefits are not now so quantifiable in monetary terms. For example, no one so far has put a benefit price on customer satisfaction, but it is a real benefit as seen by many in their nonfinancial evaluations.

Elf Aquitaine, a major public company in France, for 20 years has tried to benefit to the fullest extent from what is called in France "public research" [3]. This is research performed in the French universities or government-funded research centers. They believe in the need for access to this kind of science for several reasons. Their processes are becoming increasingly more complex, and product specifications more stringent. Often, new technologies are born in the academic world before moving to industry for exploitation. Educational institutions and government laboratories are training grounds for industry R&D staff. And, they decided they could not afford the considerable long-term investment for their own basic research facilities. "The successes achieved (notwithstanding certain failures) demonstrate that such a system requires time and patience, and the most effective technology transfer operations are often those that involve a transfer of personnel" [3, p. 24].

The themes of this brief example are many and include the following:

- There are time and cost advantages of seeking knowledge outside the firm.
- New knowledge, not only new science, to a large extent is now only available as a consequence of government funding (for example, U.S. NSF).
- Effectiveness involves bringing into the firm those who have expertise in the new science.

3.3   EVALUATING THE BUILD-UP OF COMMERCIAL KNOWLEDGE

Four tasks characterize the methodology of building up knowledge across the commercial boundary. First, a vision is needed of what the firm is trying to do. The external environment for business encompasses the three remaining tasks: the environment common to all businesses; the particular characteristics of the industry in which the firm participates; and the competitive situation in that industry. Knowledge of each of these four tasks underlies establishing a clear picture of customer needs and opportune ideas for products and services.

3.3.1   Start with Vision

How does one get vision? The methodology outlined below will help systematize the search, but one must have the ability to see what has not yet been seen by others. The following example will illustrate this need.

Christine was the daughter of the owner of a family construction firm. As a teenager, she began to work part time in the company and ended up doing their annual income taxes. After marriage and seeing her two children go off to school, she took what she had learned about the construction business, its costs, and its needs and saw an unmet opportunity. With a partner, she started a small company providing a service that many constructors wished they had available: her company provided the guards needed for road construction projects. The opportunity was there for all to see—only she had the vision to see it. Her company ended up as one of the fastest growing small companies in the country. The financial benefits came later once the customer benefits had been established.

This analysis is usually called *SWOT*—that is, *s*trengths, *w*eaknesses, *o*pportunities, *t*hreats [1]. Vision starts with opportunities, with the question "What might we do?" This is an ideal point for brainstorming sessions. There are many choices, so this question narrows down the list only slightly. Next, the question becomes, "What could we do?" Threats limit choices, as do internal strengths and weaknesses. Some needed strengths may be able to be obtained externally. Some weaknesses may be able to be offset externally. At this point, the list becomes much shorter.

"What would we do?" The values of those deciding come into play. If one is ethical, criminal acts do not stay on the list, and so on. Finally, a choice has to be made: "What should we do?" If several options are still on the list after might, could, and would, some selection has to be made.

Visionary people go through this cycle instinctively, and their success can only be evaluated retrospectively by such indicators as market share. For the rest of us, the discipline of going methodically through this cycle is necessary. To convert this selection into a detailed focused plan, the external environment needs to be analyzed.

3.3.2 Environmental Assessment

Opportunities and threats exist in the external environment. Since industries and competitors may be assessed separately, the first analysis should be of the part of the external environment that is common to all industries and competitors. This environment is economic, demographic, political, and social (including labor relations). Each of these sectors is subject to quantitative (economic and demographics) or qualitative indices (political and social). They are also always changing. To establish a base line, the existing environment should be surveyed first.

What present factors now control the environment? Based upon experience with earlier brainstorming sessions, a group tends to run out of good ideas after about 20 suggestions. These suggestions generally depend upon the character of the chosen business. Some businesses are more prone to the fluctuations in the economic business cycle. Others depend on political acts, such as the degree of government support for the information superhighway. It is important to probe deeply into the nature of this external environment to elicit as many ideas as possible from differing viewpoints. The next task is to decide which of these factors are the most important.

For example, a university needs to base its undergraduate enrollment planning on the number of 17- to 21-year olds available for forming a student body. This is a metric that can be evaluated quantitatively. The number of babies born that long ago (1976) was the lowest in the prior twenty years, resulting in a minimum in the present (1996) undergraduate student population. But the birth rate then turned up to a new peak to date in 1992, so kindergartens and lower elementary school grades are now facing a population explosion. This will happen again to universities in the early part of the next century, with a new student population peak demographically forecast at about 2012.

Again based on experience, about six of these factors will be seen to be most important after a vote of the brainstorming group.

Which future factors will dominate in the next few years? Five years is a good number for most businesses, but some are shorter term, such as less than a year for toys, and some are longer term, such as many years for mining. Again, the brainstormers will cite many of the present factors, but some new factors such as shifts in health care financing and upcoming elections will appear. Twenty or so ideas is a good base from which to develop another six most important factors.

What has changed? What impact will these changes have? A university cannot change the number of babies born two decades ago. However, it can note that the birth rate has been rising for a decade, now causing municipalities to build new high schools. Thus, it can plan for the time when these teenagers reach college age. By the time that a brainstorming group has gone through this analysis of the environment, a clear list of opportunities and threats will have emerged, and most will be in a form that can be quantitatively or qualitatively evaluated.

3.3.3 Industry Scenarios

Facing the environmental pressures that affect all industries and competitors, industries will have their own characteristics requiring analysis [4, Chap. 7]. Often, these will need to be evaluated by multiple scenarios, each with its probability of occurring. Each scenario will be based on some major, but as-yet-to-take-place, event. Some speculations include Congress passing a bill that requires employer-mandated health insurance or individuals to purchase health insurance or Congress failing to pass a bill at all. Each scenario of those most likely to happen should have a quantitative probability assigned to it. For each scenario, the question needs to be asked "which changes will be seen in the factors driving the industry?"

Each company then has to select a strategy for dealing with this uncertainty. Should all possibilities be hedged? Should the firm bet on the most probable scenario? Or should the company chose a risk-averse strategy that minimizes the unfavorable consequences of any choice? Company values strongly affect the selected strategy.

3.3.4 Competitive Assessment

The third set of constraints is that of competitors. Perhaps the best method of analysis is to create a matrix of competitors versus key characteristics. Which competitors should be chosen? The three to six competitors who have 60 to 80% of the market is a usual selection. If the industry is more fragmented than that, some logical grouping may be required—for example, all importers as a group might fit in some industries.

The other axis consists of about ten of the principal characteristics of companies that affect competition in the chosen market, best chosen because they can be evaluated in a quantitative manner. Usually this includes the four "p's" of marketing: product, price, place (market outlet), and promotion. Up to six other characteristics may include costs, finance, technology, location of plants, or any others that describe the industry's competitive conditions. For each characteristic, your firm's rating as a competitor should be rated against each other competitor, or group of competitors. The rating should be quantitative, if possible, such as 15% higher in price.

The prepared mind will translate the above analyses into a knowledge of customer needs. From this list of needs, good ideas will be generated readily for useful and economic service or product offerings, which take proper account of the environmental and competitive threats, and the strengths and weaknesses of your firm as a competitor. If it is difficult to generate such a list, help may be needed in the form of hiring new people or consultants. For most companies with which the author is familiar, however, the list of prospects usually well exceeds the available funding. It does not take a large or costly organization to run such an analysis—a handful of the right people is usually sufficient [5,6].

The flow of commercial knowledge is perceived as imperfect by many in R&D and marketing, as illustrated by the following example. A recent study of the R&D marketing interface was conducted on Zytek (a pseudonym) [7]. Engineering complaints about information received from marketing included: customers do not know what they want; marketing does not have the needed expertise; marketing's time horizon is too short; and we do not have time to wait. Marketing's replies included: engineers lack perspective; engineers do not appreciate prior customers investments; engineers do not appreciate the diverse market segments we represent; and marketing's role is to refine technically driven ideas.

This study provided only insights, not solutions. In Chapter 5, some solutions will be offered for dealing with the R&D/marketing interface.

Commercial knowledge needs to be built up using the following steps.

- Establish a vision for what the firm might, could, would, should do;
- Assess the external environment common to all competitors;
- Assess the probable swings in your own industry;
- Assess your competitors' SWOT;
- Assess the imperfections in the R&D/marketing interface.

3.4 BUILD-UP OF TECHNOLOGICAL KNOWLEDGE

The R&D manager is a custodian for the company of the gateway to new knowledge across the company's external boundary. It is not necessary for this knowledge to be technical in nature, as the initial example in this chapter made apparent. However, for a large fraction of companies, the knowledge needed for competitive advantage will be found in science and technology. Building up the technological knowledge base thus becomes an important boundary-spanning task [8]. The choices are be self-sufficient and to do it yourself or to multiply your effort with outside sources. If the latter is your choice, the sources need to be identified, quantitatively evaluated, and managed in accordance with that evaluation. Again, the form of evaluation is of the benefit-to-cost nature, recognizing that some prospective benefits cannot be quantified in money terms as are costs. Another reach across the boundary is, of course, protection of intellectual property rights—which is treated as an output from R&D in Chapter 5.

3.4.1 Technological Self-Sufficiency

The classical model of the innovative firm of the past was Thomas Edison at Menlo Park, whose example was followed by a number of early industrial technical laboratories where innovation depended entirely on internal resources. This lead to the acronym NIH—*not invented here*—as a way of saying that imports from across the external boundary were not wanted. Even with technological self-sufficiency, access to outside sources is important as a self-calibration. Consider the following example.

Hoechst Celanese has accessed the skills of others through a Scientific Advisory Board [9]. Their rationales are many: independent overview; prestige; advise on the strength of the science and technology base; add vision; review science needs; expose new thinking; and a number of other reasons.

The facts of life are now that, for all but a few firms, NIH is too costly these days. In addition, the entrepreneurial spirit has made the sources of innovation abound in small firms and in your own company's suppliers. Government spending has created a large base of technical knowledge in government laboratories, which is available to be tapped by industrial firms. The flow of advanced research funds from government is now largely to universities rather than to industrial laboratories. The growing base of scientific and technical knowledge outside the firm's own country is also there to be accessed. Evaluating whether to reach across this external boundary to technology is now central to the R&D manager's task.

3.4.2 Managing Alliances With Others

Alliances with others may take many forms. These range from simple one-on-one relationships, usually in contractual form, to multiple-company consortia focused on a common goal. Some of these are discussed in more detail below.

The boundary-spanning task begins with a fundamental commitment to multiply your company's own technical effort by some substantial factor using these external resources. There has not been much written in a scientific manner about how to manage to do this. However, there are quite a few articles and conference papers are descriptive in nature about how companies have managed alliances with partners. These all seem to point to two common principles: trust and agreed evaluation measurements.

Mutual trust between partners in alliances of all forms seems to be essential for multiplication of technical effort [10]. As one executive put it " . . . the relationship we have with our suppliers is. . . 'virtual enterprise'—it really is as if we are becoming one big, seamless value-added chain" [11]. This is diametrically opposed to the adversarial relationship that most purchasing departments have traditionally adopted with vendors of all sorts. Until and unless this shift is made to being on the same team, effort-enhancing alliances will not work.

Building trust is a difficult task [10]. It begins with encouraging friendships between key executives involved in setting up the alliance. In most countries overseas, executives stay for long periods with their company and expect the same of U.S. companies, which often is not the case. Communication between partners must be open and comprehensive as to measurable goals for the venture. Disagreements must be resolved equitably, surprises avoided, and contractual disputes worked out amiably. The people in the trenches must work in each others' facilities and not try to work the alliance just by telecommunications.

Partners bring differing evaluation metrics to any alliance. Each partner has to take back information to its management in a form that will make the alliance appear to be an extension of its own internal effort. Reconciling these evaluation metrics can be difficult in a one-on-one partnership but may end up being a major stumbling block in multicompany consortia. Resolving the factors of trust and evaluation seems to be basic to successful external boundary spanning in the search for new technical knowledge. The burden falls on the alliance management to create an evaluation system using all the metrics of all participants at the same time. If not, it must be prepared to and successfully defend a lesser set of evaluation metrics to the managements of the companies whose pet metrics are not to be used in the alliance. Of necessity, the least common denominator settles on financial metrics and those of timeliness of R&D's actions.

3.4.3 Sources of Scientific and Technical Knowledge

The potential sources of multiplying knowledge are many. Most firms, however, find there are just five most valuable places to search. Suppliers have already been mentioned. Universities in the United States are recipients of most government research grant funds and thus are the fountains of new science. Government laboratories have their areas of expertise, such as material science and massive computation facilities, which may be what an individual firm lacks. Joint ventures have been used for years domestically and are currently a leading method of tapping into research and development conducted overseas. Research consortia of many companies are the newest of the potential sources, following recent favorable U.S. government rulings on antitrust issues and the growth of similar intergovernmental-sponsored groups in Europe. Each source has its particular advantages for partnering, and each also has its own disadvantages and difficulties of evaluation. Consider the following illustration.

Two executives from the BOC Group, PLC (Public Limited Company), in association with the IRI, studied how companies benefited from external sources of technology [12]. They found that many sources can be tapped successfully, external sourcing activities must complement the strengths and weaknesses of internal R&D efforts, the success of external sourcing depends on early buy-ins from all key individuals, and successful internalization requires teamwork and communication. Failures were due to lack of strategic clarity, fluctuating commitment, short-term emphasis, weak commercial pull, people and management problems, internal resistance, and lack of the above success factors.

Suppliers have many advantages as partners. They have the industrial mentality and thus fit well with your company's values. Most use evaluation metrics similar to your own firm's metrics. Many have their own substantial research teams, such as Goodyear, a major tire manufacturer, and one of auto manufacturer Chrysler's new product team members [11,13]. Chrysler's COO puts it as follows.

> Each of these teams is made up of specialists from all the old functions, including our key suppliers. Indeed, our suppliers are critical to us, both because they provide us with no less than 70% of our parts and because they also supply us, more and more, with a whole lot of R&D. They feel safe about doing that because of the way we treat them [11].

One of the results of this strategy, coupled with decreasing product introduction cycles, is that Chrysler now seems to have the lowest combined total of innovation plus production costs of any of the U.S. automobile or truck manufacturers. Perhaps the only disadvantage of suppliers is that they have a mind of their own, which forces the procuring firm to adapt rather than dictate the terms of the relationship and the evaluation metrics to be used.

Universities, as a result of many years of government funding, are now the home of the leading edge of science in the United States. Thus, they are the logical place to obtain new technical knowledge. This may be obtained through contracts for consulting, licensing of their technology, or by applied research contracts. Some universities have specialized facilities that may be used to supplement those in-house. Finally, if you do not have close relations with universities, you will not have access to their best students when they graduate.

Barriers to using universities are many. The ownership of intellectual property rights needs to be resolved. "Publish or perish" is a university need that may run counter to company interests of keeping its technology from other competitors. Also in the security area is the need of the researchers to know about elements of the company's business strategy, which some firms may be reluctant to cede. Responsiveness, particularly short time to complete, is another issue. Companies need to have results at low investment costs due to the difficulties of capital approval. The termination procedure for the agreed program must be in place and understood, both because universities need lead times to rearrange their activities and because many research assistants graduate and want to move on to new positions, thus prejudicing the project's finish. Despite these disadvantages, universities are best used for basic knowledge, specialized facilities, and precompetitive research. But do not expect that it will be simple to evaluate the outcomes of such a relationship.

Companies are moving from NIH to AIA (*anything-invented-anywhere*) [14]. Effective knowledge transfers for university/industry collaborative research requires an effective company agent to support the program, distinct linkages used by this agent, and key indicators for the impact of these transfers. Measures of success need a mesh between business metrics (break-even, profit, numbers of licenses) and academic metrics (publications, research dollars).

Government laboratories are also advantageously used for specialized facilities, unique knowledge such as material science, ability to conduct massive computation, talented manpower, and product development skills. It is also worth getting to know the people who may in the future have the power to regulate your activities. The disadvantages are several. Government laboratories tend to lag behind universities in resolving intellectual property rights. Freedom of information laws limit their security. They are often suspicious of industry and shift with the prevailing political winds in the legislatures. Access to seed money is not readily available to explore new ideas. And due to the downsizing that accompanies the current "reinventing government," they often have plenty of internal turmoil. Evaluating these relationships is often more difficult than those with universities.

A recent study of industry interaction with government laboratories found ten ways of interacting: contract research, cooperative research, workshop seminars, licensing, sponsored research, technical consultation, employee exchange, use of laboratory facilities, individual lab visits, and information dissemination [15].

Joint ventures and other forms of partnering with single companies (other than suppliers) form another means of multiplying effort. This category ranges from simple licensing to jointly owned separate companies. Such alliances have the advantage that both companies have an industrial mind set that facilitates cooperation and common threads of evaluation. Partnering may be between firms with different specialties in the same markets, such as technology and distribution, respectively; or they may be with noncompeting or smaller firms in other fields where both partners have their own unique contribution but have their individual reasons for preserving their independence rather than merging. Evaluation is often then in terms of what improvement in financial expectations might result from an alliance?

Disadvantages include NIH; reluctance to divulge confidential strategies; skepticism about effectiveness and relevance; responsiveness; intellectual property rights; and inexperience with identifying partners, managing partnering, evaluating metrics for outcomes, and negotiating contract terms.

Research consortia are the newest form of partnering in the United States. An early example is the *Microelectronics and Computer Technology Corporation* (MCC), a consortium of some 22 shareholder companies and 48 associate members [16,17].

These consortia are established to share the costs of the evolution of new science and technology of strategic importance, on a large scale, far beyond that which individual firms could afford. Similar efforts in Europe are driven by the need to share costs of new technology across many national boundaries.

Success factors include having a vision inspired by all those collaborating. Sustaining collaboration must be learned by all partners and regularly reinforced during review sessions. This means agreement on how results will be evaluated, both financially and in selected nonfinancial terms. Individual boundary spanners from collaborators need to be rewarded for their contributions. The problems found are those already discussed, but the multiple heterogeneous voices to be heard and satisfied make the management of consortia a complex and time-consuming task. Evaluation beyond costs and milestones may be difficult to achieve.

3.4.4 Organize and Systematize Technology Acquisition

Management across external boundaries needs to be organized and made systematic. Successful use of outside sources first requires an understanding of what types of programs you are willing to place externally and how you will measure the advantage supposed to be gained. From among the sources listed above, which will best perform the task that is your firm's objective? This requires focusing on the source's true competencies. For science one might go to universities. For mature product lines, this might be consultants. This also requires deciding what to keep inside. For most firms, this is usually key core technologies, new initiatives, and strategic innovation upon which next year's breadwinners will be based.

Next comes the need to handle interpersonal relations. Dedicated personnel must be assigned as program champions and kept on that task until it has been completed. Colleague-to-colleague relations are essential to form trust. Some cultural change may be needed in your own organization, just as it will be needed in that of your partner. Speed to market, commitment, and urgency will help to give successful results quickly and establish the creditability of the alliance to both partner companies.

A consistent regular external review process will be needed to bring each colleague's peers and superiors into play. The R&D manager has to depend on the commitment of some downstream part of the organization to implement the finished innovation. Preference should be given to an activity council that includes representatives from the groups onto which the innovation will be grafted [5,6]. Groups benefit from the greater knowledge of a variety of members and the increased number of ideas generated. Participation in such a council builds commitment to the result and appreciation of the decisions that led up to it.

Finally, the evaluation metrics for alliance programs need to include all of those each partner uses for inside R&D programs. These will include financial metrics such as program costs, sales, product costs, margins, and capital. They will also have to include nonfinancial measures, such as timeliness, and hopefully also those of customer satisfaction, and measures of strategic intent. If your prospective partner is not up to your standard of metrics, or vice versa, the conflicts over metrics may keep the alliance from achieving its goals.

Technical knowledge needs to be built up by the following steps.

- Even if your firm is relatively self-sufficient, access outside knowledge through a board of scientific advisors.
- Manage alliances with others with trust, and agreed common metrics.
- Obtain scientific and technical knowledge from suppliers, universities, government laboratories, joint ventures and/or research consortia.
- Organize and systematize technology acquisition.

3.5 EFFECT OF INTERNAL ORGANIZATION ON BOUNDARY SPANNING

Thus far, this chapter has treated boundary spanning as if the organization was a single entity. In practical terms, however, the boundary-spanning tasks are different for commercial and technological boundaries. Some two-thirds of U.S. companies are organized by product lines or have their team organizations by products or product platforms. For these companies, the boundary spanners to the commercial world are correspondingly decentralized. For example, Goodyear recently "has been restructured into six self-contained crossfunctional strategic business units" [13]. The evaluation metrics then may be only a limited set of financial and nonfinancial metrics.

The technology boundary-spanning task is not quite as simple. Most decentralized companies have shown a need for some centralization of this task. The usual form for this is a central laboratory, even if the bulk of the technical effort is decentralized. For example, Chrysler keeps a small central scientific group effort of 69 people who work with the four platform teams [11]. To further avoid duplication of effort, they have also introduced an informal network of "Tech Clubs" formed by the engineers of like technologies from each of its platform teams and the central scientific research activity. The evaluation and management of such informal groups has its own set of skills [5,6]. There are no simple ways to evaluate how much value comes from retaining such a centralized core. One must ask, how much of the R&D costs, and technological disadvantage, may be increased by total decentralization? And how much of this can be saved by again recentralizing certain tasks being duplicated by decentralization?

3.6 LESSONS LEARNED ON EXTERNAL BOUNDARY SPANNING

Boundary spanning by innovation managers covers both commercial and technological external areas. The evaluation of the commercial boundary as an outcome is often measured by market share.

- The single-minded pursuit of increased market share is not the panacea presented by strategic management theory, because all other things are definitely not equal in different types of industries.
- Market share is best measured by key accounts or served markets as a percent share measurement by the input money value of tangible benefits resulting from all other metrics.
- Customer satisfaction with cost effectiveness, use of milestones, and longer product life are all positively associated with market share.

Strategy begins with a vision of the company. It also includes spanning to the general environment and to the specific industry and the analysis of competition.

- Establish a vision for what the firm might, could, would, should do;
- Assess the external environment common to all competitors;
- Assess the probable swings in your own industry;
- Assess your competitors' SWOT;
- Assess the imperfections in the R&D/marketing interface.

Technology boundary spanning involves a shift from technical self-sufficiency to a make versus buy mode of operation. Alliances with others of all forms need to be built on trust and common metrics. Sources of external knowledge available to be tapped include suppliers, universities, government laboratories, joint ventures of various sorts, and research consortia. All of these have their own specific skills and competencies that should match the company's needs.

- Even if your firm is relatively self-sufficient, access outside knowledge through a board of scientific advisors.
- Manage alliances with others with trust and consensual common metrics.
- Obtain scientific and technical knowledge from suppliers, universities, government laboratories, joint ventures, and/or research consortia.
- Organize and systematize technology acquisition.

Boundary spanning is affected by internal organization. Commercial spanning is usually effectively decentralized by groups, divisions, or teams. Technical spanning, however, needs some type of centralization to be effective, even if the bulk of technical effort has been decentralized. This leads naturally into internal organization in the next chapter.

Finally, having done the actions above, rethink how much decentralization now makes sense and what might still be centralized for cost effectiveness.

References

[1] Thompson, A. A., and A. J. Strickland, *Strategy and Policy*, revised ed., Plano, TX: Business Publications, 1981, pp. 114–115.

[2] Kaplan, R. S., and D. P. Norton, "Putting the Balanced Scorecard to Work," *Harvard Business Review*, Vol. 71(5), Sept.–Oct. 1993, pp. 134–147.

[3] Bodelle, J., and C. Jablon, "Science and Technology Scouting at Elf Aquitaine," *Research Technology Management*, Vol. 36(5), Sept.–Oct. 1993, pp. 24–28.

[4] Porter, M. E., *Competitive Advantage*, New York: Free Press, 1985.

[5] Ellis, L. W., "Effective Use of Temporary Groups for New Product Development," *Research Management*, Vol. XXII (1), Jan.–Feb. 1979, pp. 31–34.

[6] Ellis, L. W., "Temporary Groups: An Alternative Form of Matrix Management," *Matrix Management Systems Handbook* (Cleland, D. I., ed.), New York: Van Nostrand Reinhold, 1983, Chapter 10.

[7] Workman, J. P., Jr., "Engineering's Interactions with Marketing Groups in an Engineering-Driven Organization," *IEEE Trans. on Engineering Management*, Vol. 42(2), May 1995, pp. 129–139.

[8] Industrial Research Institute, "Making Innovation Happen," Meeting Summary of the IRI Annual Meeting, Washington, May 1–4, 1984.

[9] Issacson, R., R. Mitchell, and L. Starr, "Getting the Most from a Scientific Advisory Board," *Research Technology Management*, Vol. 37(2), Mar.–Apr. 1994, pp. 33–37.

[10] Wolff, M. F., "Building Trust in Alliances," *Research Technology Management*, Vol. 37(3), May–June 1994, pp. 12–15.

[11] Lutz, R. A., "Implementing Technological Change with Cross-Functional Teams," *Research Technology Management*, Vol. 37(2), Mar.–Apr. 1994, pp. 14–18.

[12] Chatterji, D., and T. A. Manuel, "Benefiting from External Sources of Technology," *Research Technology Management*, Vol. 36(6), Nov.–Dec. 1993, pp. 21–26.

[13] Gault, S. C., "Responding to Change," *Research Technology Management*, Vol. 37(3), May–June 1994, pp. 23–26.

[14] Bloedon, R. V., and D. R. Stokes, "Making University/Industry Collaborative Research Succeed," *Research Technology Management*, Vol. 37(2), Mar.–Apr. 1994, pp. 44–48.

[15] Roessner, J. D., and A. S. Bean, "Industry Interaction with Federal Labs Pays Off," *Research Technology Management*, Vol. 36(5), Sept.–Oct. 1993, pp. 38–40.

[16] Rogers, D. V., C. A. Kehoe, and S.-Y. K. Lee, "Collaborative Research as a Function of Proximity, Industry and Company: A Case Study of an R&D Consortium," *IEEE Trans. on Engineering Management*, Vol. 41(3), Aug. 1994, pp. 255–263.

[17] Gibson, D. V., and E. M. Rogers, *R&D Collaboration on Trial: The Story of MCC—America's First, Major, For-Profit R&D Consortium—And Its Quest to Enhance the Competitiveness of American High-Tech Firms*, Cambridge, MA: Harvard Business School Press, 1994.

Chapter 4

Measurements in the R&D Process

"Manage the process"—that is the key to R&D management, as a component of innovation management [1]. All the planning in the world will not get new technology implemented, so the process itself has to be managed. This chapter is about how to evaluate the process. These tasks are what organizations have to do after choosing a technical strategy. And these are not just managerial tasks, because people at the bench level really run the process. Managing the R&D process contributes to innovation performance effectiveness and makes the desired impact on downstream operations.

An analysis of the process of managing technology management begins with a choice of a model. The process to be managed changes with time along the R&D process. It also changes with the sector to be managed whether it be resources, infrastructure, or functions.

4.1. AN R&D PROCESS MODEL

Many companies now manage their overall innovation activities on a classical open systems basis, in the manner shown in Figure 1.2. This is done from inputs through processes to outputs, with minimal feedback.

Depending on the degree of R&D/Marketing coordination, the inputs may be joint from these two organizational units or commercial information may come in serial form as marketing tosses product plans or specifications over the wall to R&D. In many companies also, the output point is where design and manufacturing information is tossed over the wall to the downstream implementing organizations: manufacturing, plant operations, divisions, or subsidiaries.

In comparison to how modern companies appear to be organizing, this simple model seems to be missing the interaction with other organizational units in the company. Today, these interactions are not only in a serial interaction form with feedback but also in various parallel or reciprocal feed-forward interaction forms. Outputs from R&D have to become outcomes of value to general managers and shareholders [2]. A representation of this modified model is shown in Figure 1.4. The effect of modifying this model is that, while making it more complex, it allows a much greater variety of potential precursor or leading indicators to be evaluated. For the purposes of this chapter, this expanded model will be used to characterize the measurements of outcomes, outputs, interactions, and inputs that need to be made to make the process effective.

4.2. PROCESSES AS FUNCTIONS OF TIME

The processes to be managed vary from earliest exploration to "sales order specials" for variants of older products. Some processes remain the same, some must be added as time progresses, and some are less important at the later stages of the time scale.

For convenience, this time scale for research and development has been divided into four sectors, as shown in Figure 4.1: exploratory concepts, opportunity creation, core competency development, and product improvement [3]. Before and after each sector, there is a point (stage gate) for evaluation of the effectiveness of those processes that stay the same and the others that gain or lose importance. The effectiveness of each stage gate may also be evaluated.

This R&D process structure represents the latest (1996) thinking of the IRIMER committee [3]. For those readers not attuned to the IRI, the division of the R&D time cycle as shown in Figure 2.4 may be a more appropriate set of sectors to use. Other companies may divide the process differently. For example, an anonymous reviewer provided this sequence that may be more appropriate for certain other companies: company review, searching; evaluation and feasibility, market research, securing the technology, product development, business development, and renewal. Some companies do not do things exactly in any of these three sequences. Thus, these are the categories that may have to be considered by any specific firm to establish its own process plan, appropriate tactics, and solutions.

When the 1991 study began, the sequence was derived from the atomic submarine program at the Electric Boat Division of General Dynamics. With a long lead-time R&D process, they broke up opportunity creation into design concept, design finalization, and development. This sequence was used for the 1991 to 1995 studies covered subsequently in Chapter 7. This leads to the appropriate lesson: expand the processes and stage gates shown in Figure 4.1 as appropriate to the character of your R&D cycle.

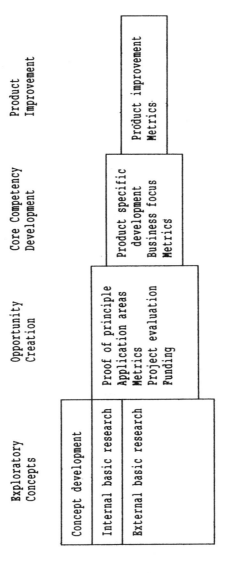

Figure 4.1. Processes as a function of time. (*After:* IRIMER [3]).

4.2.1   Processes That Are the Same From Exploration Through Extension

Some processes to be managed do not change along the time cycle. People have to be managed. Funding has to be sought. Managing requires focusing on effectiveness, which means doing the right thing, rather than on efficiency, which is measured by output divided by input. These processes are the same for all managers, not just those of technology: plan, organize, lead, measure (evaluate), control.

Managing people comes after planning, which does change along the time cycle. Once the plan is set, organizing becomes the next task. Organization involves the division of work to make effective the specialization of individuals. It also requires integration mechanisms to make whole the divided work in the interests of the entire organization. Effectiveness is best measured by a long span of control requiring fewer supervisors.

The old-fashioned division of work was by minifunction within the R&D organization. Research threw results over the wall to development, which threw models over the wall to engineering, which. . . —you get the idea. This overspecialization made best use of individual talents, but it took time. Chrysler used to take 5 to 6 years to create and first deliver a new car. It now does it in 2.5 years [4]. Thus, cycle time is a key evaluation metric.

Chrysler accelerates by project teams, which is the increasing trend in U.S. industry. Teams bring project ownership and team member empowerment. The 1993 to 1995 studies found that the use of crossfunctional project teams has now reached the 70% level in the United States. This highlights another key evaluation metric, namely, percent using concurrent engineering (this will be expanded upon in Chapter 6).

Leading follows organization. The top R&D manager used to select all department heads and project managers. Should managers continue to do this, or should teams elect their own captain? Project and program championship now becomes an issue for leadership. Launching a new team requires that management provide the initial team leader. But after that, if a natural leader develops, the manager should quietly allow her or his succession, moving the previous leader onto the next crisis.

Leadership also involves staff motivation and rewards. Morale is a consequence of motivated and rewarded team members. Rewards may be either extrinsic (for example, money and promotion) or intrinsic (such as recognition) [5]. Thus, they are input metrics, contributing to process metrics of effort and motivation. Leadership also involves the skills assessment of the quality of personnel, arranging training time each year of the proper quality, and conflict management, all of which can be at least subjectively evaluated.

Finally leadership involves top management support and commitment [6,7]. Top management needs to support the right kinds of projects. They need to get the right kind of information upward from the R&D organization. And when change is needed, they need to respond quickly.

Measuring time occurs throughout the process as covered later in Chapters 7 and 8. Many other measurements are needed depending on the stage along the time cycle. Benefit-to-cost analysis starts project selection. The percent of projects or the value passing the stage gates between the sectors and out to commercialization are measurements that evaluate the effectiveness of each stage gate design review itself.

Control is a final people management task. What you measure is that to which you control, and what you get as results. Thus, careful selection of metrics is important in order to send the right message to staff. Top-down control is necessary, but not sufficient. Peer evaluation of technical accomplishments is a desirable form of control.

Funding of the process tasks is also an activity that is conducted on the entire length of the technology process, as was addressed in Chapter 2. In the exploration phase, the technology manager may be a primary determinant of what gets funded. Business unit manager selection and evaluation of products can ensure that R&D is important in achieving the outcomes desired by management.

Key evaluation metrics covering all subprocesses are summarized briefly as follows and will be expanded upon in subsequent chapters.

- More R&D staff per supervisor;
- Short cycle time;
- Percent of projects using concurrent engineering;
- Subjective evaluation of rewards;
- Percent passing stage gates;
- Subjective evaluation of technical accomplishments;
- Percent of submitted project proposals accepted.

4.2.2 Processes Most Important in Exploration Through Development

The processes most important from exploration through development are technical planning and ensuring the quality and preservation of technical output. By the time the firm reaches the stage of product improvement, the customers and the field sales force mostly guide technical planning and the amount of technical contribution needed is less than for the earlier stages.

Technical planning for exploration involves the generation of concepts and the balancing of internal and external research efforts. Increasingly, the focus is on external alliances, as covered under managing external resources. By the time of opportunity creation, technical planning has shifted into an alliance with the business managers for the selection and evaluation of projects and the concentration on application areas. Technical planning still needs to outline what is needed to reach proof of principle. Developing core competencies brings technical planning more to a product specific mode focused on business needs. The evaluation is the same as in the previous section.

Ensuring the quality and the preservation of technical output is another task from exploration to development. Acquisition of technical knowledge is the technology manager's responsibility throughput training, hiring, or alliances. This and technical planning need metrics to guide the manager. The traditional R&D output metrics are the number and quality of patents, copyrights, and trade secrets. These fail modern needs in two ways. General managers are interested in outcomes, not in intellectual property outputs; and patent or copyright activity may be more a function of the legal department than of R&D work. Still, a common evaluation rule is "one patent per megabuck (million dollars) of sales."

Outcome metrics are of more value to higher management. These include measuring sales protected by a proprietary position secured by R&D activity. Another useful output metric that leads into outcomes is to measure at the end of each stage the percent of started ideas that are adopted by the next phase and eventually find their way into a product. Turning this into an outcome metric, the technology manager needs to show higher management how this percentage flows through to the "bottom line" (net income). The outcome *effectiveness index* (EI), discussed in Chapters 2 and 14, can be expressed mathematically as [8]

$$EI = \frac{\% \text{ New Product Revenue} * (\% \text{ Net Profit} + \% R\&D)}{\% R\&D} \tag{4.1}$$

Purists among the author's accounting colleagues point out that net profit is after interest and taxes, which have nothing to do with technology. Thus, the term in the brackets may be equivalently replaced by operating profit or by earnings before interest, taxes, and R&D.

Metrics applicable at this stage include:

- Patents and copyrights per million dollars of sales;
- Sales protected by intellectual property rights;
- Percent of started ideas passing each subsequent stage and becoming commercialized products or services;
- R&D department effectiveness index.

4.2.3   Other Subprocesses Need to be Added With Opportunity Creation

With the onset of opportunity creation, or as some call it directed applied research, new subprocesses come into play. The first of these is the need for the effort to have an alignment with the strategic direction of the firm—the "directed" part of the definition. One achieves this by bringing into the direction process those managers who have the ability to take the results and run with them, often through a group activity [9,10].

Directing opportunity creation necessitates individuals who have knowledge of customer needs. Most R&D staff have minimal coupling in this area. One such solution is to identify a lead user or teaching customer with whom both the R&D staff and the marketers interact [11]. This solution has an advantage over having marketing inform R&D of the customers' needs in that it removes one intermediate source of attenuation and distortion between customer and R&D. Whatever the method, customer contact time is the key metric to be used in calibrating knowledge of customer needs.

Opportunity creation needs goal clarity. As an old New England saying goes, "If you don't know where you are going, any road will take you there." Many R&D groups don't know where they are going, and fail to deliver as a result. This happens not only because there is insufficient knowledge of customer needs, but also because the direction from above is imprecise. This led one pair of authors to call it the "fuzzy front end" [12]. Cutting out the fuzziness is part of managing the technology management process. Goal clarity can be evaluated subjectively or by QFD.

While project selection and evaluation need technical and business input in earlier stages of the technology management process, opportunity creation is the point where such input also has to be financial, as covered in Chapter 2 [13]. If the return on an opportunity creation project in technology does not measure up to those other potential uses of that scarce commodity called money, it will not be approved.

Still another metric needed in opportunity creation is the response time to competitor moves. This is the idea-to-customer cycle time composed of the "fuzzy front end" of marketing time plus the response time through R&D and implementation, as shown in Figure 4.2.

To be competitive, companies must be able to respond to competitor moves as well as to ideas from the customer. If a company has adopted cycle time in all departments, the response time is measured as the sum of the segments. But if any one department in the chain fails to track cycle time, the overall time metric will not be precise.

Customer satisfaction is still another metric needed from opportunity creation onward. One company president put it as follows.

At Boeing, we can trace our past success to the fact that we listened closely to what our customers want in an airplane, but our future rests on also listening as a manufacturer. . . The test for all our R&D efforts to create new or better products is their effectiveness in adding value for the customer. . . Boeing's future depends on listening to our airline customers and setting our priorities by theirs. In short, our R&D efforts will continue to be customer-driven, not technology driven [14].

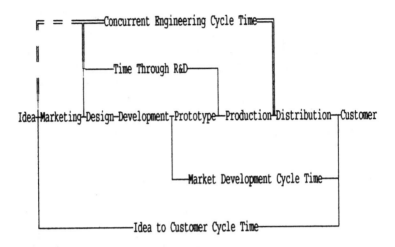

Figure 4.2. Flow of cycle-time measures through the innovation value chain.

A recent survey identified desirable forms of metrics, measuring the customer's satisfaction with your firm as well as the service or product [15]. Over half the companies use an index, market share, or a lead user to measure customer satisfaction, and often two or all three of these metrics. An overall customer satisfaction index tested had responsiveness, technology, and quality/reliability as its main components, but not cost competitiveness. For a cost competitiveness satisfaction rating, measure market share, responsiveness, and continue use of time measurements once you have started to use them. Faster or slower cycle times affect different components of an overall index, as covered in later chapters. Speedy innovation is associated with customer satisfaction with high technology and customer communication. A slower pace of innovation is associated with customer satisfaction with cost competitiveness, program/contract management, and product quality and reliability. From follow-up interviews, the customer was identified not only as the end user or consumer but also as the downstream implementation chain and the distribution chain. R&D managers should select measurements from the survey results to provide useful leading indicators for enhancing customer satisfaction in their own companies.

The following example provides a perspective on those measurements of interest to a Japanese company.

Mitsubishi Electric Corporation's Semiconductor Equipment Department uses a broad set of measures by not only section and department managers but also by their customers [16]. These include conventional metrics such as profitability, sales, delivery time, quality, number of patents, equipment downtime and yield. Also, each working group and its employees are evaluated according to their contribution, including standardization, reuse of software, and continuous improvement of the department's product development process.

Key metrics at this stage are:

- Contact time between R&D staff and customers;
- Goal clarity as evaluated subjectively or by QFD;
- Project financial evaluation;
- Response time to competitor moves (idea to customer time);
- Customer satisfaction index and/or market share.

4.2.4 New Subprocesses Begin With Core Competency/Product Development

By this point in the innovation cycle, managers need to focus on their goals for implementation. Typically, those downstream in the organization place quality, time, and cost as primary objectives [17]. Quality needs to be designed into the product or service [18]. The cost of the product or service begins to become a paramount issue. Only time in the implementers' eyes is governed in the same manner discussed earlier.

Product quality and reliability tend to be measures of customer satisfaction with the product rather than with the company as an innovator. Defect quality and reliability of an innovative offering are two distinct but complementary categories. As the customer for an innovative service or product sees it, defects are occasions when performance is not as expected. Defects per million opportunities is an appropriate measure. Reliability is the time the product is free from defects, often measured as *mean time between failures* (MTBF).

Product costs lead directly into measuring the prospective financial return versus the development and product costs. This is the main business focus.

Another new issue is that of technology transfer. The crossfunctional team metrics discussed in Chapter 6 are one way to quantify this task. Another is the degree of formality in the transfer process.

Additional key metrics needed at this stage are:

- Product or service cost estimates;
- Quality target such as defect rate or MTBF;
- Subjective evaluation of formality of the technology transfer process.

4.2.5 By Product Extension/Improvement, Some Subprocesses Decline in Importance

Strategic alignment tends to decline in importance because the markets to be served are now known. The metric then becomes one of deciding whether the extension is worth it—does the incremental profit exceed the incremental costs?

The quality and preservation of technical output also declines in importance because extensions and improvements rarely generate patents and the skills required are now known by several people.

An additional metric at this stage is incremental profit minus incremental costs.

4.3 LESSONS LEARNED ON MANAGING ALONG THE PROCESS

The key task for R&D managers is to manage the process. To accomplish this, additional evaluation metrics have been identified for the transitions stages from idea to concept and down through the chain to delivery to the customer. The subtle evaluation differences have been indicated as related to where the manager is in this sequence from conception to implementation. Summarizing the metrics identified in this section, most of which will be explained in detail in subsequent chapters, the key metrics include expanding the processes and stage gates identified above as appropriate to the character of your R&D cycle.

Throughout the R&D cycle use the following overall metrics:

- More R&D staff per supervisor;
- Length of cycle times;
- Percent of projects using concurrent engineering;
- Subjective evaluation of rewards;
- Percent passing stage gates;
- Subjective evaluation of technical accomplishments;
- Percent of submitted project proposals accepted.

In exploration through development use:

- Patents and copyrights per million dollars of sales;
- Sales protected by intellectual property rights;
- Percent of started ideas passing each subsequent stage and becoming commercialized products or services;
- R&D department effectiveness index.

With opportunity creation add:

- Contact time between R&D staff and customers;
- Goal clarity as evaluated subjectively or by QFD;
- Project financial evaluation;
- Response time to competitor moves (idea to customer time);
- Customer satisfaction index and/or market share.

With core competency/product development add:

- Product or service cost estimates;
- Quality target such as defect rate or MTBF;
- Subjective evaluation of formality of the technology transfer process.

An additional metric at the product extension stage is incremental profit minus incremental costs.

References

[1] Ellis, L. W., "Managing the Management of Technology Process," *Handbook of Technology Management* (G. H. Gaynor, ed.), New York: McGraw-Hill, 1996, Chapter 26.

[2] Brown, M. G., and R. A. Svenson, "Measuring R&D Productivity," *Research Technology Management*, Vol. 31(4), July–Aug. 1988, pp. 14–15.

[3] Industrial Research Institute (IRI), *Technology Value Program* (software diskette; and Internet World Wide Web URL: http://www.iriinc.org), Washington, DC: IRI, 1996.

[4] Lutz, R. A., "Implementing Technological Change with Cross-Functional Teams," *Research Technology Management*, Vol. 37(2), Mar.–Apr. 1994, pp. 14–18.

[5] Ellis, L. W., and S. Honig-Haftel, "Reward Strategies for R&D," *Research Technology Management*, Vol. 35(2), Mar.–Apr. 1992, pp. 16–20.

[6] Green, S. G., "Top Management Support of R&D Projects: A Strategic Leadership Perspective," *IEEE Trans. on Engineering Management*, Vol. 42(3), Aug. 1995, pp. 223–232.

[7] Farris, G. F., and L. W. Ellis, "Managing Major Change in R&D," *Research Technology Management*, Vol. 33(1), Jan.–Feb. 1990, pp. 33–37.

[8] McGrath, M. E., and M. N. Romeri, "From Experience: The R&D Effectiveness Index: A Metric for Product Development Performance," *J. Product Innovation Management*, Vol. 11, 1994, pp. 213–220.

[9] Ellis, L. W., "Effective Use of Temporary Groups for New Product Development," *Research Management*, Vol. XXII(1), Jan.–Feb. 1979, pp. 31–34.

[10] Ellis, L. W., "Temporary Groups: An Alternative Form of Matrix Management," *Matrix Management Systems Handbook* (D. I. Cleland, ed.), New York: Van Nostrand Reinhold, 1983.

[11] Herstatt, C., and E. Von Hippel, "From Experience: Developing New Product Concepts Via the Lead User Method: A Case Study in a 'Low Tech' Field," *J. Product Innovation Management*, Vol. 9(3), Sept. 1992, pp. 213–221.

[12] Smith, P. G., and D. G. Reinertsen, *Developing Products in Half the Time*, Florence, KY: Van Nostrand Reinhold, 1991.

[13] Ellis, L. W., *The Financial Side of Industrial Research Management*, New York: Wiley, 1984.

[14] Condit, P. M., "Focusing on the Customer: How Boeing Does It," *Research Technology Management*, Vol. 37(1), Jan.–Feb. 1994, pp. 33–37.

[15] Ellis, L. W., and C. C. Curtis, "Measuring Customer Satisfaction," *Research Technology Management*, Vol. 38(5), Sept.–Oct. 1995, pp. 45–48.

[16]   Funk, J. L., "Japanese Product-Development Strategies: A Summary of Propositions About Their Implementation," *IEEE Trans. on Engineering Management*, Vol. 40(3), Aug. 1993, pp. 224–236.

[17]   Hronec, S., *Vital Signs*, New York: AMACOM, 1993.

[18]   Juran, J. M., *Juran on Quality by Design: The New Steps for Planning Quality into Goods and Services*, Free Press, New York: 1992.

Chapter 5

Manage the Interaction With Other Functions

The management of interaction processes between functions or departments (other than finance covered in Chapter 2) may involve various integrating mechanisms. The first group of these concerns interfaces upstream toward the customer through marketing. The downward transfer of technology is a second group of interactions.

5.1 MANAGING UPSTREAM INTERFACES

The R&D-marketing interface, including commercial development and *quality function deployment* (QFD), constitutes the upstream area toward which R&D managers must direct their efforts.

5.1.1 Integrating Mechanisms

Organizational theory holds that two principles apply to a firm. Particularly, work is divided to gain the benefits of specialization, and the divided units must be integrated for the benefit of the company as a whole. In the smallest units, integration is achieved by the boss. As units grow, the general manager must find other mechanisms for integration, lest referring all decisions to the boss creates a super-bottleneck. Some of these mechanisms include procedures, integrating individuals, and integrating departments such as commercial development, temporary groups, and crossfunctional teams. In the growing organization, the usual integrating individual at a lower level is the project or program manager in a matrix management form [1]. Raised to the top of the firm, this individual may become a Chief Operating Officer [2]. The coordinating individual also runs into limits to what an individual can handle, and the need for coordination may grow into an integrating department [3]. These three forms are inherently top-down in structure.

The alternate approach is to structure integrating mechanisms in a bottom-up fashion. This is the logical extension of a trend that started a half-century ago to decentralizing companies "federally," like the split between Washington and the state capitals. Well over half of U.S. business is now decentralized, principally by product line; although other divisions of work are also found, such as by geographical area or key customer. What has changed in recent years is that this trend has proceeded even further down to decentralization by groups and teams [2]. First came the use of permanent or standing committees for management coordination. This was followed by the use of temporary groups, an alternate form of matrix management [1, Chap. 10; 4]. Names for temporary groups range from *ad hoc* committees to task forces. Advantages of both types of groups include the greater knowledge base from which decisions are drawn and the participation of lower level people, which increases the understanding and acceptance of decisions. Since technological innovation has so increased in complexity, with the necessary knowledge more often residing in the work force rather than in the managers, it is not surprising that the group form of organization has grown in use. Disadvantages of groups, which must be overcome by their leaders, are the conflicts they may generate and the longer time taken to reach decisions.

For the managers of innovation, a choice needs to be made for integrating the effort both upstream through marketing toward the customer and downstream through the operating chain of the firm.

5.1.2 Managing the Upstream Boundary: The R&D-Marketing Interface

The R&D-marketing interface has been shown to be important to the outcomes of research studies. To summarize what was concluded by the 1994 study, a regression model was established with this interface as the dependent variable. This choice was made for convenience in analysis rather than judging it to be an effect of other causes. Indeed, associated independent variables may themselves be causes or effects or the consequences of common causes to both variables. Two factors were most important in the R&D-marketing interface as defined by the survey question about the "extent to which there is R&D-marketing interface and involvement in the early stages of new product development in your company," with a scale from very not extensive to very extensive.

The strongest of these correlations was between extensiveness of this interface and higher new products as a percent of sales. Since the interface must take place ahead of the outcome percent of sales, it is either a cause or both factors are the consequences of the firm's strategic intent. *Concurrent engineering* (CE) use was associated with extensive R&D-marketing interface, but in a nonlinear manner. At low levels of CE use, higher use was associated with a less extent of interface, down to a minimum at 57% CE use, and rising to 100% use of concurrent engineering. While this may just be the adjustment of the firm upon introducing new management practice, since the effect never becomes fully positive, there seems to be some residual deterioration of the R&D-marketing interface when shifting to concurrent engineering.

The R&D-marketing interface is an important internal boundary. To help managers in deciding how to create a better R&D-marketing interface, three examples are given of a group approach, an integrating department, and the QFD process.

Product planning committees are a natural bottom-up grouping of marketing and R&D professionals, with the addition of other functions such as general management and manufacturing, depending on the nature of the company.

In ITT Corporation, these committees started in Europe in the 1930s, as a consequence of the need for intercountry technical coordination due to the many national subsidiaries of that company [5, pp. 94–97]. This system worked in the period just before World War II and for a number of years after the war, and the headquarters international staff expenses were kept to a minimum.

Renamed task forces in the 1960s and 1970s, a greater input was obtained of general and product line managers. The primary contribution these committees made to innovation was in the screening of new ideas from the field rather than the generation of them by committee members. This helps select a lesser number that appear attractive enough to be worth more rigorous analysis and evaluation through market assessment and financial expectations.

Only once in his career has the author found such a committee to have too few ideas—they usually have far too many, and screening is desirable to devote resources to the most promising. The one exception was funded for an outside company to organize brainstorming for them, which generated 60 ideas they had not considered, thus quickly transforming their product planning committee into a screening mode.

Commercial development of new products is a consequence of the realization that some functions are not economically able to be decentralized [3]. Commercial development is thus the creation of an integrating department of marketing and R&D while retaining a centralized operating department. Unless a business is totally labor intensive, sharing fixed assets is usually more cost effective than letting each decentralized unit have its own plant facilities. Up to a point, the close coupling of a decentralized management to its market may offset this implementation cost penalty, but as the business becomes more capital intensive, plant centralization economies of scale shape the organization structure. Thus, it is not surprising that this type of integrating mechanism is found most often in heavy industry such as primary metal and chemical manufacturing.

In the 1960s, long before the author had heard of the term "commercial development," he found that this need for centralization also applied to electronic equipment manufacturers.

Psi Radio Limited had three departments involved in radio equipment and three other nonradio product lines. While each of these needed specialty engineering and marketing, the segregation of manufacturing led to excess manpower in industrial engineering and production control, excess stocks of parts, and uneven work loading of expensive machinery in the machine shops. Combining all of these under one shop superintendent evened out machine loadings, lowered manufacturing overheads, costs, and inventories, and the company ran with fewer manufacturing staff for the same number of direct manufacturing workers. Each of the six resulting product lines kept separate combined marketing and R&D groups under a product line manager, which would now be called commercial development.

5.1.3 Quality Function Deployment (QFD)

QFD is a new product development process used to improve the integration of marketing and technology inputs [6–9]. QFD was pioneered by Japanese companies to link desired customer attributes to the functional product characteristics and technology inputs necessary for their achievement.

The QFD process starts by drawing a "House of Quality," which deploys the "Voice of the Customer" into product needs [6]. This house is shown in various forms in the references but usually has several rectangular panels capped by a triangular "roof," as shown in simplified form in Figure 5.1.

The left panel describes customer wants and needs (what?) in rows. The center panel is a relationship matrix between these needs and design attribute columns (how?) in the panel representing the second story of the house. The roof is then a correlation matrix between the design attribute columns. In the several versions are other panels representing importance, costs (how much?), customer perceptions, competitive assessments, and engineering measures. The output from the house is a flow diagram through design, operations (such as part deployment, process planning, and production planning), and process control. For those wishing for a more complete description of QFD, [7] is suggested.

The diffusion of QFD in the United States appears to have begun with Ford in 1983 [7]. By 1987, 24 U.S. companies had been identified as using QFD, of which 35 teams from nine companies were surveyed through 1989 [7]. From then until the 1994 study, the literature has not provided much more of an insight on the rate of diffusion into process use in the United States.

The Aluminum Corporation of America (Alcoa) has applied a "House of Quality" technique to identify the expectations its business hold for the technical community and to guide the Technical Center in developing a series of measures, or metrics, for use in stimulating the behaviors required to meet and exceed these expectations [10]. They define metrics as controllable actions meeting customer requirements and set target values and metric importance ratings. The central matrix of the "house" is the relationship between these metrics and the laboratory's ability to meet customer requirements.

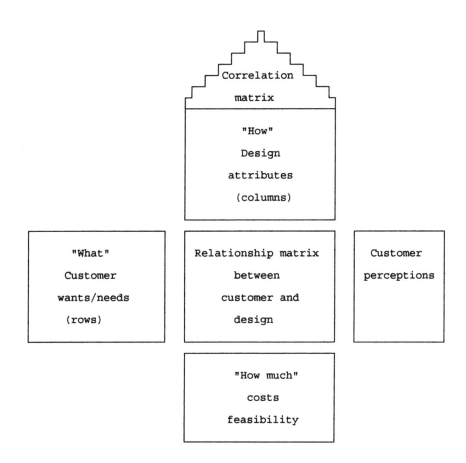

Figure 5.1 Simplified "House of Quality" (*After:* [6–8]).

The results from the 1993, 1994, and 1995 studies covered how much QFD was used, defined as "use of multidisciplinary teams in new product design to ensure that ability to be produced, quality, and serviceability dominate the design process." This was followed by a look at how QFD use compared with the use of other metrics, how correlated were these metrics, and the results of regressions involving QFD.

5.1.4 Use of QFD

The profile of QFD use among the respondents to the three studies is shown in Figure 5.2. The means of each year were not significantly different, and the

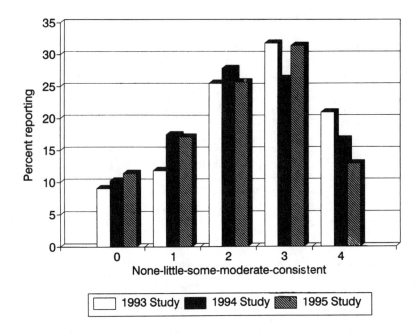

Figure 5.2 Use of QFD.

variations in percent reporting at each level were quite similar. Some to moderate use of QFD seems to have become a stable process.

5.1.5 Comparison of QFD With Other Metrics

Several other metrics mentioned earlier were compared with QFD use in 1994, as shown in Table 5.1. To bring these into a similar framework, the lowest value of QFD use was dropped, as were cycle times less than three months, use of TQM less than one year, and concurrent engineering use less than 15% of the R&D budget. The six metrics in the table were all reported from "little use" through "consistent use" by over half of those responding to the survey.

Regression analyses were tried on 1994 responses to see if controlling for other variables would yield useful results on QFD. Of these, only the outcome metrics EBIT, customer satisfaction, and idea-to-customer cycle time provided supporting associations, while new products to sales did not. Concurrent engineering was slightly associated with QFD use, while TQM years was not. An EBIT regression model showed higher use of QFD was associated with higher EBIT.

Customer satisfaction in 1994 regression models provided mixed results. Neither self-reported overall customer satisfaction nor any of the other components of

Table 5.1
Comparison of Metrics Used Little Through Consistently

Variable	Number	Percent
QFD	113	88.3
CE	110	85.9
Idea-to-Customer Time	103	80.5
New Products as Percent of Sales	97	75.8
Use of TQM in R&D	75	58.6
Index of Customer Satisfaction	68	53.1

Source: [11].

the index except cost satisfaction were associated with the use of QFD. Higher use of QFD was associated with higher self-reported customer satisfaction with cost.

A QFD regression model was the next step in 1994 regression analysis. Two models proved stable: fewer days of both R&D cycle time and idea-to-customer cycle time each associated with higher QFD use. The five other independent variables were the same in both models. Higher use of QFD was associated with companies citing cost as a reason to measure cycle times, higher customer satisfaction with cost, higher use of Taguchi methods, higher government regulation, higher use of concurrent engineering (but only among the lesser users), and a lower ratio of patents to sales volume.

At this stage in the diffusion of QFD into industry, these results may be fleeting and eventually disappear with more widespread use. Finding the positive association of QFD use and customer satisfaction with cost gives a possible clue to the reason for the improvement in financial performance (EBIT), but the survey did not explicitly track the relation of QFD and costs. This finding is also supported by the greater use of QFD in companies citing cost as a reason to measure cycle times. Use of QFD may be argued to be a contributor to this increased EBIT since its use precedes financial reporting and customer satisfaction, but all factors may merely be related consequences of the firm's strategy.

The lessons learned in organizing the R&D-marketing interface are:

- Choose an R&D/marketing interface mechanism, using a product planning committee of marketing and R&D, where manufacturing considerations are low in importance; a commercial development department, where manufacturing is a dominant well-understood concern; or QFD, where a more disciplined approach to new products is needed to integrate marketing, R&D, and downstream operations.

- Balance when decentralizing completely where evaluating the cost disadvantages overwhelms the closeness to the customer and shorter communication lines of the smaller unit.

5.2   DOWNSTREAM OUTPUT MEASUREMENTS

Another category of measurable events is the output of the innovation chain that ends in the R&D department or, in some companies, in the engineering department. This output may be in the form of R&D outputs of intellectual property, such as patents, or of a transfer of technology downward to the units making up the customer order processing or implementation chain. These are the metrics that provide a direct measure of the effectiveness of the innovation suprafunction or of the departments that comprise it. However, these are not necessarily those that top management sees or, if they are not of a technical bent, those they can clearly understand or relate to business performance. As noted earlier, some of these are cycle-time reduction in R&D (already covered), internal/external technology transfer, and patent output. At a May 1993, IRIMER meeting, discussion centered around an assessment of measurement of outputs, shown in Figure 5.3.

Figure 5.3 attempted to separate the soft measures of quality from the hard measures of quantity and put a subjective value on these measures. Some of these measures have been categorized by the author as outcomes, such as customer evaluations, *present value* (PV) of sales and cost reductions, and tracking percent of new products. Others are split between outcomes and outputs, such as key benchmarks/milestones. The remainder represent other potential measures of R&D output: media impact, consulting with operations, patents, papers, new science/technical discovery, IR&D rating, and PV laboratory estimates. Missing from this tabulation are any measures of transfer of technology downward to subsequent steps in the implementation chain.

The companies listed in Table 1.1 were also queried about their output usage other than of cycle time, which was already covered above, with the results shown in Table 5.2. Other R&D outputs were evaluated from the IRIMER committee's work. Clearly, the variety of metrics is higher and the quantity more numerous than for outcomes. The grouping shown in Table 5.2 was chosen by the author in the attempt to provide a framework for subsequent analysis.

5.2.1   Direct Outputs From R&D

Ideally, an output measure would be desirable that accurately measures the results obtained from the use of reward systems, which is clearly a choice of many as a leading indicator. Patents were used satisfactorily in an academic study of reward systems [13]. It also unsuccessfully evaluated copyrights, but found their usage then a poor third behind patents, and trade secrets. The 1993 study used both

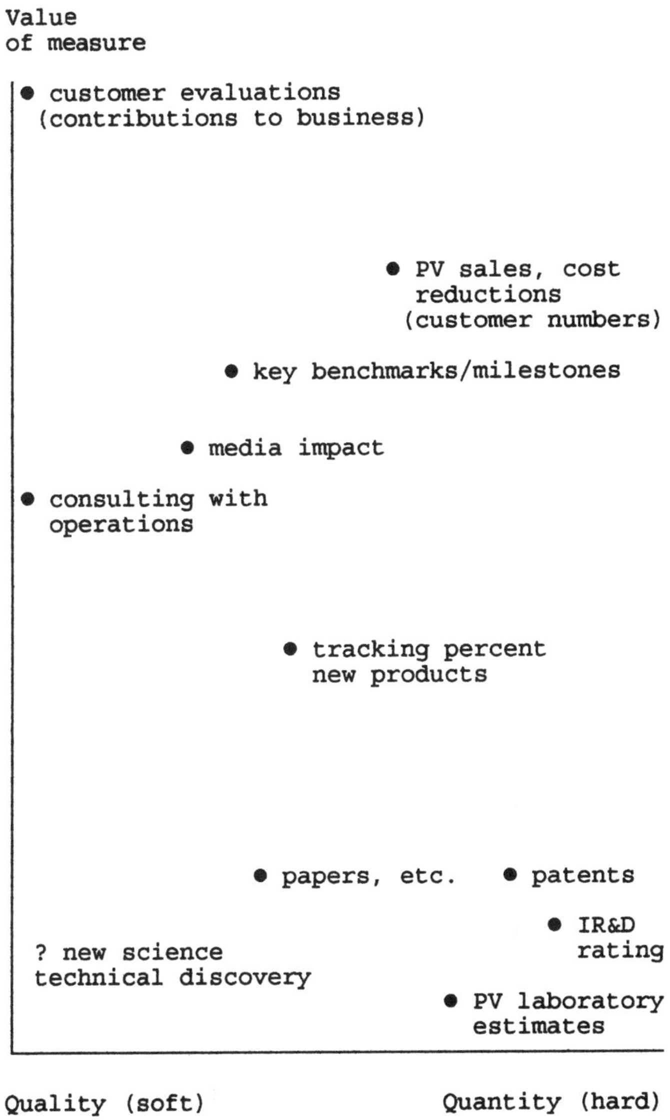

Value
of measure

- customer evaluations
  (contributions to business)

- PV sales, cost
  reductions
  (customer numbers)

- key benchmarks/milestones

- media impact

- consulting with
  operations

- tracking percent
  new products

- papers, etc.   - patents

- IR&D
  rating
? new science
technical discovery

- PV laboratory
  estimates

Quality (soft)   Quantity (hard)

Figure 5.3 Measurement of output.

Table 5.2
Use of R&D Output Metrics Other Than Cycle Time

R&D Output Metric	Number of Companies
Downward Technology Transfer	
Consulting/training to operations/customers	3
Products developed/piloted	2
Define processes/quality measures	1
Quality of products/services	1
Percent of resources on growth	1
Direct R&D Outputs	
Patents/applications/disclosures	2
Ideas adopted as projects	1
Team effectiveness assessment	1
OSHA recordables	1
IR&D rating	1
Media or Public Impact	
External presentations/publications	3
Millions of impressions in print or aired	1
Testimony to legal or standards bodies	1
Recognition	1

Source: CIMS [12].

patent quantity per million dollars of sales (to equalize between companies of vastly different size) and average patent age. The thrust of this choice was to try to measure quality in the second metric as opposed to quantity in the first.

While this has some indicative value, it should be noted that firms may have other ways of protecting intellectual property rights; such tactics include trade secrets, copyrights for software, and publication as a bar to others patenting. Many firms choose not to patent in order to keep the information a secret from competitors. Others, such as toy companies, often go for a quick profit before the product can be copied by competitors. The tradeoff is whether it is better to keep changing your product to stay ahead of competition or to patent or copyright it and protect intellectual property rights for a period of time.

Surveying recent literature, the number of scientists and engineers, as reported by the NSF, was found to measure only input in quantity, not competence [14]. This same study also noted patents as a measure of R&D output based on several earlier sources. Some negative interaction was also found between patents and publications.

The remaining direct outputs listed in Table 5.2 seem to reflect particular needs of the companies involved rather than universal output metrics. The 1992 study also sampled the output measures ranked by present use, perceived importance, and difference between these two ratings, as indicated in Table 5.3.

The 1992 study among IRIMER committee members and selected other business managers ranked a number of input, process, output, and outcome measures in use at that time and for perceived importance. The ratings of use and importance were rather lightly correlated ($r = 0.25$) and the importance ratings were consistently higher than the present use ratings, both measured on a scale of 1 to 5. The large rating difference between use and importance of cycle-time metrics brought no consistent explanations from the committee. This confirms the lesson learned that use is an imperfect indicator of the importance or effectiveness of any measurement. Figure 5.4 shows these ratings graphically.

If we compare the literature and the samples of Tables 5.2 and 5.3, the categories of downward technology transfer and R&D cycle time stand out as important to all groups. The category of media and public impact in Table 5.2 seems less important, particularly since three of the five metrics came from only one company. Added to this is a slim conceptual link of this category with any of the most mentioned results or outcome metrics. Accordingly, this and other R&D inputs were lumped into a single output group for further study.

5.2.2 Downward Transfer of Technology

Equally important to innovation is the internal organization that transfers technology downward to the implementation chain of the company. As was noted in Figure 4.2, market development cycle time is composed of the time from the start of the prototype to the completion of customer acceptance of the first delivery. This cycle time often spans several organizational units and, for many firms, is handled through teams.

In companies that have not adopted the team approach to this transfer downward, few of the cited research results give much guidance for organization.

Table 5.3
Relative Ranking of R&D Output Measures

Output	Use	Importance	Difference
Downward technology transfer	1	1*	3
R&D cycle time	3	1*	1
Other R&D outputs	2	3	2

Note: * denotes equal ranking.
Souce: [12].

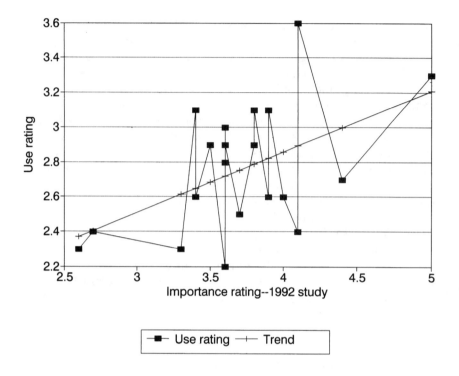

Figure 5.4 Comparison: use versus importance.

The operations side of any business is focused on repetition and process and is thus averse to change. Current accounting assigns the costs of the intermediate technology transfer organization (such as industrial engineering) into manufacturing overheads, thus providing a disincentive for manufacturing managers to devote effort to this task. Reforming the accounting treatment to allow the manufacturing department's costs for introducing new products to be separate from overheads on current production has recently been proposed [15].

As a consequence, the trend in recent years has been to demand that more of the technology transfer be done in and charged to the R&D unit. The author's only recommendation in this case is to arrange the assignment of development engineers to the manufacturing organization for as long as it takes to make sure the transfer has been made effectively. In a company managed by the author three decades ago, this was made a standard cost estimate as part of the development proposal, at 2.5% of the forecast annual manufacturing cost.

Tables 1.3 and 5.2 provide a broad list of factors that are important in the downward transfer of technology. Still another viewpoint came from the head of AT&T Bell Laboratories [16]. His output metrics included hardware and software technology and alignment with units supported, both in the category of downward transfer of technology. With such an extensive set from which to choose, it is obvious that further research is needed in this particular area. Until a clearer picture appears from such research, the individual firm needs to select measurements for downward transfer of technology appropriate to its own efforts.

From the author's own experience, at least three metrics are necessary: timeliness, cost, and quality. By timeliness is meant adherence to milestone dates for the scheduled transfer. The downstream units need to do much work themselves after receiving the transfer information before initial product or service launch takes place. The ultimate profitability is dependent on meeting or bettering the product or service cost goals. Quality in transfer means free of defects so that the downstream organization can proceed without "redo loops." These three metrics, in a different sequence, with quality first, are also guidelines used by Motorola [17].

5.2.3. Views From the Implementation Process

As the recipient (as its input) of the output of the innovation process, downstream organizational units have natural interest and forceful views on measurements. Two such studies have recently been presented [18,19]. One used four metrics: lead-time from concept to production launch and for tooling and facility preparation (output), total and post-launch *engineering change notices* [ECNs] (output), costs—total manufacturing and equipment and tooling (outcome), and overall quality on an interval scale and as measured by percent defects (outcome) [18]. The other used three similar metrics: time-to-market goals, cost goals, and quality goals (all outcomes) [19]. And it added three more: technical achievement goals (output), product feature goals (outcome), and user/market acceptance (which corresponds to customer satisfaction, an outcome) [19].

These studies also identified a large number of leading indicator metrics. Unfortunately, these were derived only by correlation analysis and do not show the magnitude of influence of each factor on cycle time. Some precursors of cycle time are shown in Table 5.4, to which descriptions corresponding to the model of Figure 1.4 have been added.

5.2.3.1 *Some Cycle-Time Metrics; Most Significant Positive Correlations in Rank Order [18,19]*

Please note the following conventions that were adopted for the ranking. (1) All variables showed positive correlations with reduced cycle-time metrics in original texts [18,19]. (2) Months concept-to-production launch reported by design engineers was converted to percent reduced lead-time [18]. (3) Months for tooling and facility preparation was converted to percent reduced lead-time [18]. (4) Time to market was measured on a five-point performance attribute scale [18].

1. Use of concurrent engineering [18] (interaction);

2. Crossfunctional teams—early design stage meeting frequency [18] (interaction);
3. Manufacturing influence on design release [18] (interaction);
4. Process control for online monitoring of production [19] (process);
5. Common goal rewards on speed ramp-up time [18] (process);
6. Design standards [18] (process);
7. Improved design documentation [18] (interaction);
8. Design reviews used at all on projects [18] (interaction);
9. Design of experiments [18] (process);
10. Concurrent engineering awareness training [18] (process);
11. Project manager role [18] (process);
12. Design/manufacturing data bases [18] (interaction);
13. Less levels to common report [18] (process);
14. Elimination of fasteners [19] (process);
15. *Design for assembly* [DFA] or *Design for manufacturability* [DFM] [19] (process);
16. Design reviews—frequency of manufacturing participation [18] (interaction);
17. Approved parts and materials [18] (process);
18. Dotted-line reporting [18] (interaction);
19. Crossfunctional teams used on all projects [18] (interaction);
20. DFM software [18] (input);
21. Group-based rewards [18] (process);
22. Concurrent engineering methods education [18] (process);
23. Design—manufacturing job rotation [18] (interaction);
24. Colocated design-manufacturing group [18] (interaction).

A similar list with some differences could be extracted for other outputs or outcomes. In any case, these represent a formidable number of potential leading indicators, especially considering that those conjectured and found not statistically significant have been eliminated. Taking those highest ranked provides the following key actions for R&D to improve the downstream interface:

- Use concurrent engineering/crossfunctional teams with manufacturing sign-off on design release (interaction);
- Use common goal rewards and on-line monitoring of production (process).

5.3 LESSONS LEARNED ON MANAGING THE INTERACTION PROCESS

The upstream process through marketing to the customer may be managed by product planning committees, commercial development, or QFD. In these cases, evaluation is both by outcome metrics and by the efficacy of the process. The latter is best measured as a progressive yield by the percent of ideas initiated that pass each subsequent stage. QFD is in sufficiently stable use among those responding to the most recent studies to be a contender for managing the upstream process, particularly since it shows a favorable association with financial performance (EBIT). The lessons learned in organizing the R&D-marketing interface are:

- Choose an R&D/marketing interface mechanism, using a product planning committee of marketing and R&D, where manufacturing considerations are low in importance; a commercial development department, where manufacturing is a dominant well-understood concern; or QFD, where a more disciplined approach to new products is needed to integrate marketing, R&D, and downstream operations.
- Balance when decentralizing completely where evaluating the cost disadvantages overwhelms the closeness to the customer and shorter communication lines of the smaller unit.

In the downstream direction in the organization, the actions are:

- Measure the yield percentage passing each stage gate in addition to more financial ones.
- Use concurrent engineering/crossfunctional teams with manufacturing sign-off on design release (interaction).
- Use common goal rewards and on-line monitoring of production (process).

The use of concurrent engineering involving crossfunctional teams from marketing down through delivery to the customer, as shown in Figure 4.2, seems the appropriate way to manage the entire process. This will be further justified in the next chapter.

References

[1] Cleland, D. I., ed., *Matrix Management Systems Handbook*, New York: Van Nostrand Reinhold, 1983.

[2] Lutz, R. A., "Implementing Technological Change with Cross-Functional Teams," *Research Technology Management*, Vol. 37(2), Mar.–Apr. 1994, pp. 14–18.

[3] Duerr, M. G., *The Commercial Development of New Products*, Report No. 890, New York: The Conference Board, 1986.

[4] Ellis, L. W., "Effective Use of Temporary Groups for New Product Development," *Research Management*, Vol. XXII(1), Jan.–Feb. 1979, pp. 31–34.

[5] Deloraine, M., *When Telecom and ITT Were Young*, New York: Lehigh Books, 1976; *Des Ondes et des Hommes: Jeunesse des Telecommunications et de l'ITT*, Paris: Flammarion, 1974.

[6] Hauser, J. R., and D. Clausing, "The House of Quality," *Harvard Business Review*, May/June 1988.

[7]   Griffin, A., "Evaluating QFD's Use in U.S. Firms as a Process for Developing Products," *J. Product Innovation Management*, Vol. 9(3), 1982, pp. 171–187.

[8]   Griffin, A., and J. R. Hauser, "Quality Function Deployment: Improving the Product Development Process Through Linking Marketing and Technology Development," unpublished research proposal, M.I.T., Cambridge, MA, Oct. 31, 1987.

[9]   Sullivan, L. P., "Quality Function Deployment," *Quality Progress*, Vol., 19(6), June 1986, pp. 39–50.

[10] O'Neill, P. H., and P. R. Bridenbaugh, "Credibility Between CEO and CTO—A CTO's Perspective," *Research Technology Management*, Vol. 35(6), Nov.–Dec. 1992, pp. 25–33.

[11] Ellis, L. W., and C. C. Curtis, "Measuring Customer Satisfaction, *Research Technology Management*, Vol. 38(5), Sept.–Oct. 1995, pp. 45–48.

[12] Bean, A. S., "IRI R-o-R Effectiveness Survey (1992): A Summary Report," CIMS, Lehigh University, Bethlehem, PA, Oct. 8, 1992.

[13] Ellis, L. W., and S. Honig-Haftel, "Reward Strategies for R&D," *Research Technology Management*, Vol. 35(2), Mar.–Apr. 1992, pp. 16–20.

[14] Chakrabarti, A. K., and C. L. Anyanwu, "Defense R&D, Technology, and Economic Performance: A Longitudinal Analysis of the U.S. Experience," *IEEE Trans. on Engineering Management*, Vol. 40(2), May 1993, pp. 136–145.

[15] Ellis, L. W., and R. G. McDonald, "Reforming Management Accounting to Support Today's Technology," *Research Technology Management*, Vol. 33(2), Mar.–Apr. 1990, pp. 30–34.

[16] Mayo, J. S., "R&D in the Third Millennium," Presentation to IRI Seminars, Washington, DC and Bedford, MA, June 9 and 22, 1992.

[17] Gill, M. S., "Stalking Six Sigma," *Business Month*, Jan. 1990, pp. 42–46.

[18] Liker, J. K., and F. Hull, "What Works in Concurrent Engineering? Sorting Through the Barrage of Practices," *1993 Academy of Management Conference*, Atlanta, GA, Aug. 11, 1993.

[19] Lee, D., and L. Heiko, "Adoption of Innovations and Product Development Performance," *1993 Academy of Management Conference*, Atlanta, GA, August 11, 1993.

Chapter 6

Evaluating Crossfunctional Teams

The management practices noted in earlier chapters were a mixture of internal processes to the departments concerned. The now widespread use of crossfunctional innovation teams, including concurrent or simultaneous engineering, is seen as the best overall innovation management practice. Incorporating the degree of use of this with other process and outcome measurements into a best set of innovation precursor metrics is a modern method for evaluating team effectiveness.

6.1 WHY CROSSFUNCTIONAL INNOVATION TEAMS?

The best overall management practice for effective innovation, including not only the innovation chain but also part of the implementation one, is clearly now the use of crossfunctional innovation teams. These incorporate R&D, engineering, manufacturing, and usually but not always marketing. This use of crossfunctional teams for innovation is usually called concurrent engineering in the United States and often simultaneous engineering in Europe.

Crossfunctional teams, however, are not limited only to concurrent engineering and innovation management. Many other teams involving the same functional members are used in industry for other business goals. For example, quality circles are widely used for improving the quality of the implementation process, with members of the circles coming from many of the same functional departments as for concurrent engineering teams.

Concurrent engineering appeared on the scene a few years ago as a conceptual solution to the time delays encountered in the traditional manner of serial engineering, whereby a project moved in a steady but slow progression from marketing down through functional stages of research, development, and engineering and finally out through manufacturing to a customer. Concurrent engineering was conceived as an overlapping, crossfunctional process, allowing each function to begin earlier as a result and thus contributing to reducing the overall time from conceiving an idea to delivering it to a customer. This chapter will address how some experienced companies are successfully evaluating and managing this concept.

Arguments in favor of this practice are that it solves these upstream and downstream coordination problems, lowers costs as shown in Figure 6.1, reduces cycle time, shortens lines of communication, and brings those most knowledgeable into the decision path [1]. Cycle time has previously been highlighted as a key outcome metric of interest to higher management.

Against this practice it is argued that the will to stay with concurrent engineering had faded at many of the firms surveyed who had initially followed this practice [3,4]. Where it had been enthusiastically sustained, the organizations had been transformed with shorter cycle times and fewer engineering changes. Thus, numbers of such changes are additional team evaluation metrics. The management of human resources was the most difficult issue in two areas: balancing team preservation against the demands for staffing newly initiated projects and linking teams back to the unchanged parts of the organization, particularly functional executives. Despite these concerns, concurrent engineering is now widely used, as explained in a subsequent section.

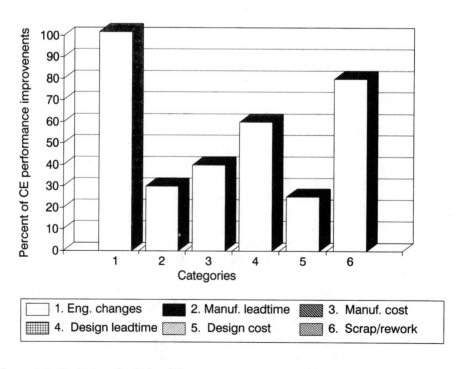

Figure 6.1 CE: the benefits (*After:* [2]).

6.1.1 Some Background

The term "concurrent engineering" was put forward by the *Defense Advanced Research Projects Agency*'s (DARPA) *Defense Initiative on Concurrent Engineering* (DICE) at the University of West Virginia [5–7]. These sources summarize a number of efforts at cycle-time reduction, stressing that many redesigns come because the development has not been reviewed for manufacturability, quality, serviceability, or testing before being "thrown over the wall" into manufacturing. This view held that paralleling of engineering and manufacturing would alleviate the problem, but the cited sources clearly neglected marketing, as might be expected where the supplier was expected to respond to a government specification. At about the same time, the Department of Defense also adopted TQM as an objective, so both initiatives interacted in companies doing defense business. As an engineer in an aerospace company put it in a follow-up interview to the 1994 study, "to meet the Defense Department's requirements for TQM for a new (airframe) model, a totally new concept has been initiated called Integrated Product Development Teams, marking the first time in the company's history that a genuine 'concurrent' engineering effort has been implemented."

TQM has been adopted also by many nondefense companies. As an engineer in a food company laboratory put it in a follow-up interview to the 1993 study, "We must measure concurrent engineering activities as part of the total quality initiative, and cycle time is an almost ideal metric."

Managers used to call concurrent engineering "common sense," emphasizing teamwork based on trust, confidence, and broad representation as well as the team choosing a leader to act as project coordinator [8]. Thus, there appears the issue of parallelism versus teamwork as the preferred implementation of concurrent engineering. Organization theory addresses the three forms of task interdependence—serial, parallel, or pooled/reciprocal—and uses the analogy to the sports of baseball, football, and basketball, respectively. However, rarely are the actual tasks so clearly differentiated. Most are often a continuum from parallel to reciprocal or a hybrid of serial and concurrent engineering [9]. This latter article argues that where there is a step that cannot start before another is completed, serial engineering of that phase is less costly than starting both steps in parallel, and no more time consuming. Thus, a hybrid serial/parallel development approach is preferable. This is supported also for "make to order" products where concurrent engineering seems to be well suited and effective for incremental innovations, since internal functions and suppliers are more comfortable with the technology, whereas breakthrough products have to progress serially down the experience curve in mastering the new technology [10].

New product development cycles were addressed in financial terms by the author some years ago, showing the improvement in project return if development was advanced [11, pp. 22–23]. Another view from a financial basis showed both the benefits of a fast cycle and the poor financial consequences of too long a cycle and extended this to speed-to-market accelerators in engineering, production, sales response, and customer service, thus bridging the gap between innovation and implementation [7]. Other authors broadened the development speed focus to customer loyalty and market share, involving a major shift in culture from a cost orientation to one based on time [12]. However, for the most part, the financial returns promised by these authors have not been achieved, as benefits came down as fast as costs.

On the commercial products front, the R&D-marketing interface was the focus of a competitive analysis counseling against having marketing "throw it over the wall" to R&D [13,14]. This was expanded by the notion that traditional barriers between departments need to be torn down by including sales and marketing functions in the new product development team. Thus, the issue of where concurrent engineering begins seems distinct between firms dealing directly with the end user and those supplying government bodies, particularly the Defense Department.

Three comments from follow-up interviews for the 1993 study with commercial products companies also highlight some of the issues involved with the manufacturing interface: "For us, concurrent engineering results in lower defect rates in manufacturing (automotive components);" "concurrent engineering helps avoid the kind of mistakes that negatively impact manufacturing (consumer products industry);" "it takes time to run a complex concurrent engineering project, but that time is made up in manufacturing (chemical industry)."

These comments focus in on the key evaluation metrics of crossfunctional teams, all of which have been discussed earlier: reduced overall cycle times, not merely those in R&D; quality as measured by lower defect rates, fewer technical mistakes, fewer engineering changes; and effective downward transfer to manufacturing.

6.1.2 How Companies Actually Manage CE

More recently, several authors have begun to address good management implementation practices [5, 15–17]. These have identified the critical management tasks: team formation, innovative techniques, computer-based technologies, measurable evaluation and improvement goals, a supportive organization, anticipating customer needs, keeping a system view, strong leadership, colocation, dedication, isolation, and concentration. While giving some unidentified and limited examples to support these views, missing from these articles were indepth studies of how managers actually manage.

One of the clearer views came from Chrysler, based in Detroit, MI. CE at Chrysler started in January 1989, on the Dodge Viper car, with a volunteer crossfunctional team of just 85 people [1, p. 16]. Yet the Viper team was just a small testbed for the four larger platform teams now in place (a platform is a chassis and drive system common to several different models). For example, three 1993-model sedans—the Chrysler Concorde, Eagle Vision and Dodge Intrepid—were done simultaneously by a platform team of 744 people. The minivan heavier weight platform team, however, was assigned the electric vehicle project because of high battery weights and the larger numbers of prospective passengers. These teams not only blur the lines between advanced R&D, designers, engineers, and manufacturing people, but also the lines to outside suppliers.

The Neon project for a small car gives another example [18, p. 25]. The small car platform team had a core group of 150 people but mobilized more than 600 other internal and external engineers, 289 suppliers, and many shop people. In 42 months a new model was in production at a sufficiently low cost to make it profitable against competing small imported cars. The total development cost was $1.3 billion as compared with Ford's $2 billion and five years for the Escort, and General Motors' $5 billion and seven years for the Saturn.

To avoid duplication of effort and hoarding of information with R&D people spread over four teams, an informal network was established of "Tech Clubs" [1, p. 17]. These might include brake engineers from the four platform teams, some one from purchasing and one or two suppliers. In addition, a small scientific research activity of 69 people was kept to look at advanced fabrication, transmissions, and bodies and to provide expertise to back up platform team R&D.

A second example comes from another manufacturing company based in two locations in the Midwest. A detailed study of Deere & Company stressed the need for a lean, flexible, and barrierfree organization based on teams, concluding it to be more difficult and protracted than managers realize [19]. Deere began in 1984 with parallel or simultaneous engineering but found that parallel tracks rarely meet. As a consequence, two different but more advanced forms are proceeding in different divisions of a more reciprocal form of integrated engineering in two separate testbeds: construction equipment since 1988 in Dubuque, IA, and Harvester equipment since 1984 in Moline, IL.

At Dubuque, four-fifths of the engineers have been shifted out of their function into one of four self-contained businesses (product lines) where they remain through early manufacture of their product [19]. The reasons for the shift were to bring the R&D staff into closer contact with their marketing and manufacturing counterparts and to couple them more closely with business needs. The results were evaluated by lower costs and shorter cycle times. Even with this success, there are still pulls from the twin masters of the self-contained businesses. The business heads, with a natural interest in the bottom line, seek continued lowering of costs and cycle times. The R&D functional director at headquarters is somewhat more concerned with maintaining the technical enhancement of the engineers and the longer range core competencies of the R&D groups, which have their costs and divert some attention from costs and cycle times.

The Harvester division has gone even farther into a nonhierarchial multidisciplinary organization [19]. Their shift was to solve the twin pulls between business heads and their functional directors that had also been found at Moline as they had at Dubuque. There they have learned that fully integrated engineering has to go beyond concurrent engineering. Effective teamwork at Harvester required abandoning matrix structures and the multiple lines of responsibility. They also found that teamwork does not work with too many layers of hierarchy—Harvester is down to three layers between the general manager and operators by combining some of the functions and broadening the scope of the managers and supervisors in each of the three layers.

Neither division has abandoned functions completely, preserving some to ensure that others learn and advance in their disciplines [19]. Differences still exist between the two locations in the degrees of integration and of moving away from pre-integration functional directors. This is in part due to how long each has been at it and because engineering and manufacturing at Harvester have yet to become colocated. Differing circumstances will always make multiple experiences desirable.

From this discussion, several issues appear. First, the currency of many of the cited sources indicates this shift to a time orientation is rather recent. Several threads relating to application of concurrent engineering seem to have been identified. There is a need to address the innovation management issue of reducing the cycle time from concept to product introduction into the implementation process. The inclusion or exclusion of marketing seems dependent on the closeness of the business to the end user. Last, the most effective method of implementation—parallel or by teams—and the management techniques are imprecise [20]. Evaluation of time, quality, and cost stands out in all examples.

6.1.3 Use of CE

The 1993 to 1995 studies documented the use of concurrent engineering in a large number of companies. The questionnaire asked "What is the approximate percent mix between the (serial and concurrent engineering) approaches of your company's total R&D budget?" In all three surveys, the median value for concurrent engineering was at least 65%. The distribution of responses is shown graphically in Figure 6.2.

When responses to the 1994 study were compared by industry groups, no significant differences were found. Thus, concurrent engineering is well established as an innovation management practice despite the concerns expressed in several studies cited earlier. Its use has not, however, grown appreciably in the three years, giving support to the proposed hybrid argument [9].

6.1.4 Correlation of CE and Other Factors

From the uniformity of the curves in Figure 6.2, the reader might infer that there was a stable relationship between other factors over the three years. This was not

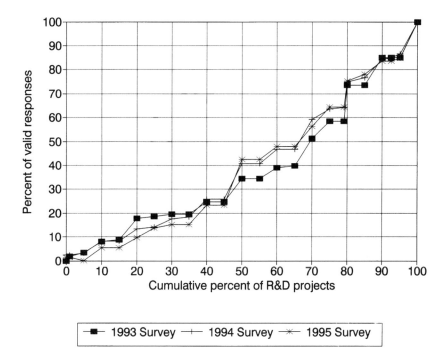

Figure 6.2 Use of CE.

the case, however. Several factors were correlated in one or two years, but not in all three, as shown in Table 6.1. In particular, a shorter idea-to-customer cycle time was correlated in 1993 when only 20% of the responses measured both that time and the use of CE and thus cannot be considered a reliable result for the longer term. In the later two years, with over 80% of the responses measuring both, the correlation was far from being significant.

To establish a composite view of these factors, the three years were pooled. Testing for differences between the three years and the pooled value showed no significant year-to-year factor. After controlling for idea-to-customer time, higher use of concurrent engineering was associated positively with higher use of value engineering, lower percent of the R&D budget on product extensions (and thus higher percentage on major and minor new products), and higher patent numbers. Value engineering is a discipline that breaks down product cost into its constituent elements and analyzes each of them for necessity.

These findings from pooled years support the single year results in Table 6.1. The first and second results imply a consistent management strategy, focused on medium to large cost-effective R&D projects. The evaluation metric suggested is

Table 6.1
Factors Correlated Positively With CE

Factor	1993	1994	1995
Shorter idea-to-customer time	x		
Center of gravity close to customer	x		x
Extensive R&D-marketing interface	x	x	
More years TQM used in R&D		x	
Use of value engineering		x	
Low percent of R&D budget on extensions		x	
High numbers of patents			x

Notes: Statistically significant at $p = .05$.

that used in the surveys: percent of the R&D budget on major projects, minor projects, and product extensions.

The last result seems principally to be a proxy for the larger firms' R&D organizations being more into concurrent engineering than smaller ones, since the correlation with sales volume was nearly as high, and that with patent intensity (patents/sales) not significant. In contrast to the 1994 result, fewer years of use of TQM in R&D were associated with higher use of concurrent engineering in the pooled data. Surprisingly, a center of gravity close to the customer and an extensive interface between marketing and R&D did not retain their importance.

The factors not significantly correlated in this or any of the other models include profitability as measured by earnings before interest and taxes, new products as a percent of sales, and R&D cycle time. It may be interpreted that the extent of the use of concurrent engineering has now become so high among competitors that using it no longer gives a visible competitive advantage in these outcome metrics.

Still another model was attempted, both to use a more linear portion of the concurrent engineering use curve and to identify what was related to higher levels of serial engineering use (lower levels of concurrent engineering use). This model was made using only the values of serial engineering use above the median of 30% use. This point was chosen judgementally as a compromise between linearity and retaining enough samples for statistical significance. Higher use of concurrent engineering in this higher serial engineering use group was still positively associated with a higher use of value engineering but not with any of the other factors in Table 6.1 except product extensions. Higher use of concurrent engineering was associated with both a higher percentage of extensions, rather than a lower one for the full group, and a higher percentage of major new projects. It would appear that the addition of marketing and/or manufacturing team members has had an effect shifting R&D priorities away from the middle ground of minor projects. Also, a higher use of concurrent engineering in this higher serial engineering use group was associated with an increased new product percentage to sales and an increased use of QFD.

To summarize the correlation findings, managers who use concurrent engineering highly are also likely to be large in size, focus on major and minor new products, and use value engineering. High users of serial engineering still benefit from a greater use of concurrent engineering, from a higher new product-to-sales percentage, a focus also on both major projects and extensions, and a higher use of QFD. All of these are self-reinforcing around the theme of fostering innovation through the use of concurrent engineering. This supports the contentions that while concurrent engineering may be good with incremental projects, serial engineering has a role in breakthrough products [9,10]. Although this may enhance shareholder value through increased growth, the use of concurrent engineering is now so prevalent that there is no reliable correlation in the responses with profitability or fast cycle times.

6.1.5 CE and Throughput Maximization

The argument has been advanced that apart from return on sales, concurrent engineering should also improve the return on assets even more because the shorter cycle times maximize throughput or the output per unit time, which is the reciprocal of cycle time [21,22]. This is quite a plausible argument. However, nothing in the research studies on which this book is based has shed any light on this contention. Thus, this remains an area for further study.

6.2 LESSONS LEARNED IN TEAM EVALUATION

The use of crossfunctional teams, including concurrent or simultaneous engineering, is now widespread and is seen as the best overall management practice. Higher concurrent engineering use is associated with the higher use of value engineering, several other factors that differ between all responses, and just those of the group of companies with higher serial engineering use. However, its use is not in recent years reliably correlated with profitability or cycle time.

The author still recommends evaluating crossfunctional teams by overall (idea-to-customer) cycle times because of the high level of general management interest in competing on time. Cost evaluation must still also be done to communicate with financial managers. A selection of quality metrics such as lower defect rates, fewer technical mistakes, and fewer engineering changes are also appropriate in evaluating teams. Subjective evaluation should be done of the effectiveness of downward transfer to manufacturing. Measuring the level of use of serial engineering will help raise questions of whether shifting to increasing use of concurrent engineering might enhance the new product-to-sales percentage and improve the interfaces with the balance of the company. Finally, there is a need to continue to follow the fast changing literature in the field [23].

References

[1]   Lutz, R. A., "Implementing Technological Change with Cross-Functional Teams," *Research Technology Management*, Vol. 37(2), Mar.–Apr. 1994, pp. 14–18.

[2]   Lucas/Artemis, Presentation to Industry, Trumbull, CT, 1992, Dec. 12, after: "Changing Your Way to a Better Business," *Engineering Computers*, May 1991.

[3]   Center for Innovative Management Studies, Technology Management Review, Lehigh University, Bethlehem, PA, Summer 1993.

[4]   Lee, D. M. S., "Management of Concurrent Engineering: Organizational Concepts and a Framework of Analysis," *Engineering Management J.*, Vol. 4(2), 1992, pp. 15–25.

[5]   Rosenblatt, A., et al., "Special Report: Concurrent Engineering," *IEEE Spectrum*, Vol. 28(7), 1991, pp. 22–37.

[6]   Ellis, L. W., and C. C. Curtis, "Practices in Concurrent Engineering," *Managing in a Global Environment: 1992 International Engineering Management Conference*, IEEE Catalog No. 92CH3222-7, Piscataway, NJ: IEEE, 1992, pp. 115–118. This document has an extensive bibliography covering prior articles on concurrent engineering and cycle-time reduction.

[7]   Vesey, J. T., "The New Competitors: They Think in Terms of 'Speed-to-Market,'" *Executive* (Academy of Management), Vol. 5, 1991, pp. 22–33, and "Speed-to-Market Distinguishes the New Competitors," *Research Technology Management*, Vol. 34(6), 1991, pp. 33–38.

[8]   Cousins, R. E., "Rules for Concurrent Engineering—Parts I & II," *Computer*(IEEE), Vol. 24(11), 1991, p. 112, and 24(12), 1991, p. 136.

[9]   AitSahalia, F., E. Johnson, and P. Will, "Is Concurrent Engineering Always a Sensible Proposition?" *IEEE Trans. on Engineering Management*, Vol. 42(2), 1995, pp. 166–170.

[10] Handfield, R. B., "Effects of Concurrent Engineering on Make-to-Order Products," *IEEE Trans. on Engineering Management*, Vol. 41(4), 1994, pp. 384–393.

[11] Ellis, L. W., *The Financial Side of Industrial Research Management*, New York: Wiley, 1984.

[12] Smith, P. G., and D. G. Reinertsen, *Developing Products in Half the Time*, Florence, KY: Van Nostrand Reinhold, 1991.

[13] St. Charles, D., "Don't Toss It Over—Break Down the Walls," *Automation*, Vol. 37(6), 1990, pp. 68–69.

[14] Wolff, M. F., "Teams Speed Commercialization of R&D Projects," *Research Technology Management*, Vol. 31, 1988, pp. 8–10; "Metanoic Society Helps Shell Commercialize Product Ideas in Half the Time," *Research Technology Management*, Vol. 34(6), 1991, pp. 9–11; "Working Faster," *Research Technology Management*, Vol. 35(6), 1992, pp. 10–12.

[15] Zangwill, W. I., "Concurrent Engineering: Concepts and Implementation," *Engineering Management Review*, Vol. 20(4), 1992, pp. 40–52.

[16] Wheelwright, S. C., and K. B. Clark, "Competing Through Development Capability in a Manufacturing-Based Organization," *Engineering Management Review*, Vol. 20(3), 1992, p. 37.

[17] Reddy, Y. V., et al., "Special Issue: Computer Support for Concurrent Engineering," *IEEE Computer*, Vol. 26(1), 1993, pp. 12–16.

[18] Dess, G. G., A. A. Rasheed, K. J. McLaughlin, and R. L. Priem, "The New Corporate Architecture," *Academy of Management Executive*, Vol. IX(3), Aug. 1995, pp. 7–20; *IEEE Engineering Management Review*, Vol. 24(2), Summer 1996, pp. 20–28.

[19] Lorenz, C., "Team-Based Engineering at Deere," *McKinsey Quarterly*, (4), 1991, pp. 81–93.

[20] Liker, J. K., and F. Hull, "What Works in Concurrent Engineering? Sorting Through the Barrage of Practices." *1993 Academy of Management Conference*, Atlanta, GA, Aug. 11, 1993.

[21] Morbey, G. K., "Accelerating the Product Development Process," *Business Success Through New Product Success*. Bloomington, IN: Product Development & Management Assn., 1991, pp. 34–37.

[22] Goldratt, E. M., and J. Cox, *The Goal*, 2nd ed., Great Barrington, MA: North River Press, 1986.

[23] Gerwin, D., and G. Susman, eds., "Special Issue on Concurrent Engineering," *IEEE Trans. on Engineering Management*, Vol. 43(2), May 1996, pp. 118–217. (Received in final editing too late for inclusion in this chapter.)

Part II

Time to Market: Measurement and Management

Of the various general outcomes measured by the companies in Part One, timeliness stood out as that most often selected. However, time evaluation was addressed in multiple terms that were not really sufficiently specific for the primary level R&D manager to make operating decisions. Thus, time needs to be broken down into specifics and submeasures to really be useful for evaluation purposes at this lower managerial level. This was begun by initiating a new round of survey research—the 1994 and 1995 studies, as described fully in Chapter 14 and summarized in Chapters 7 and 8.

This second part of the book addresses measuring, evaluating, and managing time in much greater detail. Chapter 7 reviews timeliness evaluation measurements: cycle time, milestones, and others. Chapter 8 goes into how time needs to be managed once it has been evaluated.

Chapter 7

Cycle Time: Outcome and Output Evaluation Metrics

In developing a pattern of measurements, a split has been made by the author between the outcomes, which are those viewed by top management after an innovation has gone through the implementation chain and has been delivered to a customer, and the outputs from the innovation chain in a company, usually from the research, development, or engineering departments, that have been sent downstream toward the implementing or order handling part of the organization.

As mentioned in Chapter 2, the economic measure of TFP, while theoretically correct, did not correspond to what companies were accustomed to using and was viewed as too retrospective to provide timely guidance. Obviously, the actual usage by companies would be a better place to start, even if it is an incomplete indicator of effectiveness. The work of other researchers and the responses to the survey in Table 1.1 provide a convenient although not necessarily unbiased sample. In reviewing metrics mentioned in previous chapters, that most frequently mentioned for both outcomes and outputs is cycle time, thus giving it pride of place in analysis.

7.1 INTRODUCTION TO CYCLE-TIME MEASUREMENT

Because cycle time through R&D is such a large component of overall cycle time, and thus highly correlated with it, it is convenient to examine them together as overall outcome and R&D output measurements, respectively. In addition, the 1993 study begins to do what the R&D manager desires, that is, to identify precursor or leading metrics that may be potentially useful for management because they occur earlier in time, allowing more prompt controlling actions to be taken. In addition, this study has noted the low contribution of reduced cycle time to financial performance, which will be discussed below under cycle time's relation to financial evaluation.

7.1.1 Cycle Time as an Outcome Measurement

In previous chapters, the terms used to describe cycle time as an outcome measurement were overall time, time to market, idea-to-customer time, and concept-to-production launch time. The metric most frequently used was calendar days, or those derived from the same base, such as percent time reduction. The image is clear from these descriptions that not only is the beginning of the innovation chain to be included (that is, idea, concept, customer, and marketing) but the initial time through to the end of the implementation chain as well (that is, market development and production launch).

On the other hand, the 1991 and 1993 studies found that idea-to-customer time was then only about one-fourth as likely to be measured by respondent companies as time through R&D, an output measurement (This changed in later years, as will be discussed.) Thus, we had the paradox that what was then most important to measure—the outcome, was far less often measured than what was easier to use as a measurement—the R&D output, which was within the responsibility of a single functional department head.

Although idea-to-customer cycle time was from a smaller and less-representative sample than that for R&D cycle time, it is useful to see what factors were then associated with it. A graphical representation of these factors associated with decreased idea-to-customer time is shown in Figure 7.1 (from the 1993 study [1]).

External factors in this chart are roughly equivalent to what was designated earlier as inputs. Of these, private ownership has a minimal effect, company age increasing by a year corresponds to a 10-day shorter overall time, and each additional year of average product life slows overall time by 37 days. None of these have much leverage for management action.

Of Figure 7.1's factors labeled "internal," extent of early R&D-marketing interface and emphasis of R&D in the value chain have minimal effects. Each percent of R&D budget shifted into projects using concurrent engineering is associated with an 11-day decrease in overall time. Since firms can easily make such shifts in the tens of percents, this seems the principal indicated management action. Patents per million dollars of sales also has a strong accelerating effect, suggesting that proprietary technology is an important management action.

Finally, each percent shift of the R&D budget into major new projects is associated with an 8-day longer overall time, which is not unexpected—larger projects take more time. Rather than using this as an excuse to retreat from major new projects, the positive financial impact from them shown under cycle time's relation to financial evaluation should be considered.

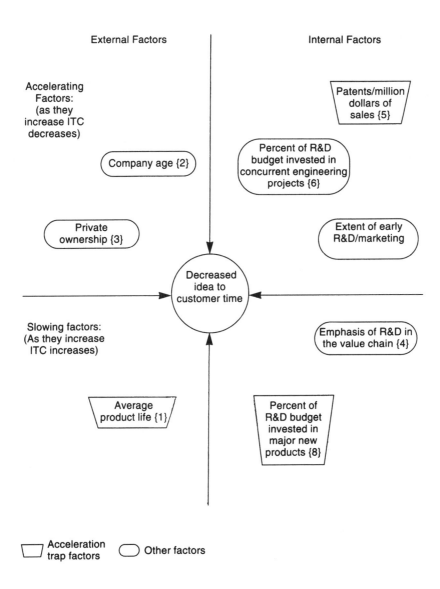

Figure 7.1 Factors related to idea-to-customer time. (*Source:* [1]. Reprinted with permission.)

7.1.2   R&D Time as an Output Measurement

In previous chapters output measures of cycle time included reduction in R&D time and tooling and facility preparation as a narrower measure of interest to manufacturing engineers. The companies who answered the questionnaire covered in Table 1.1 were queried as to the their use of time as an output measure, with results shown in Table 7.1.

Stage-gate tracking is a formal process requiring management approval to proceed past each step or gate in the development process [3]. While stage-gate tracking is widely used, it is most effective when bottom up control (as in concurrent engineering) allows those closest to the program discretion in proceeding past the gate if only a limited amount remains to be done on the critical path to the gate. In either case, appropriate metrics are those such as percentage of dates met on time or percent accomplishment of what had been planned by scheduled dates. In addition to the milestones achieved on time measurement noted in Table 7.1, another approach has merit: time ahead or behind schedule expressed as a percent of estimated time.

Milestones are the estimated target dates for reaching the various stages or gates in an R&D program. Even for companies not using stage-gate tracking, metrics that evaluate how much of these phases has been completed by scheduled dates or how much of enabling technological results has been achieved.

Milestone dates are often reported on Gantt charts, named early this century after the American industrial engineer Henry Gantt. But even Gantt's original chart included estimated and actual labor hours as an aid to analysis. Without this, it is difficult to ascertain whether any project slippage is due to insufficient applied time, to low estimates, or to the disease of "creeping elegance" as the original targets are expanded during the project. If labor hours were below estimate, adding people would be a solution; if hours were on estimate, more work had to be done to complete the project than had been estimated originally.

Stage-gate tracking and milestone measurement, when they are combined into a category that might best be called "timeliness of R&D's actions in meeting promised commitments," were more frequently used in 1993 than cycle-time

Table 7.1
Time Metrics Used in R&D

	Number of Companies
Stage-gate tracking/milestones achieved on time	5
Cycle-time reduction/analytical turnaround	2
Objectives/technology milestones	2

Source: [2].

measurements. For example, companies interviewed as part of the 1993 IRIMER study gave about a two-to-one preference for the totals of use of stage-gate tracking and milestones over the use of cycle-time measurement.

The 1993 study also considered time through R&D as an output measurement. Since many more companies used this metric then, the results are more robust than for idea-to-customer time. Figure 7.2 shows the factors this study found associated with decreased time through R&D [1].

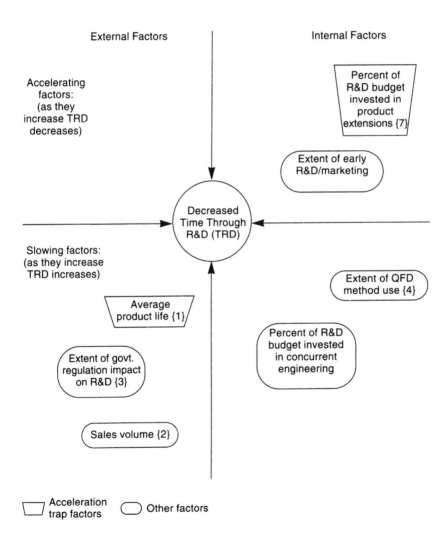

Figure 7.2 Factors related to time through R&D. (*Source:* [1]. Reprinted with permission.)

As with idea-to-customer time, an average product life increase delays R&D cycle time. While not delaying overall cycle time, the extent of government regulation and company size as measured by sales volume delay R&D cycle time. These input factors are manageable to the extent of ensuring that their presence does not unnecessarily flow through into overall time.

In contrast to overall cycle time, concurrent engineering is associated with a minimal increase in R&D time. While not reflected more than minimally in overall time, each one-step increase in rating the extent of R&D/marketing interface has a substantial effect in decreasing R&D time. Also, the extent of QFD use is associated with longer R&D time, but not with overall time. In the past there was often the complaint "We never have time to do it right, but always have time to do it over." The message for management action seems to be do it right the first time, even if it delays R&D time, and you will be compensated in overall time by avoiding the "do-it-over" time, as shown graphically in Figure 6.1 [4]. Finally, shifting into product extensions by one percent of budget decreases R&D time, but it is not an action to be taken without considering the negative effect on profitability shown under cycle time's relation to financial evaluation.

7.1.3 Cycle Time's Relation to Costs

While much has been written suggesting that cycle-time reduction leads to cost reduction, most examples given have been far less rigorous in keeping track of the "before" costs and times than they have of the "after" costs and times. As a result, one needs the proverbial grain of salt about claims both of the amount of cycle-time reduction and of cost reduction. If nothing else had happened, cycle-time reduction by paralleling activities need not have reduced cost at all—a greater number of people working for a shorter time period yields the same work hours and costs on the project.

What does happen, however, is that people work differently under concurrent engineering and do different things, so overall fewer work hours are used and less cost is incurred. However, the cost reduction percentage is not always equal to that of the time reduction, as shown graphically in Figure 6.1.

R&D costs may tend to increase despite claims to the contrary. Doing it right the first time means more front-end R&D expense. Procedures such as QFD and concurrent engineering increase R&D costs. Closer integration with marketing also raises R&D costs. And if team members are transferred to R&D from marketing and manufacturing, their former functional superiors will most likely want their labor costs transferred too.

Overall costs, however, often decrease. Some of this is cosmetic as people transferred to teams do not now show up in their former department expenditures. However, many real costs are reduced, principally in the "do-it-over" area, as also shown in Figure 6.1. With fewer changes, the costs of redesign are reduced, tooling is not reworked, parts are not made surplus, and many other costs previously incurred prior to and often after product launch are not now needed. Due to the differences between companies who have tried cycle-time reduction, no precise guidelines are readily available. However, believable cycle-time reductions of 20 to 40% have been achieved by many companies, with equally believable overall cost reductions achieved of the order of half of the corresponding cycle-time reductions. However, these cost reductions apparently do not flow through to the bottom line, which will be discussed in the next subsection.

7.1.4 Cycle Time's Relation to Financial Evaluation

How does cycle time correlate with the financial evaluation discussed in Chapter 2? Part of the problem in answering this question is that there are so many financial metrics used in industry that research has not looked at them all closely.

Six different financial metrics were suggested in an early survey [2]: NPV, ROI, IRR, cost reduction of operations, process savings, and throughput (direct expenses/development). R&D return on development costs, as measured in a post-audit, was a measure put forward in an earlier IRI study [5]. As that study defined the term, it was a discounted benefit-to-cost ratio, a measure often used in the analysis of projects for government agencies. The specification of "post-audit" suggests that perhaps a better term for this section might be "financial post-evaluation" to separate the outcome measure from the use of financial selection in the project approval stage. Thus, there is no shortage of candidates for the exact metric, with company preference being the determining factor. What is clear, however, is that some measurement of financial results or outcome is needed to be compared to cycle time, despite the low ranking given this metric by the 1992 study of IRIMER members and the similarly low rankings by technical executives in Chapter 2.

The 1993 study found no correlation of cycle time with ROI or return on sales. EBIT in ratio to sales was used, therefore, as a financial measure free of the firm's capitalization and tax structure. The 1993 study found results as shown in Figure 7.3 [1].

The external factors shown correspond roughly to inputs, while the internal factors include internal processes, interactions, and one output (time through R&D). The surprising finding was that cutting time through R&D in half only yielded a one-percent increase in EBIT! In view of the extent of cost reductions previously indicated to be associated with cycle-time reduction, either costs did not reduce as much as indicated or benefits also declined proportionately to the declining costs. Declining benefits could have come from price reductions associated with competition, and this is hinted at in the factor entitled "ROI/cost control reason given for using time metric in new product area," summarizing five different reasons given by respondents. This group had EBIT's 5% lower than the remaining

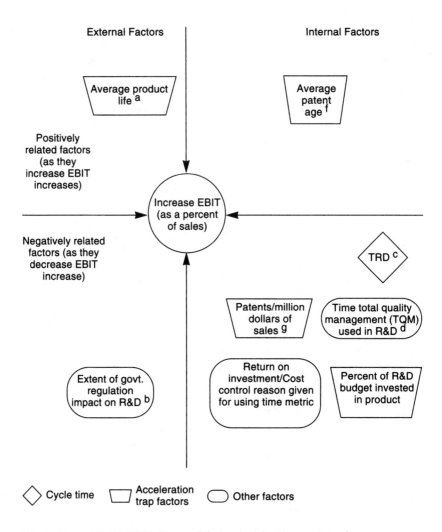

Figure 7.3 Factors related to EBIT. (*Source:* [1]. Reprinted with permission.)

responses, seeming to indicate they had already experienced strong pricing pressures.

Having advocated for a decade that time is money in R&D project selection [6; 7, Fig. 3], it is humbling to be shown that this does not hold true in practice. Looking back with 20:20 hindsight, it becomes clear the earlier position assumed that all other things were equal; this is just not true. Since most of the evidence is that the cost reductions were estimated accurately, it appears that a wrong assumption was made; namely, that given a speeding up of the project, no change would be realized in the benefits from it.

Clearly, for any one product, being first-to-market has many benefits. There is an initial period when the product has no competition and can be priced profitably. When competition appears, the firm that was first-to-market is somewhere further down the learning curve and, thus having lower costs, can be more profitable than the competition at a competitive price. Equally, being late-to-market due to slower R&D cycle time might have meant less profitability as competitors took over the market.

Since this outcome is not reflected by the 1993 research, it seems clear that some management actions must have eaten into the benefits then-assumed to be available. Since this measurement was over an entire company, and not just one product, these actions may have been on products other than the newly introduced first-to-market products. Whether this is because there was an acceleration trap and the benefits did not last as long as earlier estimated—or competitive pressures did not allow recovering the full price anticipated—presents a worthwhile task for future research-on-research.

The acceleration trap is a term coined by Von Braun [8] to describe the contradiction between financial performance failing to improve with increasingly shorter cycle time. He suggests instead the existence of a point at which further time reductions will not only fail to add to lifetime product revenue streams but may also contribute to financial deterioration. He also suggests the following four possible explanations:

1. At a certain point, further acceleration yields no further lifetime revenues for the product.
2. The benefits last for a shorter time, because the product life cycle starts or ends sooner.
3. Additional costs are incurred, but the customer sees no value and won't pay more.
4. Competition forces lower prices.

A recent study also found that "rapid development times are not correlated with expected commercial success"[9], ascribed to difficulties in technology integration and the need to develop new channels of distribution.

The first-to-market concept also fails to take into account the time required to penetrate the market until the innovative product is accepted, as shown in the following example.

Apple Computer Inc. introduced its personal computer well before IBM and had to spend its marketing resources introducing the concept. By the time IBM came into the fray, using Microsoft's operating system that was widely endorsed by software creators, it quickly gained market acceptance and for a time led in PC sales. Then IBM PC clones came in even later, driving prices down and leading both Apple and IBM in sales. In both of these cases of late-to-market, the customer acceptance, first, of the different operating system's software availability, and then subsequently of the lower prices, offset the first-to-market advantage held by Apple.

Many similar cases have been noted where the perceived attraction of being first with shorter R&D cycle times has not yielded the purported profit advantage. Since the first 1% of financial gain (EBIT) requires cutting the R&D cycle time in half, it is futile to expect getting large profit gains from shortening cycle times. This means that compressing the cycle to improve profits is practical perhaps only once in a major effort. Therefore, a critical place for management to begin reconsidering their motives for reducing new product development cycle time is to ensure that these reasons include compelling nonfinancial considerations.

The 1993 study has characterized possible acceleration trap factors in Figure 7.3 by *trape*zoids [1]. For example, it was found that increasing the average product life by 1.3 years would increase EBIT by one percent, and the converse is true that shorter product life lowers EBIT. Under time pressure, one would be inclined to invest in product extensions rather than in major new products. However, each such 4% shift of the R&D budget lowers EBIT by 1%. Longer lived patents, usually associated with major projects, increased EBIT; while increasing the numbers of patents per million dollars of sales, more likely to be associated with many smaller projects, was associated with lowered EBIT.

Summarizing cycle-time measurement, the principal management actions to reduce cycle time are:

- Shift an increasing percent of the R&D budget into projects using concurrent engineering.
- Raise proprietary technology, as measured by patents per million dollars of sales.
- Do it right the first time, even if it delays R&D time, and you will be compensated in overall time by avoiding the "do-it-over" time.
- Compressing cycle time to improve profits is practical perhaps only once in a major effort. Management should reconsider their motives for reducing new product development cycle time to ensure that these reasons include compelling nonfinancial considerations.

7.2 EXPANDED DIMENSIONS OF TIME TO MARKET

While timeliness was treated previously, that earlier discussion was principally in relation to overall and R&D cycle times. The rest of this chapter will cover measuring and evaluating the individual component time segments as well.

7.3 MEASURING AND RECORDING TIME

What time to measure? Earlier in this book, cycle time was usually measured in terms of calendar days. A stage-gate or milestone measurement tends to focus in time measured as forecast and actual dates. Financial measures of time focus on costs, which means measuring time as labor hours. Also, to use any one of the many available project management computer programs for evaluation, all three of these time dimensions tend to be required as input measurements. Thus, measuring and recording time as days, dates, and labor hours becomes a precondition for successful management. These are needed both in estimates and records of overall time and in the time segments into which the overall measures are divided.

For managers of all levels who deal in a variety of daily tasks, still another time recording is appropriate; that is, record how your day was spent so as to be able to apply the time management lessons later in this book to your own work.

7.4   MEASURING OVERALL TIME

Previously, overall time was analyzed in terms of idea-to-customer time and R&D time. Another overall measure for those companies that have adopted concurrent engineering is to measure the time through that part of the organization that forms the innovating team. The 1994 study adds still another overall dimension, namely, market development cycle time. Figure 4.2 shows how these cycle-time metrics relate.

Table 7.2
Responses Relating to Use With New Product Development

Factor Measured	Percent Measuring	Days of Cycle Time		
		Min.	Mean	Max.
Concurrent Engineering (1)				
Product design	66	10	166	360
Product development	60	10	155	360
Prototype to manufacturability	66	7	96	186
Production	69	1	82	360
Testing	66	3	48	357
Other Functions Reporting				
Marketing	31	17	123	180
Ship to customer	29	3	6	10
Service request	37	1	11	50
Aggregate Measurements				
Idea to customer	17	103	261	360
Time through R&D	31	23	187	360

Note: (1) Functions usually considered to be part of concurrent engineering.
Source: 1991 study, as presented in [10].

The respondent means reported in the 1991 study are shown in Table 7.2, and the progression of overall measurements through 1995 are shown in Figure 7.4.

7.4.1 Idea-to-Customer Time

Idea-to-customer time is usually defined as the time between initiation or identifying customer need and the delivery of the first product or service to an end user. Thus, it encompasses all steps in the innovation chain, and all those in the implementation chain involved with first product or service delivery. These steps may be grouped into two other constituent aggregate measurements: R&D time, which with marketing makes up the innovation cycle, and market development cycle time, which makes up the innovation chain's transmittal to the implementation chain.

Idea-to-customer time should be a primary aim of a measurement system. It was not so considered by the majority of responses to the 1991 survey, shown in Table 7.2, where only 17% reported using it as a measurement. For the 1993 to 1995 studies, however, the percentage of respondents using this metric had

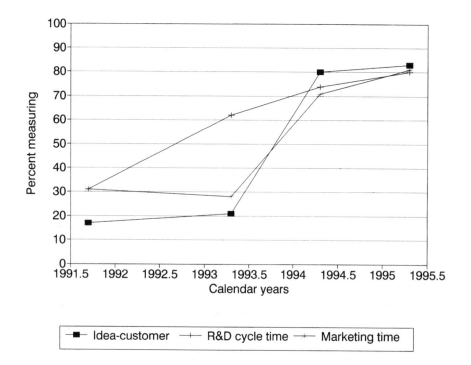

Figure 7.4 Time measurement growth.

climbed to 21, 80, and 83%, respectively. As explained more completely in Chapter 14, in a 1994 model that used idea-to-customer time as the dependent variable, this factor was explained by many independent variables. Customer satisfaction ratings provided five of these factors in a pattern that seems to indicate dual philosophies of innovation management. First, speedy innovation involves customer satisfaction with high technology and customer communication; alternatively, formality in measuring satisfaction with innovation management and cost competitiveness go with slower idea-to-customer cycle times. Greater use of in-house benchmarking was associated with a longer idea-to-customer cycle time—does looking at your own company mean looking away from timeliness in serving the customer? Longer R&D cycle time was associated with longer idea-to-customer time—apparently the more the R&D group does, the more time has to be taken in other segments.

Measuring idea-to-customer time requires that the entire organization be set up to measure time. This is a difficult task because of the many different departments involved. Thus, for idea-to-customer time to be measured adequately, general management has to have timeliness as a priority for strategic purposes.

7.4.2 R&D Cycle Time

R&D cycle time begins when a new product or service designed to meet a customer need has been identified and defined. In a company dealing with multiple customers, this definition is the function of marketing; or if the idea originates in R&D, it needs to be validated by marketing and the customer. For companies dealing with government bodies or original equipment manufacturers, this definition usually comes in the form of a specification and request for bid. In some companies with good relations with the end user or lead user, there is participation in defining what is required so that this onset is less precise. However, for most companies, a clear go-ahead signal is given in the form of a project approval or contract receipt from which R&D time can be measured.

The task of the R&D or team organization is usually considered complete when a prototype is handed over to the downstream organization together with all necessary information for manufacture if a product or software if a computer-based service. Implicit in this transition is that technical feasibility has been established—for software to be sold, there is even an accounting definition of what is required [11]. For many companies, the R&D task does not stop there—R&D stays responsible until the bugs are out of the manufacturing information or software. This time may be unplanned or built into the time estimates as "assistance to manufacturing" [6].

Chrysler calls these the redo loops [12]. As noted in the previous chapter, they reorganized the company around concurrent engineering platform teams. The following example shows some of their results in time and cost from making this transition.

Concurrent engineering at Chrysler started in January 1989, on the Dodge Viper car, with a volunteer crossfunctional team of just 85 people [1, p. 16]. Exactly three years later, actual production Vipers were on the streets, against the traditional five to six years. Time to market was thus reduced by nearly half as compared with earlier developments. This was clearly a revolutionary one-time reduction that was then spread to the rest of the organization. However, subsequent time savings on newer cars have been more evolutionary and modest in amount. For example, the four models of the LH sedans required 3.25 years, and the small Neon 3.5 years. This demonstrates that once the time-consuming "throwing the design back and forth over the wall" between functional departments has ended, there are still tasks that must be done serially within the team, thus limiting further cycle-time savings.

The costs in the early months of the Viper were higher due to paralleling of design, engineering, and manufacturing, to the dismay of the company's financial executives. However, these costs were later offset by having done it right the first time and thus avoiding costly redo loops as changes continue to be made to cars coming off the line. This resulted in lower total development costs of the Viper. Similarly for the LH series sedans, total development costs were $1.6 billion for a team of 744 people, compared to $2.5 billion seven years earlier for the comparable Ford Taurus/Sable family.

The Viper team members were rewarded in the usual monetary sense. They were also rewarded in nonmonetary ways. Many articles praising their accomplishments were written. Also, the CEO and COO frequently went to visit them.

Before design and development start, there may be a need to accomplish some applied research. The design cycle may be broken down further into time to finalize the concept and time to finalize the design. Development may need to include both product and process development. All of these segments of R&D time will be discussed later.

Research and development cycle times were measured in the 1991, 1993, 1994, and 1995 studies by 31, 62, 74, and 80% of the respondents, respectively. Since these functions are usually under a common leader either as a department or as part of a concurrent engineering team, there is less of an organizational barrier to obtaining adequate time measurements than in the overall case. Thus, it is not surprising that the increase in use of this metric has evolved at a more deliberate pace than for idea-to-customer time, as shown in Figure 7.4.

As expanded in Chapter 14, in the 1994 study, R&D cycle time was used as the dependent variable in a model. While this cycle is correlated with idea-to-customer time, of which it is a component, this overall metric was omitted to help identify which other independent factors would help explain what may drive the R&D time. Many factors were replicated with those in the 1993 study, possibly reflecting the greater experience industry has had with R&D time measurement. Sales volume is still a slowing factor that may reflect more the scale of projects attempted in larger companies rather than that they are more bureaucratic than smaller firms. This finding highlights an area for R&D management attention to counteract this slowness with firm size. Higher use of milestones is associated longer R&D time. Financial outcomes are not significantly related—as a recent article asks "Is speedy R&D really beneficial?" [13]. It is not financially beneficial on findings to date.

These results suggest some additional lessons learned.

- Larger companies need to watch their R&D cycle times, numbers and age of patents, and milestone management, lest these factors unnecessarily lengthen idea to customer times.
- QFD, concurrent engineering, gaining experience with time metrics, and rewards based on the business unit show as useful strategies for shorter cycle times.

7.4.3 CE Time

A philosophical discussion occurs in the literature as to whether or not marketing time is part of CE, as shown in Figure 4.2. Which alternative is true obviously depends on the particular firm's business structure. Most analysts agree, however, that CE always includes what has been defined previously as R&D time plus production and testing of the initial product or service offering. As can be seen in Table 7.2, these latter time segments in 1991 also had over 60% of the respondents measuring their times, while marketing time was then only measured in about half as many responding firms. By 1995, all segments were measuring times equally well, at more than 80% of the responders. The starting point of CE time is as defined earlier dependent upon the company's structure, while the end point is either the delivery of the first production product or software or the end of the redo loop cycle. A few companies are fortunate to have managed so well that these last two dates are coincident.

7.4.4 Market Development Cycle Time

In the pretesting of the 1994 study, one company added a fourth overall time measurement that was added to the questionnaire, that is, market development cycle time. This time begins from the start of the prototype through manufacturability, production, testing, shipping to the customer, and ends with the completion of customer service time on the first delivery. Conceptually, this aggregate time measures how long after development is complete has the first customer been satisfied.

Organizationally, since market development cycle time spans R&D, production, testing, and the two departments of shipping and service that are often part of marketing, the same coordination problems exist as with measuring idea-to-customer time. As a newly defined overall metric, the fraction of companies who are using it was found in the 1994 study to be a substantial 72% of the respondents.

A 1994 model was formed using market development cycle time as the dependent variable, as covered in Chapter 14. A shorter cycle time was associated with a greater share of the R&D budget that product extensions have, which is logical since the choice of extensions precedes the time cycle, and less effort is required to learn to handle extensions than for new products. Users of this route still have to deal with the aforementioned negative profit impact. A longer cycle time was associated with longer R&D time—the effect of more R&D effort apparently spills over into more time to market.

Summarizing measuring overall time, the principal management actions are the following:

- Idea-to-customer time should be a primary aim of a measurement system.
- Larger companies need to watch their R&D cycle times, numbers and age of patents, and milestone management, lest these factors unnecessarily lengthen idea-to-customer times.
- QFD, CE, gaining experience with time metrics, and rewards based on the business unit are useful strategies for shortening cycle times.
- A shorter market development cycle time may come from a greater share of the R&D budget that product extensions have, but this may have a negative profit impact unless disciplined project selection procedures are used.

7.5 MEASURING TIME SEGMENTS

All of the overall measurements may be done directly or consist of the measured time segments of which they are composed. From the prior description of aggregate time measurements, the individual time segments include: marketing, applied research, design to finalize the concept, final design, product or service development, process development, prototype to manufacturability, redo loops, production (fabrication and assembly, or the equivalent in software), testing (alpha and beta), shipping, and service. The purpose of this section is to single out the beginning and ending milestones of each of these segments.

7.5.1 Marketing Time

One part of the idea-to-customer time is marketing time, defined as time between initiation or identifying customer need and identifying a new product or service to meet that need. As can be seen in Table 7.2, 31% of companies responding measured this time in 1991, rising to 81% by the 1995 study, paralleling that of idea-to-customer time.

The end of this time period is when the definition of customer need is handed over to R&D or the CE team that will develop the needed product or service. The beginning, however, is rather less precise, leading one source to call it the "fuzzy front end" [14].

An Allied Signal project's research objective was to design a material based upon specific physical properties [14]. This would allow candidate molecules to be selected faster, thus reducing time to market. The NIH problem was relative as the material was not known to chemists—it was solved by deeper investigation of theory. Sufficient effort was addressed by a select team and by contract research. The needed skills were obtained from universities and consultants. End user input removed barriers to transfer to the business unit who also identified many intermediate deliverables enhancing the value of research. TQM proved to be the most effective tool in bringing team members together with a shared goal.

Several examples of the starting date being properly recorded have been noted by the author in earlier studies. For example:

- The need is stated in a field salesperson's trip report on a visit to the customer.
- The concept is documented in the minutes of a product planning meeting.
- The customer raises the need in a visit to the firm, a letter, or an acceptance report on a completed contract.
- A formal specification is received from the customer—if this is your firm's start, usually you are behind the competition who has had wind of the need from one of the other three sources.

A marketing time model was created using this time segment as the dependent variable, as explained in Chapter 14, considering that the leading factor of marketing time was most important to innovation managers. One slowing factor is R&D time; although marketing occurs timewise ahead of R&D, it is more likely that both time segments are consequences of a common strategic intent regarding speediness rather than a cause and effect of each other. A second slowing factor was the use of CE out to 63% use—above that point, an increased use of CE was associated with a less-extended marketing time. Four accelerating factors of marketing time were the use of NPV in project selection, percent of new product sales, a center of gravity closer to the customer, and specifying a reason for using time measurement in innovation. The impression is that a speed-to-market company strategy is most visible in speediness in the marketing department, which spills over into speed in R&D. Some comments of respondents to the 1993 study on this point are as follow.

7.5.1.1 Responses on the R&D-Marketing Interface

- I call this the Dump and Run Syndrome—a marketing person coming in with a new product idea, a lot of arm-waving, and disappearing. This company has found the investment in extra time (acknowledging the cost) very worthwhile, however—we have a much higher ratio of successful-to-total new products when we insist on intense early R&D-marketing involvement (consumer goods industry).

- Seems to fit the NPV analysis model—more costs up front offset against time saved (chemicals and energy industries).
- It is more important that R&D and the customer have an interface than there be an intermediary, especially if the intermediary cannot make a contribution to clearly defining the customer's need (automotive components).
- We have an extensive early R&D-marketing interface because marketing is close to the customer. By involving them early, we ensure that the requirements are established early and do not get changed (energy).

7.5.2   Applied Research Time

The applied research time, or advanced technology section contribution time, is shown in Figure 1.1. In practical terms, it is assumed that some scientific base is available to the company, either from its own basic research or from some external source. Thus, the start date of applied research or advanced technology can be measured from the same project start date of the balance of R&D or team effort. As indicated in Figure 1.1, the end date is when either the effort is stopped due to obtaining the necessary technology elsewhere or when the effort is transferred to the mainstream development activity.

Alcoa identified four factors that lead to a research project's cancellation: lack of market potential, lack of company support, technical barriers, and economic barriers [15]. Attributes that led to success were: congruent technical and business agendas, market pull, early business unit involvement, focused development, proper anticipation of post-development work, clear perception of production start-up, and clear customer communication from the start.

7.5.3   Design Time to Concept Finalization

Team or R&D time begins when there has been an identification and definition of a new product or service to meet a customer need. From this idea, a technical concept must be developed and reviewed for validity. This design review may include higher management in a stage-gate process and should include both upstream and downstream representatives to assess adequacy to meet the customer needs and ability to be produced, as indicated in the earlier example of Chrysler. The finalization of the concept occurs at the date of this design review, which is the start date of the next phase.

7.5.4 Design Time to Design Finalization

From the finalization of the concept, the next stage is to complete the design to the satisfaction of the same upstream and downstream representatives. The output of this phase is often a technical specification matching the commercial specification provided by marketing or the customer. Again, a design review is called for, and the review approval date is the meaningful measure.

7.5.5 Development Time and Process Design

Product development begins officially with a sign-off on the design and ends with an in-house (alpha) tested prototype meeting the technical specification. A new service offering needs a similar period of in-house development and testing. Software and firmware development starts with the design approval at the end of systems analysis and goes through coding to testing on the host computer system. If both hardware and software or firmware are involved, development only ends when both are alpha-tested jointly. Testing on the customer's premises, or beta-testing, is covered in Section 7.5.9.

In metallurgical or chemical industries, there is a need for process design to accompany new product developments. This cannot realistically start before the design sign-off and may start sometime later. Finalization of the process design usually has to await testing of the prototype. Thus, process design will tend to have a time scale of its own.

From the discussions in the several preceding sections, it will be seen that the design review is the key to establishing start and completion dates of the design and development time segments. These dates may either be set by the team or R&D department or from higher management as a stage-gate process. Between each set of dates, there is effort to be expended that can and should be estimated in terms of labor hours and costs.

7.5.6 Time from Prototype to Manufacturability

The time from prototype to manufacturability in the case of hardware or to deliverable software will vary by industry. Process development will also be part of this time period, including any required scaling up of the prototype to a production size. In a team-based company, this work will most likely be conducted within the teams. If not team-based, depending on the type of the firm this responsibility will either be in the R&D department or often in a separate industrial engineering or engineer of manufacture department under the director of manufacturing. In most industries, this will include preparing the documentation necessary for succeeding departments and customers to use the product or service. This category can be summarized as being composed of all the one-time tasks that need to be done in the transition from innovation to implementation and that usually do not need to be done again to handle subsequent customer orders. The calendar time necessary can be minimized by a team-based organization or careful overlap of activities between development and manufacturing.

7.5.7 Redo Loops

How often has the author heard the plaintive comment "we never have enough time to do things right, but always have time to do them over!" These wasted activities go by many names, such as debugging in software, or redo loops in manufacturing, as in the earlier example from Chrysler [12]. As shown in Figure 6.2, these may include the costs of engineering changes and of scrap and rework to correct errors found. In job shop manufacturing that the author supervised some years ago, these activities were built into the planning and costing cycle because preparation of errorless documentation was not affordable. However, for any reasonable production volume, there should not be things that need to be done over because there was not time to do them right first.

The principal benefit of closer engineering-manufacturing interaction is the reduction of the redo loops in both time spent and costs incurred. As a continuous improvement effort, a well-run team organization should be able to reduce these to nearly zero. One author, however, counsels that "no engineering time spent on such effort is probably too little" [14, p. 50]. The optimum level is a function of the particular firm as a balance between spending too much for customer satisfaction and the costs being too high in effort for the rewards obtainable in reducing such activities to near zero. The measurement can best be made by the time spent by the R&D team on such redo activities as a percent of its total available time. The time and effort required in redo activities should be measured and built into future time-cycle planning so that accurate forecasts can be made.

7.5.8 Production

Having separately estimated the previous two time periods, the time through first production of a new innovation still will not be as fast as later production because it will take place at the beginning of the learning curve. The author has seen this estimated by rule-of-thumb methods at the simple end through full calculation of learning curve effects at the other end.

The prototype is usually fabricated using model-shop methods. Initial production is often from soft tooling. Serial production is usually done with hard tooling. Each of these methods has its own time cycle and differences in both fixed costs and variable costs. Since the time cycle of interest to innovation managers is that of initial production, most likely the time of interest in the market development cycle is through soft tooling only. The assembly of first production deliveries is in general by methods akin to those used to assemble the prototype and, thus, labor intensive rather than dependent on tooling.

The equivalent of production in software is making copies, which is only a minor time-cycle issue in the initial deliveries. If firmware is to be delivered, it is usually "burned" into the programmable read-only memory at the factory, which is not a time-consuming task. However, some firmware needs to be designed into the semiconductor "mask," and this is often done before finalizing the prototype.

7.5.9 Testing

Initial production needs to be tested to see if it is in conformance with test results on the prototype. This set of initial tests is often more comprehensive and, thus, takes more time and labor hours than subsequent deliveries.

In some industries, further tests are made on the first or lead user's premises. In the computer industry, these are often called "beta" tests to distinguish them from the "alpha" tests in the company on the prototype. This time period needs to be estimated as part of the innovation group's total project effort.

7.5.10 Shipping Time

As can be seen for the U.S. companies who answered this item in Table 7.2, the time from available to ship to the customer's door is not an important factor. For those companies dealing with export business, however, the shipping time to an overseas location may be an important time to measure if the first user is not in the same country.

7.5.11 Customer Service Time

Customer service time is measured from the arrival on site if part of the contract with a first user or from a customer request to completion of service. Again, if the first user is overseas, careful pre-estimation should be done.

7.5.12 How Often to Measure Time?

Time measurement and evaluation in industry is often governed by the accounting cycle. Thus most companies measure time only every week or month. Is this frequently enough? One author has traced the need to measure time to the sampling theory of Nyquist [16]. This theory states that the sampling interval needs to be at least twice as frequent as the highest rate of change expected. Thus, if changes are expected no more frequently than every two months, sampling monthly will do. In a fast-moving field, more frequent sampling may be needed to keep track of and manage time.

7.5.13   Key Attributes of Metrics

The large number of metrics defined may at first glance seem to be excessive for many firms. Individual managers need to choose from this list those metrics key to their organization's performance. One author's criteria for this choice are relevance to the aspect being measured, minimum number to be complete, timeliness (as in the previous section), and maximum insight with minimum data [16].

7.6   LESSONS LEARNED ON EXPANDED TIME MEASUREMENT

The lessons learned so far on time measurement can now be expanded with some newer insights.

Timeliness of the entire innovation process is meeting schedule commitments to be measured by stage-gate tracking, percentage of milestones attained, or percent ahead or behind schedule; or time from idea to the customer's door, to be measured by cycle time in calendar days from notification of the need by the customer until delivery of the product or service to the customer's premises; or other customer cycle-time span.

When you measure idea-to-customer cycle time—as a cautionary lesson for cycle-time reducers—make sure your objectives are right and not just hoped for financial results before going all out on cycle-time reduction.

Timeliness of R&D's actions is measured by stage-gate tracking, percentage of milestones attained, or percent ahead or behind pre-estimated elapsed time; or cycle time in calendar days from notification of the need from marketing until delivery to manufacturing, subsidiaries, divisions or other cycle-time span.

To get good measurements of aggregate times, each of the applicable segments must be subjected to the same measurement discipline. Even without full company participation, good time measurements, where they can be obtained, enable increased effectiveness of innovation management.

Measuring and recording time as days, dates and labor hours becomes a precondition for successful management. These are needed both in estimates and records of overall time and in the time segments into which the overall measures are divided.

Larger companies need to watch their R&D cycle times, numbers and age of patents, and milestone management, lest these factors unnecessarily lengthen idea to customer times.

QFD, CE, gaining experience with time metrics, and rewards based on the business unit are useful strategies for shorter cycle times.

A speed-to-market company strategy is most visible in speediness in the marketing department, which spills over into speed in R&D.

Starting and ending points for each intermediate stage gate or milestone are best marked by design reviews.

Measure time at least twice as frequently as the highest rate of change expected.

Select metrics for relevance, with the fewest to be complete and timely, and maximum insight with minimum data.

References

[1] These diagrams from the 1993 study were subsequently published in Curtis, C. C., "Nonfinancial Performance Measures in New Product Development," *J. Cost Management*, Vol. 8(3), 1994, pp. 18–26.

[2] Bean, A. S., "IRI R-o-R Effectiveness Survey (1992): A Summary Report," CIMS, Lehigh University, Bethlehem, PA, Oct. 8, 1992.

[3] Cooper, R. G., "Stage-Gate Systems: A New Tool for Managing New Products," *Business Horizons*, May–June 1990, pp. 44–54.

[4] Lucas/Artemis, "Presentation to Industry," Trumbull, CT, Dec. 12, 1992, citing "Changing Your Way to a Better Business," *Engineering Computers*, May 1991.

[5] Foster, R. N., L. H. Linden, R. I. Whitely, and A. Kantrow, *Improving the Return on Research and Development*, New York: Industrial Research Institute, 1984; summarized with the same title in *Research Management*, Vol. 28(1), 1985, pp. 12–17, and Vol. 28(2), 1985, pp. 13–22.

[6] Ellis, L. W., *The Financial Side of Industrial Research Management*, New York: Wiley, 1984.

[7] Ellis, L. W., "Viewing R and D Projects Financially," *Research Management*, Vol. XXVII (2), Mar.–Apr. 1984, pp. 29–34.

[8] Von Braun, C.-F., "The Acceleration Trap," *Sloan Management Review*, Vol. 32 (1), 1990, pp. 49–58.

[9] Meyer, M. H., and J. M. Utterback, "Product Development Cycle Time and Commercial Success," *IEEE Trans. on Engineering Management*, Vol. 42(4), Nov. 1995, pp. 297–304.

[10] Ellis, L. W., and C. C. Curtis, "Practices in Concurrent Engineering," *Managing in a Global Environment: 1992 International Engineering Management Conference*, IEEE Catalog No. 92CH3222-7, Piscataway, NJ: IEEE, 1992, pp. 115–118.

[11] Financial Accounting Standards Board, *Statement of Financial Accounting Standards No. 86: Accounting for the Costs of Computer Software to Be Sold, Leased, or Otherwise Marketed*, Stamford, CT, August 1985.

[12] Lutz, R. A., "Implementing Technological Change with Cross-Functional Teams," *Research Technology Management*, Vol. 37(2), Mar.–Apr. 1994, pp. 14–18.

[13] Ellis, L. W., and C. C. Curtis, "Speedy R&D: How Beneficial?," *Research Technology Management*, Vol. 38(4), July–Aug. 1995, pp. 42–51.

[14] Smith, P. G., and D. G. Reinertsen, *Developing Products in Half the Time*, Florence, KY: Van Nostrand Reinhold, 1991.

[15] Burkart, R. E., "Reducing R&D Cycle Time," *Research Technology Management*, Vol. 37(3), May–June 1994, pp. 27–32.

[16] Patterson, M. L., *Accelerating Innovation: Improving the Process of Product Development*, New York: Van Nostrand Reinhold, 1993.

Chapter 8

From Time Measurement to Time Management

Chapter 7 summarized what is now known about measuring times of cycles, dates, and staff hours. Once these times are recorded, they must be further diagnosed and managed by reducing times, consolidating time, concentration, and measuring contribution.

8.1 TIME MANAGEMENT PRACTICES

The philosophies of time management covered in this section derive from some four decades of use by the author in practice and in the business school classroom. However, underlying these experiences are the classroom teaching of Peter F. Drucker to a green R&D manager attending New York University in the 1954 to 1955 academic year and Drucker's subsequent writings [1]. His primary injunction was as valid then as it still is today: "Time is inelastic—you can throw money and people at any project, but you can't make more time!"

8.1.1 Diagnosing How Time Is Spent

Once time has been recorded as days, dates, and labor hours, one must diagnose: Where did time go? Even for projects close to schedule, answering this question will be helpful in understanding how effective the organization is. Where schedules are not being met, diagnosis is essential to understand what management steps must be taken to correct the problem.

To show an example, Table 8.1 summarizes where one software project using only milestone management was reported to be at a scheduled revision date nine months after the original project plan's starting date.

Table 8.1
A Project Milestone Schedule Revision

	Dates		Months		
Milestone	*Original*	*New*	*Planned*	*Late*	*Percent Late*
Plan Start	1/28/92	1/28/92			
End Part 1	5/20/93	9/7/93	16.7	3.5	21
End Part 2	1/20/94	6/25/94	23.7	5.2	22
End Part 3	1/20/95	9/1/95	35.7	7.3	20
End Part 4	9/18/95	4/9/96	43.6	6.6	15

From: A customer's own schedule revision (first 3 columns); balance calculated by the author.

Milestone dates shown in the table are often reported in bar chart from, usually referred to as a Gantt chart, named after the American industrial engineer Henry Gantt. But even Gantt's original chart also included pre-estimated and actual labor hours as an aid to diagnosis. Since this was not done for this particular project, it is difficult to ascertain whether the slippage was due to insufficient applied time, to low pre-estimates, or to the disease of "creeping elegance" as the original targets were expanded during the project. If labor hours were below estimate, more people would have been a solution; if hours were on estimate, it would have quickly been seen that more work was needed to complete the project than had been estimated.

Since these revised estimates were from only nine months into the plan, they did not give much confidence in achieving project timeliness. Some indication of the problem may be diagnosed, however, by calculating the slippage as a percent of planned time, as was done by the author in the final column in Table 8.1. The relatively similar percentages for each project part argue for pre-estimates that were too low rather than a too slow build-up of staff that would tend to show up in a more constant months of lateness. In post-evaluation, the latter turned out to be the case, as work in each part was moved forward from the next later part.

One author defines "performance-to-commitment" time as the months of progress per month of activity [2]. Had the slip of Part 1 of 3.5 months been calculated as performance to commitment, a progress of 5.5 months would have been shown, which is 61% of the 9 months elapsed time. A cynical forecast might therefore have been for a 40% slip of completion date or 6.7 months late finally for Part 1 rather than 3.5 months late.

Some authors argue for milestone management alone [3]. Based on experience as exemplified by Table 8.1, the author favors using both milestones and project labor hours to provide the best opportunity for diagnosis.

For the multitask manager seeking to manage her or his own time, recording personal time during the day may be required to effect an adequate diagnosis. Who wasted my time? Whose time did I waste? Were meetings effective? These are only a few of the questions an adequate personal time record may help answer.

A summary of diagnosing time includes:

- Measure time against milestones and labor hours for ease in diagnosis.
- Keep track of your own time through the day to identify that which is not productive.

8.1.2 First, Prune Time Wasters

Once time has been recorded and diagnosed, proactive time management must begin. Classification into a matrix form with urgency across and importance down is one source's prescription for such time management [4, p. 151]. His fourth category includes time wasters, among other tasks. This author's experience has been that eliminating time wasters is the easiest way to gain free time for other needed activities. Thus, the first task is to prune out time wasters.

Accountants tend to split time into applied time and unapplied time, which is not the same as wasted time. Time applied to specific tasks may include productive time and time that is wasted because the tasks are unproductive. Unapplied time as viewed by the accountants is time not applied to job tasks. Some of this time is unavoidable as time paid, but not worked—holidays and vacation time are examples. Training time is classified by accountants as unapplied but may be an investment in the future and thus not wasted.

Better than using the accounting classification is to ask yourself "if we were not doing this already, would we start out doing it now?" Applied time to unproductive specialties falls into this category just as much as waiting time in the unapplied category. Controls that do not control waste time—is the cost of applying the control a good investment as compared with the potential of loss if not controlled? Common sense pruning can free up time for more productive uses, as in the following example.

Basiltown Electronics Company (not its real name) had a 400-person engineering department. Working through the applied time records, it was discovered that only the equivalent of 135 full-time employees were charging time to approved projects. The balance of charges were to unapplied time or to supervisory accounts. A review of its organization showed seven levels from the bench engineer to the Chief Engineer. Restructuring into a flatter organization and pruning unapplied time to the essentials justified a 270-person department. The balance of 130 people were reassigned to other short-handed groups in the company. In postevaluation one year later, slippages on less than 5% of the development projects were attributable to the reduced staffing.

For the innovation group, redo time discussed earlier is one of the easiest places to begin pruning time wasters. Time to do things right needs to be allocated to prevent redoing activities. Time payback, analogous to cash-flow payback, is an easy way of low-level decision making. Break-even time, or time from the beginning of the project until product introduction has generated enough profit to repay the development investment, is another version of this metric [5].

For the busy manager, pruning wasted hours during the day is just as important. Who could do this as well as I could? Too often the diagnosis shows the boss to be the bottleneck. One of the big advantages of empowered teams is that the R&D manager is freed of many decisions that should never have been sent up to that level in the first place.

Prune the time that other people waste, that you waste, and that you cause others to waste.

8.1.3 Consolidate Time to Use It More Efficiently

After time wasters are pruned, the productive time remaining needs to be regrouped into larger time blocks to enable time to be used effectively. This is particularly true in a multitask environment, including the productive time of supervisors. The time that is freed up may be in such small increments that it does not allow effective use; while regrouped schedules may not only free up larger blocks of time but may also prune away the time lost in dropping one task and picking it up later.

In short, consolidate time into larger blocks so that it may be used more effectively.

8.1.4 Concentration on First Things First

"Do first things first" is the guiding principle of concentration [6, p. 57]. The 80/20 rule is the principal guideline of how to concentrate: 80% of results are produced by 20% of effort. The corollary is also true: 80% of effort produces only 20% of results. The lesson of the 1993 study is that profitability is aligned with the proportion of effort spent on major new projects. Thus, the action needed may be summarized concisely as: Feed the stars. This requires finding some effort that was not previously available, some of which can be supplied by reducing time wasters.

The second part of the 80/20 rule shows where to look for the rest of the extra effort needed to feed the stars. Every organization that has been around for a while has many of the low-result activities on its plate. Older and once-successful products, unproductive specialties, and unnecessary specialties are such categories. Product extensions were shown in the 1993 study to be in this profit-lowering category, despite their attraction in lowering idea-to-customer time. Similar negative results on extensions showed in correlation analysis in the 1994 study but were found to be offset by a number of newly introduced factors measuring the degree of management attention to time and costs. Apparently, requests in many companies for such extensions and specialties have not been thought out well enough in terms of how they will affect financial returns. Cash-flow payback or break-even time is a quick method to identify such activities [7]. Another is to set a low amount of the budget for these tasks and thus force rationing of numbers of requests for sales-order specials. The management task in concentration is also clear: Cull the dogs, and yesterday's successes that no longer merit high levels of support.

Concentrate on first things first.

8.1.5 Measure Innovation Contribution

In place of the vague term *results*, in time management *contribution* needs a more complex definition: Time saved, at little or no impairment of financial performance; or improved financial performance needing little or no extra time. It is often easy to reduce cycle time by tackling incremental projects, but this has been shown in the 1993 study to cause worse financial results.

The focus on innovation contribution needs to be outward from the R&D organization, not inward and downward. Contribution results mostly from satisfying a customer, who then will pay a remunerative price for the service or product.

Inward to the organization is the task of making the average person productive in the sense that she or he works toward the definition of contribution. Human resources contributions need also to be focused not on making individuals happy but on what will aid their own contributions. Contribution from meetings also needs to be focused on time effectiveness, at minimum cost in time away from assigned tasks.

To recollect, measure contribution in time saved at minimal cost, cost saved at minimal time lost, and on actions that will increase customer satisfaction.

8.1.6 Build Upon Strength in Core Competencies

The organization should make its strengths relevant to time performance of the assigned tasks. This means primarily staffing with just the number of people needed, each with their own appropriate expertise. The necessary degree of empowerment needs to be given to the innovating group so that it can conduct its work rapidly, with the minimum of delays to coordinate with external interfaces.

One key task is identifying and selecting talented people [8, Chap. 8]. They are the firm's most important asset.

Several years ago IBM established a program to focus on the development of outstanding technical people by surveying 25 senior professionals [8, p. 58]. They clearly felt that outstanding people were best identified by the respect of his or her peers and managers. The most frequently mentioned leading indicators of superior technical performance were special assignments, technical memos, publications, awards, and presentations.

Industrial psychologists also profess to be able to contribute to this selection of talent through psychometrics. Where they are most useful, however, is in understanding personalities who are unlikely to be effective participants in group or team activity.

The task of the R&D manager is not to personally direct all work but to neutralize weakness, personality, and conflict in the organization that might lower its contribution. This does not mean suppressing conflict, but keeping it sufficient to build creativity, and not too much to impair effective cooperation. The evaluation of this optimum level is best left to human resource professionals or skilled consultants. Equally, the task of the group is to make its boss productive by keeping up the flow of information needed to satisfy higher management.

In short, build strength in competencies by employing enough outstanding people and by neutralizing weakness, personality, and potentially destructive conflict.

8.1.7 Decision Making

In an empowered innovation organization, the R&D manager makes few decisions. The team, closer to the task, makes many decisions on the spot, freeing the manager to make the most important decisions. In this environment, the managerial effort is to define effective decisions and make decisions effectively.

The effective managerial decision is one that addresses a generic problem. Most such problems are masked by symptoms that should not be treated individually. If the project is late, a symptom, is the generic problem a bad estimate or understaffing? The manager must realize that the required knowledge rests at the lower level of the group and seek out the problem from the symptoms. Also, the group needs to participate in making the decision so that they will understand and respect the decision.

Development cycle time and risk are interrelated [7, Chap. 12]. Speedy R&D entails some increased risk, but taking risks does not always save time. Usually this is technical risk, from failure to perform or meet cost targets. There is an optimum cycle time where the lowering of risk through design reviews can shorten time, but where excessive reviews with too high level executives can take away enough development effort and contribute to lengthening cycle time without much additional risk reduction. There is also market risk, which can best be lessened by increased involvement of the customer.

Making decisions effectively at the R&D manager's level is an example of the scientific method. Which alternatives are there to address the generic problem? How does each address the need, and what new risks does it entail? Which criteria should be used to make the decision? How does the choice among alternatives get made? Once made, how does the choice become adopted? Who changes? What does the manager do if they won't change? All of this is easy to say but hard to do.

To summarize, make effective decisions that address generic problems, lessen risk at no cost or time delay, and make them effectively by the scientific method.

8.2 ACCELERATING THE INNOVATION PROCESS

Accelerating the innovation process needs actions to improve the upstream end (the "fuzzy front end" [7]), the downstream end (usually in manufacturing or service operations), and in R&D or the team during the process of product development.

8.2.1 Improving the Upstream Process

Improving the upstream process involves two tasks, specifically, improving the R&D-marketing interface and improving the flow of information to the development team. The R&D-marketing interface involves the trade-off of time against financial performance. In the 1994 financial model, the center of gravity of the company closer to the customer and use of QFD at this interface are associated with improved financial results. This is offset by a closer R&D-marketing interface in the early stages of design being associated with slightly worse financial performance.

Management should expect more work up front in adopting QFD and Taguchi methods. The use of QFD is associated with a shorter time through research and development in the 1994 study. Since use of QFD raises financial performance, offsetting a lower result from Taguchi methods, according to the 1994 study, apparently the front-end costs are made up elsewhere in the organization. Thus, implementing QFD methods appears to be a good investment. An example of the use of QFD by Alcoa was given in Section 5.1.4.

The actions required to improve the upstream of information processes have been rather well summarized by one executive in [2] and are as follows.

- Select the best available opportunities;
- Align the projects well;
- Provide visionary leadership;
- Do most valuable tasks first;
- Design effective experiments;
- Increase rate of experimenting;
- Use all available information.

In essence, improve both the R&D-marketing interface and the flow of information to the development team.

8.2.2 What R&D Can Do to Reduce Manufacturing Cycle Time

A full discussion of reducing manufacturing cycle time is beyond the scope of this book and may be found elsewhere [2]. Nevertheless, many actions can be taken by R&D that have a downward impact on manufacturing or service operations. The first of these is designing in quality so as to minimize scrap and rework and to improve customer satisfaction.

A second area is in the area of "prototype to manufacturability" shown in Table 7.2. In that survey, the range of times was from 7 to 186 days with a mean of 96 days. Clearly, this is an area where combined R&D and manufacturing managers can make a difference. Rapid prototyping is one part of this cycle that the R&D manager can do much to influence.

Psi Radio Limited had consolidated its manufacturing for all product lines. The four product line and R&D managers were concerned that this left them at the mercy of manufacturing's priorities for prototyping. An accord was negotiated with the shop superintendent for expedited handling of prototype manufacture in the machine shops, or in the tool room if necessary. The motivation for the shop superintendent was clear—faster prototyping meant earlier first manufacture, which in turn kept the shops busy with production work. Also, by having the prototypes manufactured as much as possible by production people, the learning curve was advanced, with fewer redo loops.

Achieving overlapping activities, as in this example is discussed in detail in [7, Chap. 9]. From this source comes another example:

Neles-Jamesbury manufactures quarter-turn valves for heavy industry. Defective castings, including those needing time-consuming ECNs, were once returned to the foundry to await a second batch of castings. This delayed debugging the machining process. They now accept and pay for the initial defective castings, use them to debug machining operations, and thus save time by overlapping processes.

Implementing CE, or simultaneous engineering, is a management practice effective for shortening cycle time that does not involve tradeoffs with financial performance. In the 1993 study, the extent of CE use was measured by the percentage of the R&D budget directed to projects involving CE. Considering the short time this practice has been in use, the median response was a remarkably high 65% of R&D budget in all three surveys.

The idea-to-customer time model in the 1993 study shows that a shift into CE projects shortens the cycle time, but this effect was not seen in the 1994 study. In the 1994 R&D time model, the greater the use of CE, the shorter the cycle time. An upward shift of the average CE percentage of the R&D effort might therefore provide large potential savings in time as long as the pacing tasks are not sequential in nature. No significant relationship was found between CE use and financial performance in either the 1993 or 1994 studies. This suggests that the costs of using this method are more than offset in the overall innovation cycle, most probably in reduction of ECNs and scrap and rework in operations. This hints at a "do it right the first time" R&D management task. The once plaintive cry "we never have time to do it right, but always have time to do it over," seems to have diminished with CE.

In short, improve the downstream interface by designing in quality, reducing the prototype to manufacturability time, and using CE.

8.2.3 Sources of Product Development Speed

Product development speed involves a tradeoff between faster development and financial results. There is no advantage for a company to deliberately speed up development if financial performance deteriorates as a consequence [9]. One explanation is that there is an acceleration trap [10] because financial results questioned the assertion that financial performance improves with increasingly shorter cycle time. He suggests instead the existence of a point at which further time reductions will not only fail to add to lifetime product revenue streams but may also contribute to financial deterioration.

The acceleration trap makes great sense in the consumer products industry [9]. The landscape is littered with products that were ahead of their time. Later entrants proved that the right products at the right time are the way to gain market dominance, equaling better financial results. Major new products take longer to create. If they also have high margins, getting them sooner to market may simply result in attracting competition even sooner, unless you have some countermeasures in place. Then you may be forced to compete on price. The acceleration trap exists.

Another author, based upon his experience directing R&D at the highly successful Hewlett Packard Company, addresses time management in innovation with a different set of steps related to the cash flow wave form in [2]. These steps are summarized in the following:

- Reduce the time to perceive opportunities;
- Reduce the time to begin the project;
- Decrease development time;
- Speed up release time;
- Speed early customer cash flow;
- Increase maximum cash inflow;
- Extend product life.

These steps are relatively self-explanatory, except perhaps for decreasing development time. That author recommends, without detailed explanation, sufficient engineers on the project, available expertise, size and nature of the task, clarity and definition, level of risk, available development tools, quality of development processes, and information resources available.

Many companies, however, do not have the resources that Hewlett Packard has to meet the aforementioned requirements. The acceleration trap leads to the conclusion that companies should have other and more compelling strategic reasons for shortening their new product development cycles than as a means to improve their financial performance. Suppose a company truly has no choice in adopting a fast cycle-time strategy just to remain in the industry as a key competitor. Is there a way out of the acceleration trap? There appear three ways to approach speedy R&D time management in innovation without "shooting yourself in the foot" financially [9]:

- Use concurrent engineering approaches in all projects;
- Increase the closeness of the R&D-marketing interface during the early stages of product design;
- Focus your R&D patent policy on quality rather than quantity.

8.2.4 Control of Product Development Delays

Many R&D managers are not so much faced with speeding up R&D as with preventing it from dragging on beyond the scheduled dates. To control delays in product development, first the R&D manager must do the converse of each item listed in Section 8.2.3.1. For example, do not let opportunities take time to get started, and so on.

More than just these recommendations, however, the manager must change the culture of the organization. Time must be made one of the goals of all individuals. This is done by top-management commitment and the management of change covered in Chapter 10. Time control must emphasize meeting schedules, with penalties both for slippages and for padding estimates just to be safe. Stage-gate tracking processes have been shown (in the research covered earlier) to be the preferred form of milestone reviews.

One more control is needed—the control of changes. The delays in the first two phases of the project described in Table 8.1 were found in post-evaluation review to have been in part due to changes in scope after initial project approval. At least, this organization had a formal change procedure that had been followed. Thus, the project manager could show that the real slippage in Part 1 was only 3 months from the revised date after the change and that he had been relatively effective in his management task. Thus, the final control is a change procedure, that is, a change review process in which the whole organization has a voice in approving proposed changes once a project is under way.

In short, control project delays by doing the converse of each item listed in Section 8.2.3.1, change culture to one of time commitment, and control changes in scope.

8.3 TIME MANAGEMENT LESSONS LEARNED

This chapter has covered steps in time management. After times have been recorded, they should be further diagnosed and managed by reducing time, consolidating time, concentration, and measuring contribution.

- Measure time against milestones and labor hours for ease in diagnosis;
- Keep track of your own time through the day to identify that which is not productive;
- Prune time that other people waste, that you waste, and that you cause others to waste;
- Consolidate time into larger blocks so that it may be used more effectively;
- Concentrate on first things first;
- Measure contribution in time saved at minimal cost, cost saved at minimal time lost, and on actions that will increase customer satisfaction;
- Build strength in competencies by employing enough outstanding people and by neutralizing weakness, personality and potentially destructive conflict;
- Make effective decisions that address generic problems and, lessen risk at no cost or time delay, and make them effectively by the scientific method.

Accelerating the innovation process requires first improving upstream processes toward the customer, next improving downstream toward operations, and finally managing internally to the innovation organization itself.

- Improve both the R&D-marketing interface and the flow of information to the development team;
- Improve the downstream interface by designing in quality, reducing the prototype to manufacturability time, and using CE to couple to operations;
- Speed R&D without financial impairment by using CE approaches in all projects, increasing the closeness of the R&D-marketing interface during the early stages of product design, and focusing your R&D patent policy on quality rather than quantity;
- Control project delays by doing the converse of the items listed in Section 8.2.3.1, change culture to one of time commitment, and control changes in scope.

These steps in time management are the foundations of measuring the results of strategic intent of the firm, which will be reviewed in the next chapter.

References

[1]   Drucker, P. F., *The Effective Executive*, New York: Harper & Row, 1967. See also earlier books by the same author and publisher: *Managing for Results*, 1964, and *The Practice of Management*, 1954.

[2]   Patterson, M. L., *Accelerating Innovation: Improving the Process of Product Development*, New York: Van Nostrand Reinhold, 1993.

[3]   Van Remoortere, F., and R. Cotterman, "Project Tracking System Serves as Research Management Tool," *Research Technology Management*, 36 (2), Mar.–Apr. 1993, pp. 32–37.

[4]   Covey, S., *Time Matrix Management: The 7 Habits of Highly Effective People*, New York: Simon & Schuster, 1990.

[5]   Ellis, L. W., *The Financial Side of Industrial Research Management*, New York: Wiley, 1984.

[6]   Maccoby, M., "The Human Side: Personal Change in the Information Age," *Research Technology Management*, Vol. 37(3), May–June 1994, pp. 56–58.

[7]   Smith, P. G. and D. G. Reinertsen, *Developing Products in Half the Time*, Florence, KY: Van Nostrand Reinhold, 1991.

[8]   Humphrey, W. S., *Managing for Innovation: Leading Technical People*, Englewood Cliffs, NJ: Prentice-Hall, 1987.

[9]   Ellis, L. W., and C. C. Curtis, "Speedy R&D: How Beneficial?," *Research Technology Management*, Vol. 38(4), July–Aug. 1995, pp. 42–51.

[10] Von Braun, C.-F., "The Acceleration Trap," *Sloan Management Review*, Vol. 32 (1), 1990, pp. 49–58.

Part III

R&D Process Evaluation Measurements

R&D processes need to be measured and evaluated. Throughout the first two parts of this book, lists have been given in several places that show which of these metrics have actually been used. What is most important to the R&D manager, however, is to have these more quantitatively rated as to how they impact on outcomes of interest to general managers.

Survey research and recent literature have given some guidance in answering this need. However, the explanatory power of any one metric in relation to another that occurs later in time tends to be rather low. Thus, combinations of several metrics tend to be needed to lead the way to higher levels of outcomes. Chapter 9 looks at these sources from interaction and input metrics. Chapter 10 addresses these sources from the internal viewpoint of the R&D organization (department or team).

Chapter 9

Interaction and Input Metrics

This chapter continues looking backward down the feedback and feed-forward paths. It begins by describing metrics that occur earlier in time and have a close association with results. The interaction with other organizational units becomes the first promising place to look for precursor or leading indicators of outcomes and outputs. Input metrics are also an equally promising source of early indicators.

9.1 INTERACTIONS WITH OTHER ORGANIZATIONAL UNITS

Two researchers cited earlier addressed interactions in terms too general to use practically: enterprise integration (coordinating R&D with all other corporate activities) and formal mechanisms for interactions. Combining all of the sources previously cited into one list of desirable interactions cannot be done scientifically because of the diverse methods that were used by the originators.

However, the number of times mentioned by different researchers gives a rough indication of the value seen by them. This may be used as a guide for discussion and for more detailed research. However, a caution must be given that the degree of association of the use of metrics and their perceived importance, satisfaction, and effectiveness is only moderate. The most frequently cited of these interactions concerned internal organization.

9.1.1 Internal Company Organization

Thirteen of the studies previously cited in this book used issues of internal organization as leading indicators—more than any other topic. The specific terms used were crossfunctional participation, teams, CE, training, education, collocation, manufacturing influence on design release, approved materials and parts, design documentation, and data bases. Most of these had positive correlations with one

141

or more outcome metrics. This seems to indicate a broad-based concern with the effect of organization on the desired outcomes covered in earlier chapters. The specific metrics group naturally into those concerning teams, individual development, and downstream interfaces.

A 1992 study of a small nonrepresentative sample of technical executives used an interval scale from "not important" to "very important." Since this scale did not result in normal distributions, only the ranking of interactions from highest to lowest in importance is shown in Table 9.1. To facilitate comparisons between interactions, internal processes, and inputs, the numeric rank following each entry is the rank it has among all three of these categories.

Upwards and downwards coordination were rather moderate terms used in the 1992 study. Transfer of technology, treated as an output of the innovation activity, is shown for comparison in Table 9.1. Perhaps, if the three downward coordination questions had instead been only one question, the downward ranking might have been equal to or higher than that for upstream coordination with marketing.

Measurements in these cases can only be facilitated with a formality type of scale. Care should be taken to define the upper end of the scale in low probability terms to avoid the bias that was found in the 1992 study toward too many things being "very important." A suggested approach might be based upon a comparison with competitors or world-class companies.

Honda began a new style of product development in 1981 with a 1200-cc engine city car [2]. The project team from R&D, production, and sales (average age 27) were told to develop a car that the youth segment would like to drive, including such features as efficiency in resources and fuel and quality at a low price. The

Table 9.1
Importance Ranking of Interactions

Interaction	Ranking
Coordination of R&D and marketing	1
(Transfer downward of technology*)	
Coordination of R&D and engineering	3
Coordination of R&D and downstream departments	6
Cross-functional participation	9
Support to the rest of the company	12
Conflict level and its management	13
Coordination with higher executives	14

*Treated as an output in the 1992 study rather than as an interaction, but included for comparison at the point where it would have ranked as an interaction. (*Source:* [1].)

team broke with conventional wisdom and designed a short, tall car, instead of a long, low one. When the project hit a dead end in developing the concept, several members went to Europe and took ideas from the Mini-Cooper small car developed years earlier in the United Kingdom. The team stayed together until the factory was up and running.

Honda, in its day, was a good example of a world-class competitor in the 1980s. It began crossfunctional teams in 1981; Chrysler began the Viper car this way in 1989. Honda broke with the traditional way of designing a car. They sought input from firms in other countries, and the team saw production happen rather than throwing the design over the wall.

Of course, all these actions are now done with the use of teams in the 1990s. The task is now to identify which companies are now at the leading edge and use them to calibrate the top end of the rating scale. Staying world class is an evanescent state—somewhat like *Alice in Wonderland*, where you have to run as fast as you can to stay in the same place. Within this state at present are, for example, companies who have recently won the Baldridge Quality Award—Motorola's "Six Sigma" (only a few defects per million opportunities) program comes to mind. General Electric and its (almost) "boundaryless organization" is another.

The few results available show a minor positive correlation of downward coordination and transfer with customer satisfaction and output from R&D. The extent of early R&D-marketing interface shows positive correlations with speedy R&D and idea-to-customer times. These moderately support upward and downward coordination and transfer measurements as precursor or leading indicators. They seem to indicate that attention to these aspects of internal organization moves in the right direction but needs to be accompanied by other management actions as well.

- For speed in R&D and idea-to-customer times, measure the extent of early R&D-marketing interface.
- For customer satisfaction and R&D output, measure the extent of the downward interface from R&D.

Crossfunctional participation was described by other researchers in terms of bridging linkages with other departments. This was in general a more positive term than coordination, as used above. Depending on the firm's industry, these included a number of specialized units such as, for example, styling in the automotive industry. Most of the references, however, were to participation of downstream units such as manufacturing departments. These might most likely be industrial engineering, purchasing, and assembly in the typical product firm. In general, all who have to implement an innovation have a natural interest in participation in decisions, coordination of activities, and specifying the details of technology transfer.

It might seem strange that marketing was not so often mentioned as a cross-functional interaction. As shown in Figure 7.4, the 1991 and 1993 surveys noted that the percentage of respondents measuring time through marketing was only about half of those measuring time through production and a quarter of those measuring R&D cycle time. This confirms the downstream bias of companies studied in 1992. The only clear reason came from companies dealing with the government or with original equipment manufacturers, who define the requirements rather than the firm's own marketing department. Nevertheless, upstream cross-functional interaction plays as important a role as that being done downstream. Comments on coordination and measurements made in the previous section apply here also.

Teams and CE represent an even tighter interaction mode. Again, the team structures most often focused on downstream units, with less emphasis on including marketing. Figure 6.1 shows reduced design and manufacturing costs with CE. In the 1993 study, the percent of the R&D budget invested in CE reduced idea-to-customer time, despite increasing R&D time, and showed no measurable impact on EBIT. As a simple and straightforward metric, it certainly rates as a useful precursor or leading indicator of timeliness.

In short, for lower costs and reduced idea-to-customer cycle times, measure the percent of R&D in concurrent engineering projects.

Collocation of teams correlated positively with results in only one study reviewed but is a measure worth considering. The case for collocation is forcefully made in an article on teams at Deere [3]. Even with advances in telecommunications, teamwork is difficult to achieve at a distance.

Chrysler started team activity in 1989 with the Viper car [4]. Although the teams included marketing people, they were not colocated with R&D, styling, and manufacturing engineering who were at a technical center some distance out of Detroit. After assessing the problems this caused, part of the product management staff was moved to the technical center. The layout meant that the maximum distance between any two team members was up or down a stairwell. There is one residual problem still to be solved—marketing people have an intense need for coordination early in the cycle and close to product launch, but not so much in the middle of development.

Therefore, measure the distance, or travel time, to the farthest team member, as a negatively correlated metric of team interaction effectiveness.

Training and education lead to the issue of coordination with the human resources department, which in most firms has these responsibilities. It also appears as an internal process in some studies and as an input to staff competence in others. For example, the Baldridge Award criteria on human resource utilization and interaction include human resource management, employee involvement, *quality education and training* (emphasis added), employee recognition and performance measurement, and employee well-being and morale [5]. An outcome-based measurement for training and education would be desirable. The more typical metric, however, is input-based, such as costs of training and education as a percent of payroll or sales. The extent to which this input correlates with outputs and outcomes is far from clear. However, it is accepted as an article of faith in most discussions of how to effect change in a company.

Measure internal personnel development by training and education costs as a percent of sales against a goal set internally or against world class competitors.

9.1.2 Less-Cited Interaction Metrics

A number of other interactions are worth mentioning as special cases for measurement of certain limited results. These received only one or two mentions in other studies or were in the lower portion of Table 9.1.

Quality assurance of products and services in the innovation stage is best achieved by design reviews. For companies using a stage-gate process, design reviews accompany the gates and are measured accordingly. Other companies should schedule design reviews at important transition points defined by the nature of the innovation chain. Measurements might be in the form of design review dates met on schedule or a portion of technical objectives met by design review date. The Baldridge Award criteria include "design and introduction of quality products and services, documentation, and supplier quality," which pertain to the innovation process [5]. These are measured by that award's own type of formality scale. Coordination with the quality department may also be measured by a formality scale.

In the 1993 study, TQM in R&D was negatively correlated with EBIT. An increase of the use of QFD was associated with slower R&D time, but not with idea-to-customer time nor EBIT. Measuring innovation quality using TQM or QFD has thus not been shown to be much assistance as a precursor or leading indicator. Since QFD's extra time in R&D was made up sufficiently not to lengthen idea-to-customer time, and did not affect EBIT, it seems the better technique to use in R&D management.

- Measure design review dates met on schedule, or the portion of technical objectives met by design review date, as a metric of timeliness.
- Measure QFD rather than TQM in R&D as an interface metric which does not impair EBIT not idea-to-customer cycle time.

Support to the rest of the organization is rather low in the importance rankings of Table 9.1. In the author's experience, this is a nonlinear measurement: Too little support lowers the coupling of R&D to the rest of the organization and results in problems downstream; too much support takes R&D's attention away from its basic task of innovating. No organization had a good measurement tactic; and most used subjective rules, such as "X percent of budget is about right" [6, pp. 46–51]. In most cases, this budget was the R&D budget, with percentages in the range of 10 to 30%.

In one New Jersey research laboratory of Rayonier Company, visited by the author some years ago, the support effort was about 50% of the R&D budget. This clearly handicapped the lab in its main mission of carrying out R&D in applications for chemical cellulose.

Another example concerned R&D in a manufacturer. In Psi Radio Limited, the support rule was 2.5% of factory cost. This was treated as a standard cost by accounting, which measured variances against this goal. The distribution of results was similar to that shown in Figure 2.6. This rule was equivalent to about one-sixth of Psi Radio's R&D budget.

Conflict level and its management involve another nonlinear metric. That is, too little conflict indicates a stagnant organization; too much conflict is destructive and reduces the effectiveness of innovation. A discussion of this subject may be found in any standard text on management. While low on the list of importance in Table 9.1, a strong positive correlation was found in the 1992 study between conflict level and its management and new products and services as a percent of sales. Measuring conflict level and management might best be done only if there is a suspicion that it is a problem. In view of the nonlinear nature of this category, separate questions about both extremes, using a scale from strongly agree to neutral to strongly disagree would best be phrased in terms of "do you agree with the following statements: 'The organization is too stagnant to stimulate creativity,' and 'The conflict level is too high to let me do my job properly.'"

Coordination with higher executives is a natural preoccupation of innovation managers. As Table 9.1 shows, however, it was not rated very high in importance in 1992. Correlations were small and not significant with all outputs and outcomes, with only a nearly significant negative correlation with customer satisfaction. It may not be polite to tell the big boss that she or he does not matter in the measurement of innovation effectiveness, but that seems to be the result in the studies done to 1993.

Strategic planning was cited in three instances: integration of strategic technology planning with corporate strategic planning (including utilization of core technologies), strategies well defined, and funding of research from corporate. Attempting to use strategic planning in the 1992 study, however, failed to clearly distinguish it from marketing. For those innovative organizations that have a clear distinction in interaction relationships between strategic planning and marketing, measuring coordination with the former directly may make sense.

9.1.3 Interaction Measurement Lessons Learned

This outline for using interaction metrics as precursor or leading indicators yields a few clear guidelines.

- For speed in R&D and idea-to-customer times, measure the extent of early R&D-marketing interface.
- For customer satisfaction and R&D output, measure the extent of the downward interface from R&D.
- For lower costs and reduced idea-to-customer cycle times, measure the percent of R&D in concurrent engineering projects.
- Measure the distance, or travel time, to the farthest team member, as a negatively correlated metric of team interaction effectiveness.
- Measure internal personnel development by training and education costs as a percent of sales against a goal set internally, or against world-class competitors.
- Measure design review dates met on schedule, or the portion of technical objectives met by design review date, as a metric of timeliness.
- Measure QFD rather than TQM in R&D as an interface metric that does not impair EBIT nor idea-to-customer cycle time.

9.2 INPUTS TO THE INNOVATION PROCESS

Inputs to the innovation process may be in the form of knowledge of a technical or nontechnical nature. Technical inputs may take the form of access to new science. Nontechnical inputs may be an understanding of customers or markets. Inputs may be in the form of guidelines set down by management to which the innovators must conform. The 1992 study ranked inputs to the innovation process as shown in Table 9.2, with rankings in the composite with interactions in Table 9.1.

Counter intuitively, generation of new ideas had a strong negative correlation with output from R&D in the 1992 study. More predictably, financial project selection also had a strong negative correlation with output from R&D. Do too many new ideas or the restraints of a quantitative selection process interfere with the things researchers would themselves prefer to do? On the other hand,

Table 9.2
Importance Ranking of Inputs to the
Innovation Process

Input	Rank
Knowledge of customer needs	2
Generation of new ideas	5
Financial selection of R&D projects	8
Competence of R&D staff	11

Source: [1].

generation of new ideas and financial project selection both had a moderate positive correlation with new products/services as a percent of sales. And competence
of staff had a moderate positive correlation with output from R&D. Other studies
showed a mixture of input measures, which are grouped below to correspond to
those of the 1992 study.

Knowledge of customer needs drew the support of two other studies: customer focus of R&D and competitive intelligence. Both of these are related to coordination with marketing and lead users previously discussed in Section 9.1. One
potential measure of the former would be percent of innovation budget devoted to
customer-originated projects. The percent of technical features equaling or exceeding competition would measure whether competitive intelligence was being acted
upon.

The generation of new ideas also drew support from two studies: extent of
control over product specifications and degree of regulation encountered. Companies directly reacting to customers specifications might show a low percentage of
control, while those creating customer wants should show higher values for this
category. Degree of regulation encountered would measure constraints imposed
on the firm, usually by government. This latter factor was found, in the 1993
study, to increase time through R&D, particularly in pharmaceutical and biotech-
nical companies, and to decrease earnings as compared with firms not so
constrained.

The financial input area received five additional mentions in other studies reviewed: analytical project selection, R&D intensity as a percent of sales, company
size in dollars or employees, average product life, and investment in major new
products versus investment in product extensions. The 1993 study, looking at analytical or financial project selection as an important metric, supports the findings
of the 1992 study and those by this author a decade ago [6]. A simple metric is the
percent of the R&D budget allotted by financial project selection methods.

R&D intensity was found to be nonlinear and thus have an optimum
value—too much or too little R&D lowers earnings; the estimation of this optimum may be derived from industry data [6]. While the calculation of an optimum
is straightforward mathematics, a first approximation may be derived from the average industry R&D intensity. Because of its nonlinear nature, the absolute value of
the difference between actual intensity and the optimum intensity, or the industry
average, may be used as a metric with negative implications—the further below optimum, the less is being invested in the future, and the further above optimum, the
likelihood is that current earnings are being penalized for at best marginal projects.

Company size, measured by sales dollars or number of employees, was found
to increase time through R&D in the 1993 study and to lower the patent output ratio to sales in other studies [7–11]. Longer average product life, measured in calendar time, was found to increase cycle times in the 1993 study, but less than
proportionally, and to increase earnings. The 1993 study also found that more investment in major new products, measured by percent of budget allocated to

them, raised earnings while product extensions decreased them. Each of the four financial metrics discussed in this section have value as precursor or leading indicators.

- Measure the generation of new ideas, and the percent of the R&D budget allotted by of financial project selection, as precursors of the percent of sales in new products and/or services.
- Measure the percent of the R&D budget devoted to customer-originated projects as a metric of knowledge of customer needs.
- Measure the percent of technical features equaling or exceeding competition as a metric of whether competitive intelligence was being acted upon.

The competence of staff was highlighted in one study that asked core technologies be defined. Due to its low ranking in the 1992 study and minor correlation only with R&D output, and not with other outcomes, this does not rank highly as a precursor or leading indicator. The 1992 study used an interval scale to measure importance. Others have used various indices of the percent of staff with degrees beyond the baccalaureate level or with terminal degrees.

Technical design standards was one area not covered by the pilot study. Three studies mentioned positive correlations with outcomes in this area: *design for assembly* (DFA), *design for manufacture* (DFM), and software. The source of all of these were researchers from the field of production and operations management. Thus, these represent concerns from the output of the innovation chain and should not be ignored. An interval scale measuring the extent to which these, or any other appropriate standards, are used seems the proper metric. However, this may also be measured as for downward interface/transfer.

The technology base is an important input factor not mentioned in the above studies. For technology focused companies, access to the necessary base is essential. It is, however, not an easy-to-measure quantity. Thus, its presence must be inferred by output or outcome metrics.

9.2.1 Input Measurements Lessons Learned

Some of these input measurements were most noted for correlations with intellectual property output from R&D. At this point, one might ask whether this is what the innovation process is about, as these outputs do not track highly with outcomes of interest to general management. A theme common with upward interactions, however, is that increased new products and services, in which general management is interested, are associated with the following two input metrics, measured on formality scales:

- Measure the generation of new ideas and the percent of the R&D budget allotted by financial project selection as precursors of the percent of sales in new products and/or services.
- Measure the percent of the R&D budget devoted to customer-originated projects as a metric of knowledge of customer needs.
- Measure the percent of technical features equaling or exceeding competition as a metric of whether competitive intelligence was being acted upon.

While financial project selection has some signs of negatively impacting customer satisfaction and output from R&D, its pluses for higher management are many. Companies run on financial results, and this measure also is a precursor of new products and services. Financial metrics of value in justifying the R&D budget to general and financial managers are:

- What percent of projects is subjected to financial discipline?
- What proportion of projects is on major new products or services?

References

[1] Internal study within IRIMER. The results were not submitted for publication until inclusion in this book.

[2] Takeuchi, H., and I. Nonaka, "The New Product Development Game," *Harvard Business Review*, Vol. 64(1), Jan.–Feb. 1986, pp. 137–146.

[3] Lorenz, C., "Team-Based Engineering at Deere," *McKinsey Quarterly*, (4), 1991, pp. 81–93.

[4] Lutz, R. A., "Implementing Technological Change with Cross-Functional Teams," *Research Technology Management*, Vol. 37(2), Mar.–Apr. 1994, pp. 14–18.

[5] U.S. Department of Commerce, *Application Guidelines for Malcolm Baldridge National Quality Award*, Gaithersburg, MD: National Institute of Science and Technology, 1991.

[6] Ellis, L. W., *The Financial Side of Industrial Research Management*, New York: Wiley, 1984.

[7] Honig-Haftel, S., and L. R. Martin, "The Effectiveness of Reward Systems on Innovative Output: An Empirical Analysis," *Small Business Economics*, Vol. 5(4), Dec. 1993, pp. 261–269.

[8] Ellis, L. W., and S. Honig-Haftel, "Reward Strategies for R&D," *Research Technology Management*, Vol. 35(2), Mar.–Apr. 1992, pp. 16–20.

[9] Ellis, L. W., and S. Honig-Haftel, "Reward Strategies for R&D: A Comparison of Contemporary Industrial and Academic Research," Faculty working paper, University of New Haven, West Haven , CT, March 1991.

[10] Honig-Haftel, S., "The Effect of Reward Systems on the Development of Patents in High Technology Firms," Sc.D. diss., University of New Haven, West Haven, CT, 1990.

[11] Smayling, M.-M., "Incentive Systems for Research and Development Scientists and Engineers," Ph.D. diss., University of Minnesota, Mineapolis, 1987.

Chapter 10

Evaluating Internal R&D Processes

Internal R&D processes are actions taken within the principal organizational unit most responsible for innovation. In the serial engineering organizational structure, this is usually the R&D department. In crossfunctional teams or CE, this structure may include assigned employees of other departments. In some companies, suppliers' personnel join the teams; and in consortia, people come from a number of companies. All of these are considered internal processes for this discussion since the team leadership has powers over processes like those of a R&D department head in serial engineering. Where R&D is used in this section, it thus applies to team structures as well.

The 1992 study ranked a few internal processes as shown in Table 10.1, with rank numbers in a total list including outcome, output, and interaction rankings.

Using the simple criterion of number of mentions, it is possible to group findings of research into a limited number of headings. Management of human resources had a leading position, with motivation as its largest component. Technical design standards, quality, and performance received multiple mentions. Planning and management issues also brought a diverse set of categories.

Table 10.1
Importance Ranking of Internal Processes

Process	Ranking
Motivation of R&D staff	4
Quality and performance of R&D	7
Planning and management of R&D	10

Source: [1].

10.1 MANAGEMENT OF HUMAN RESOURCE ISSUES

When considering human resource issues as potential precursor or leading indicators, researchers have settled on a broad variety of topics: diversity, rewards in R&D, motivation of employees, team rewards, ramp-up time, job rotation, effective career development, training and education, outside recruiting in universities and other companies, and leadership. This list sounds like a standard text book on human relations and, for the most part, represents items with too little direct impact to provide much management guidance.

Training and education was mentioned in Section 9.1.1 under interactions. A company whose staff has limited training, as an internal process, may offer incentives for self-improvement via training and education. The growth of evening graduate and undergraduate programs at U.S. universities reflects this as an indirect consequence of companies externalizing what was once an internal process.

On the other hand, this may not provide much of an incentive to a highly educated staff, and different efforts must be taken to motivate them. Thus, motivation and reward systems are the most important tasks in human relations.

10.1.1 Motivation and Reward Systems

Top management's commitment to a course of business action is reflected, in part, by its choice of reward systems for its managers and employees. As technical executives view R&D, they are influenced in their decisions by the rewards that have been selected by those managers above them. Thus, reward strategies for R&D are part of the basic management systems used in R&D management.

Evaluation measurements should look at the existing reward systems and determine what is worth motivating and either demotivating or not worth continuing, as illustrated by the following example.

George (not his real name) was in his last MBA class, his research project. He proposed reviewing reward systems in his own division. After counseling him on both the ethics of such a study and the probable company politics involved, he obtained clearance from his human resources director and conducted a simple survey of engineers at his division. His report was potential dynamite—seven of the eight existing reward systems were scathingly panned with comments such as "do they really think we would fall for that!" He was advised to go over the report with his human resources director and work out a strategy to keep him from "being shot as a messenger" while communicating the results to both general management and the engineers who responded.

The moral of this tale is that if you want to find out about your reward systems, go ask the potential recipients. But be careful—there is a need for care with the intermediary chosen. If the intermediary represents management, there is the presumption that responses will be heeded. If they are not, morale will suffer. A management outsider, such as the student above or one of the author's current doctoral students [2], may get freer comments. She or he is, however, in a rather exposed personal position with higher management. Perhaps, this is where a neutral consultant might be an advantage.

The measurements used can be simple interval scales, preferably with "neutral" or "no impact" as a midpoint. Suggested end points for measuring importance might be "very important" and "detracts from effectiveness." A second set of end points might measure intensity of the reward with an interval scale "too little to motivate—about right—excessive for the intended result."

Intrinsic and extrinsic rewards that are substantial have a positive impact on the generation of patents [3–7]. In the 1992 study, motivation was also found to have a large positive impact on the inclusive measure of output from R&D (of which patents is but one metric) but a minor (although statistically significant) negative impact on new products and services as a percent of sales. The implication is that reward systems currently in use may have traditionally focused on what is interesting to R&D staff (output) to the detriment of results for the firm (new products and services).

Given the nature of the engineers and scientists in the typical research laboratory, it would be natural to expect that not all of the strategies thus far investigated for general management applications would be applicable and effective to such professionals. Thus, implicit in studying rewards is to identify which were most used, which were considered to be most motivating, and which produced the best results. Rewards are viewed by many as necessary to motivate technical people.

The methodology used in gathering information on this topic was dual. First, the IRI held several meetings on the subject, including a special interest session at its Fall 1990 General Meeting [8]. Second, and in parallel, the topic was being investigated in academic research [3–7].

The first findings on this topic were those from the IRI [8]: positive experiences included public recognition by management of outstanding performers; public achievement awards; frequent use of small recognition tools such as dinners, tickets, and photos on bulletin boards; membership in in-house societies for distinguished contributors (with or without big dollar rewards); mementos for patents; awards that provide research time/money to explore new concepts; stock options/grants; scientific ladder promotions; and others. Two companies were covered in detail.

Reward Systems at DuPont are an investment in future behavior [8]. They are used to foster self-esteem and to accelerate change in the units to which those rewarded belong. Their reward system is based on team recognition as well as individual recognition. The use of reward systems is broad-based, with about 25% of people awarded each year. They have surveyed internally to find how people feel about their jobs but not to evaluate the impact of rewards.

Minnesota Mining and Manufacturing (3M) found that its major needs were innovation (the introduction of 25% new products each year), productivity, quality, and a global approach to business [8]. They use small teams, informal methods, and corresponding recognition. Team awards were emphasized over individual awards, and hundreds of awards are given each year.

This highlights that even between manufacturing sectors there are differences in the use of rewards. DuPont is in heavy industrial chemicals and petroleum products, which tend naturally to large organization structures within which individual recognition is important. In the multiproduct businesses of 3M, the team structure is a natural organizational pattern, and team rewards are more appropriately stressed.

In service industries, there are correspondingly divergences between large monolithic R&D organizations and those organized for close service to the customer at multiple locations. In telecommunications and electric utilities, recognition of individuals plays the same role as at DuPont. Banking and insurance companies also tend to run large centralized software development groups. But for retailing, the R&D for point-of-sale systems is most often done by the manufacturer, many of which are small team-based companies.

From other companies (mostly in manufacturing), negative or less positive experiences were high monetary rewards for patents, lack of public announcement of achievement awards, annual awards/bonuses that become seen as entitlement, team awards that included noncontributors, peer-nominated awards that were too nondiscriminating, and individual awards that demotivated teams.

Two recent academic investigations both used patents issued as an output measure. The first of these two studies used a model that employed an employment term, a squared employment term (to measure diseconomies of scale), small sum awards, large sum awards, and recognition [7]. His results based on primarily large firms showed that small per-patent or per-application payments were of little value as incentives, while large sum awards and recognition had positive effects. The second study, in attempting to replicate the first, had to reduce the predominately small- and medium-sized firm sample to those 53 firms having a "patent culture," that is, those having had patents issued during the study period [3–6]. This confirmed the high value of large sum awards and the little value of small sum awards, but failed to confirm the value of recognition as had the earlier model.

In the more recent study, the range of reward systems was broadened and a more comprehensive model was used [3–6]. Various analyses were conducted with differing combinations of input variables in search of a more descriptive model. The results are shown in Table 10.2 for those reward systems with a statistically significant result (shown in parentheses) in any of these trials, with the apparent mean increase in patents associated with the reward system.

To what does this lead us? The 80/20 rule seems to apply: Much of what the 80% of companies are doing is not producing results. Only a few of the strategies appear consistently in the results column. Reviewing what these investigations have found, one would conclude that there are only a few productive strategies.

Table 10.2
Effective Reward Systems from Analysis of Patent Culture Firms

Reward Systems (% Used)	Mean % Increase in Patents	Number of Times (Significant)
Large sum awards (13.0%)	48	4(2)
Informal or unpublicized award program	34	9(9)
Variable bonuses based on issue of patent	30	8(4)

Source: [3–6].

1. Use monetary rewards that register strongly in the minds of recipients and colleagues, that is, large sums, shares in the venture or company, or variable bonuses.
2. Intrinsic rewards produce best results if they are also seen to be a strong reflection of top management's commitment; are made very visible, spontaneous, prompt, informal; and the awarding is seen as fair and nondiscriminatory.

Diseconomies of scale were found in the two academic studies, as the quantitative models used attempted to adjust the outputs for all of the other factors involved as inputs [2–5]. One of these, which appeared in both studies, was the effective size of the firm. Like earlier studies, both demonstrated that there are diseconomies of scale in patent issuance. Doubling the size of the firm does not result in a doubling of the number of patents issued; in fact, doubling the number of employees only increased patents by about 75%, while doubling R&D expenditures per employee increased patents by about 25% [3–7]. Thus, size in sales volume or employees and R&D intensity are needed input measures as control variables in quantitative analysis.

Team rewards may be very touchy to measure by questionnaire, as the balance is controversial between rewarding individuals for personal achievement and rewarding teams for group accomplishment even though some group members have been undercontributors [2,9]. Again, however, it is necessary to speak to the potential recipients in order to get realistic answers unfiltered by the biases of R&D leaders.

The objective of research currently in progress, and endorsed by the firm's human resources director, is to clarify the role of team rewards [2]. First, the responders were asked to give their impression of the current reward structure between individual, team, and organizational rewards. Then they were asked to indicate the mix they preferred–even in a team environment the mean of responses was for increased individual rewards. Next, they were asked for the value to them (e.g., benefit and valence), and the attainability, of a long list of rewards.

These included both those in use and those selected from earlier studies as potentially valuable. The intent of analysis now in progress is to assess the following [2].

- Is the current mix of rewards between individual, team, and organizational rewards more effective than the responders' preferences, or not?
- Which rewards are highest ranked on a scale of the crossproduct of benefit times attainability?
- Are the highest ranked rewards correlated either with stated effort or effort imputed from motivation theory?
- Are the highest ranked rewards correlated with milestone achievement?
- Are the answers to the above questions affected by demographic factors such as age or gender?

Summarizing common reward themes, only 20% of the reward systems actually used in earlier studies correlated at all with patents issued as a measure of output. There is a need to control for company size (an input), which has an effect, as does R&D intensity (a process). And motivation as a process must be measured more broadly than just by reward systems alone–perhaps by the formality scale mentioned earlier, or by a subjective scale from low to high.

10.1.3 Leadership

Leadership rounds out the list of traditional human resource concerns. The Baldridge Aaward metrics (on their formality scale) of this internal process are senior executive leadership, quality values, management for quality, and public responsibility [10]. The academic leadership literature covers overall leadership thoroughly but is rather silent on leadership applied to innovation. However, effective leadership by the CEO can have a major impact on the strategic position of the company [11,12]. When the CEO focuses on R&D and innovation, it sparks the whole company to respond.

Thus, while there is an intimation that leadership counts as an internal process, so far there is insufficient research background to define recommended process metrics directly applicable to innovation. The effect of leadership is of course visible in selected output and outcome metrics.

When Stanley Gault was CEO at Rubbermaid, he thought that in a five-year period, at least 30% of sales should come from products that had been in the line less than five years [12, p. 26]. For CEO leadership, that was a very demanding objective. Not only did Rubbermaid meet the new product goal but exceeded it. In many years they would have 32, 33, and 34% annualizing in a five-year period.

10.1.3 Managing Major Cultural Change in R&D and Marketing

For those not yet into CE or having difficulties in handling the changes required by introducing it, a few comments can be made on the change process. First, this change requires a behavioral change for which many innovation managers are poorly prepared and texts or experts should be consulted [13]. Having an experienced facilitator available to the team leader should be a regular practice. These facilitators are available in many companies' human resource departments or can be obtained via outside consultants.

Managing major change in the innovation area has been compared to reshaping an ice cube [13]. First, the old shape must be melted down. Then the liquid is sloshed around, poured into the new mold, and finally the cube is refrozen into the new shape. The melting takes place through temporary groups, education, and training. Then the change is put into place, and a period of adjustment takes place, with the facilitator easing over the rough spots. Refreezing is encouraged by setting benchmarks and goals, revised procedures, new measurements, and rewards based on the new metrics. This leads into commitment building between the project teams and their leaders and general management.

The success factors in managing major change in R&D were recently studied [14]. The most dominant success factors started with top management's quick recognition of the need to change and being fully committed to it. In U.S. companies, the use of change champion was next most highly rated as a success factor, followed by teams. In Japanese companies the use of teams was rated third. Since CE is a team activity, it seems logical to emphasize teams in the future over the use of a change champion. However, the latter may be appropriate in larger firms. Piloting the change in part of the organization builds experience in making the change and provides a source of missionaries to preach to those needing to be converted, as was done at Chrysler in the transition from the Viper car pilot to the current four platform teams [15].

10.1.4 Internal Organization of the Innovation Effort

Four studies showed a positive correlation between results and internal structure: organization and the role of R&D in centralized and decentralized organizations, less levels to common reports, dotted line (functional) reporting, and the project manager's role. Levels to common reports is an evaluation measure of a vertical organization. Thus, fewer levels improves effectiveness. This can be turned into a positive metric as the greater average number of staff reporting to a single individual, the flatter the organization with less levels. A calibration from history may help: The Roman legions under Caesar had one *dux* for every ten legionnaires and one *centurion* for every ten *duces*. Rarely has the author seen such a flat R&D organization. Unfortunately, no such simple metrics address the other organizational attributes.

A derivative financial metric to this staff numeric is the R&D department overhead rate. This is the sum of all costs the department incurs besides salaries and wages divided by these salaries and wages [16, Chap. 3]. Thus, it includes the costs of excess supervision, clerical and support staff, plus associated labor benefits (fringes), allocated costs, and department spending. While thus a less-precise metric of organizational flatness, it has the benefit of easy communication with the financial management community. The R&D manager should evaluate the "lowest possible overhead rate." [16, p. 47]. However, if achieving this rate requires cutting out longer term beneficial actions such as training and education, the R&D manager should be prepared to fight the accountants.

10.1.5 Quality, Performance, Planning, and Management

While rated rather low in the 1992 study, selected items in these areas were found to be statistically significantly associated, each by a different single study: balancing long-term/short-term R&D objectives, optimization of R&D spending and employment in slow economic conditions, strategic quality planning process, quality goals and plans, benchmarking of the R&D organization, R&D portfolio management, globalization of R&D, multinational R&D, central facility or a small number of them, university and third-party relationships, formal monitoring of external R&D activities, information and analysis, scope and management of quality data and information, competitive comparisons and benchmarks, and analysis of quality data and information.

From this list, it seems clear that R&D management is an important internal process factor, even if not highly rated in the 1992 study. This study found no correlations with quality and performance; but a strong negative correlation appeared between planning and management, on the one hand, and output from R&D, on the other hand. Speculatively, is it possible that too heavy-handed managers may impair creativity? However, no other clear metrics of a type that working managers could use are immediately apparent. To measure any of these for a specific organization, an interval rating scale might be used, as was done in the 1992 study.

10.2 LESSONS LEARNED ON INTERNAL PROCESS METRICS

The most important evaluation measurements of internal processes are thus to measure the rewards in use, the degree of flatness of the internal organization, and top and R&D management commitment.

- Are rewards seen as important? Are they producing results aimed at business objectives? Or are some seen by staff as inconsequential, and thus candidates for pruning?

- How flat is the internal organization, measured by the average number of direct reports of managers?
- Are both top and R&D management aware of the need to change the existing organization to match technological change? Are they committed to making the change happen? Are teams involved in preparing for and implementing the change?

References

[1]   Internal study within IRIMER. The results were not submitted for publication until inclusion in this book.

[2]   Buckta, B., "The Effect of Reward Systems on Team Performance: A Case Study at a Greenfield Company," Sc.D. dissertation research in progress, University of New Haven, 1996.

[3]   Honig-Haftel, S., and L. R. Martin, "The Effectiveness of Reward Systems on Innovative Output: An Empirical Analysis," *Small Business Economics*, Vol. 5(4), Dec. 1993, pp. 261–269.

[4]   Ellis, L. W., and S. Honig-Haftel, "Reward Strategies for R&D: A Comparison of Contemporary Industrial and Academic Research," Faculty working paper, University of New Haven, New Haven, CT, March 1991.

[5]   Ellis, L. W., and S. Honig-Haftel, "Reward Strategies for R&D," *Research Technology Management*, Vol. 35 (2), Mar.–Apr. 1992, pp. 16–20.

[6]   Honig-Haftel, S., "The Effect of Reward Systems on the Development of Patents in High Technology Firms," Sc.D. diss., University of New Haven, New Haven, CT, 1990.

[7]   Smayling, M.-M., "Incentive Systems for Research and Development Scientists and Engineers," Ph.D. diss., University of Minnesota, 1987.

[8]   Industrial Research Institute, Minutes of ROR and SIS meetings, and tapes of the SIS meeting at the Fall General Meeting, Tape Productions, Phoenix, 1990.

[9]   Mower, J. C., and D. Willemon, "Rewarding Technical Teamwork," *Research Technology Management*, Vol. 32(5), Sept.–Oct. 1989.

[10] U.S. Department of Commerce, *Application Guidelines for Malcolm Baldridge National Quality Award*, Gaithersburg, MD: National Institute of Science and Technology, 1991.

[11] Taylor, W., "The Business of Innovation: An Interview with Paul Cook (CEO of Raychem)," *Harvard Business Review*, Vol. 68(2), Mar.–Apr. 1990, pp. 96–106.

[12] Gault, S. C. (CEO of Rubbermaid and Goodyear), "Responding to Change," *Research Technology Management*, Vol. 37(3), May–June 1994, pp. 23–26.

[13] Weisbord, M. R., *Productive Workplaces: Organizing and Managing for Dignity, Meaning and Community*, Jossey-Bass, 1990, pp. 21–41.

[14] Farris, G. F., and L. W. Ellis, "Managing Major Change in R&D", *Research Technology Management*, Vol. 33(1), Jan.–Feb. 1990.

[15] Lutz, R. A., "Implementing Technological Change with Cross-Functional Teams," *Research Technology Management*, 37(2), Mar.–Apr. 1994, pp. 14–18.

[16] Ellis, L. W., *The Financial Side of Industrial Research Management*, New York: Wiley, 1984.

Part IV

External Evaluation of R&D

Besides financial evaluation, a number of nonfinancial metrics help evaluate the effectiveness of R&D processes. The most important of these is the area of customer satisfaction covered in Chapter 11. New products and services and various forms of benchmarking are covered in Chapter 12. These are compared with the financial evaluation metrics in Chapter 13. Chapter 14 addresses the research methods used and provides quantitative summaries of the multiyear research studies. Chapter 15 summarizes the outcome evaluation process and gives the author's recommended list of best evaluation metrics.

Chapter 11

Customer Satisfaction Evaluation and Measurement

The literature is rather sparse on the subject of evaluating and measuring customer satisfaction. Equally, research is largely lacking on precursor or predictor measurements that affect the measured results of customer satisfaction. What literature there is dwells mostly on measuring the customer's satisfaction with ongoing products or services, similar to the Baldridge Award criteria [1], rather than on measuring satisfaction with innovation. The reader will quickly notice that its descriptions are those of manufacturing organizations. Yet, equivalent functions exist in purely service organizations, particularly those dependent on IT [2]. Service companies need measurements also, as this source makes clear:

> An important common finding was that, in the companies surveyed, decision-making processes for IT projects were comparable to those used for other complex advanced-technology projects. In many instances, decisions about investments in IT are like decisions about R&D. Payoffs from both R&D and IT are likely to be uncertain in both scale and timing [2, p. 13].

It goes on to state: "Service companies in particular have taken a leadership role in developing customer-oriented measures of quality" [2, p. 183]. The author, as a consequence of this advice, makes no distinction in what follows between manufacturing companies' innovation and that of technology dependent service companies.

11.1   DEFINING THE CUSTOMER AND SATISFACTION

This chapter is a summary developed by the author from his experience, the literature, and the multiple elements covered in the 1994 and 1995 research studies on the effective management of innovation. First, one asks who is the customer? Then what is satisfaction? These are followed by strategies for measurement and finally by a limited summary of research results, which are discussed more completely in Chapter 14.

11.1.1   Who is the Customer?

The consumer or end user is normally thought of as the customer, and she or he certainly is the important one. Yet, there are two other customers whose satisfaction must be measured, as depicted in Figure 11.1.

Obviously, there is the internal customer to the innovation chain, which is the firm's implementation chain. However, for many firms, beyond the output of the implementation chain is also often a long and fragmented distribution chain. Satisfaction here also must be measured and evaluated if distribution is to perform satisfactorily and effectively.

The end user of an innovative product or service sees it as a change from before, or not used at all. To be a successful innovation, this customer must be lured into the outlay of cash to remunerate the innovator. Some perceived value must result from such a purchase. This value is either in differentiation from alternatives or in lowered costs to the end user. More recently, writers have begun to add two additional criteria, namely, perceived quality of the good or service and timeliness of the service's or product's availability [3,4].

End users may be large and concentrated, such as governmental bodies, or may go all the way to the other extreme and represent millions of individuals, or any group in between. Not under the control of the innovating firm, their views must be obtained by persuasive interrogation or observation.

The distribution chain involves all organizational units, whether internal or external to the company, between the output of the implementation chain, where the product or service becomes a distinct entity, to the point of sale to the end user. In satisfying a government customer, or an original equipment manufacturer,

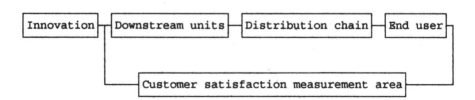

Figure 11.1 Steps from innovation to the end user.

there may be no external distribution involved, with all customer relations handled internally. In a consumer or industrial product, however, a whole class of distributors, wholesalers, retailers, and other intermediaries are involved, with their number and variety dependent on the industry's characteristics. In services, travel agents, insurance agents, and other intermediaries are also often involved.

The distribution chain, while usually not under the control of the innovating firm, is nonetheless dependent upon it. Thus, it is more responsive than the typical end user when probed for its views. Also, the number of organizations to be queried is often more manageable than the number of end users.

Downstream units are those organizational elements of the implementation chain who receive the innovation chain's output and deliver it to the distribution chain or directly to the end user. Manufacturing in product companies, or computer operations in service companies, represent units under control of the innovating company, and even fewer units in number than those of the distribution chain.

In summary, there are three customers for the firm to address when measuring satisfaction:

- End users;
- Distribution;
- Internal operations.

Each of these has differing levels of ability to be controlled and numbers of individuals about which to be asked or observed as to their satisfaction.

11.1.2 The Lead User

Many studies of the diffusion of innovations into the market place have shown that there is a category of end users who are pioneers by nature [5]. That is, they actively seek to be the first to use a new innovation in their field. For the R&D manager, the advantage of measuring and evaluating customer satisfaction first through a lead user (also called by some as a "teaching customer") is timeliness of feedback. The probability is that many of the subsequent adopters of the innovation will follow the choice of the lead user.

The concept of dealing with a lead user is shown graphically in Figure 11.2, indicating a balance between four organizational units, with the principal leaders of the innovation effort being shown as R&D and market research.

Implicit in using a lead user is that the firm is comfortable with the following necessary organizational realities.

- Discussing the details of the company's product planning at the user's level;
- Letting R&D talk to the customer jointly with marketing rather than having marketing be the sole interface with the customer;

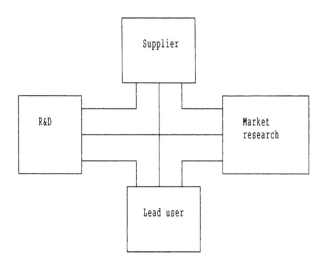

Figure 11.2. The lead user concept (*After:* [5]).

- Being willing to change, modify, and field test (also called beta test) the product or service on the user's premises.

For many firms, this would require such a cultural reformation that it could only be contemplated after commitment to CE as discussed in Chapter 6 [6].

11.1.3   What is Satisfaction?

A broad definition of satisfaction begins with the same two measures that are the basis of defining quality, namely, conformance to requirements and value as perceived by the customer [7, pp. 9–13].

Conformance to requirements as a metric implies that the requirements be spelled out clearly and correctly. This is a standard problem when dealing with a product or service that is well launched in the implementation chain. But when an innovative product reaches the customer for the first time, often the words used in specifying mean different things to the innovator and to the customer. An example from the author's experience may serve to illustrate this point.

The telephone rang late in the afternoon in the Chief Engineer's office. It was the project manager (who had been with two of the customer's engineers all day in acceptance testing of a new process control system) requesting an urgent meeting. At this meeting, the customer's engineers acknowledged that the product had performed exactly as specified, but there was a problem for them with the alarm system; that is, it logged all alarms and, when the storage was full, flashed a signal that no more alarms could be taken and recorded, all as specified. Their normal procedure, however, was to use an alarm system not for alarms, but for prompting the plant operators. Thus, they stated, "If the alarm storage gets full and no more alarms are received, we could blow up the plant!" They were advised that due to the late hour, nothing could be done to address their problem until the following morning. Fortunately, a fix was quickly found to keep alarms being received, so contractual arguments were unnecessary.

What this type of misunderstanding shows is that relying on written specifications for innovative products may not be an adequate substitute for thorough knowledge of the customer's needs. Thus, measuring conformance may not be the best choice for measuring innovation.

Value as perceived by the end customer, however, is a much more difficult measurement to make and, most importantly, often a costly one for the company. Thus, a tradeoff is required between accuracy and cost. Value also has many different meanings to different customers, so a few actual companies' approaches are worth reviewing.

A recent article analyzed three of these firms' approaches [8]. The first used (1) a pricing index as a measure of cost competitiveness; (2) a customer rank survey against competitors, done annually by an independent organization; (3) a customer satisfaction index done monthly; and (4) market share by key accounts as a measure of tangible benefits. The second measured customer satisfaction and market share. And a third measured on-time delivery, lead time, and performance-to-schedule, all measures of timeliness. These measures differ greatly among the three companies. It should be noted that for the purposes of this chapter, market share is not a direct customer satisfaction metric but rather a strategic results metric (which is covered in Chapter 12), and thus only indirectly a measure of customer satisfaction. What is clear, however, is that value in all three cases is in satisfaction with the supplier to a greater extent than satisfaction with the product or service.

11.1.4 Motorola's Satisfaction Criteria

While using quality as a primary basis for determining customer satisfaction, the example of one defense contracting division (GEG) of Motorola serves to set value perception in perspective [9]. For this division, "Customer Satisfaction Assessment" is 20% of the weighted total system performance assessment. The measurement used is "percentage of customers surveyed ranking GEG in the top 20% compared to other defense contractors." The specific ratings are shown in Figure 11.3 and the categories in Table 11.1, from the "1989 GEG Customer Satisfaction Survey."

For illustration in this table, the author has organized those measures in a classification scheme showing those that measure customer satisfaction with (1) service as an innovator and (2) the innovative product or service itself. Perhaps one of the advantages of this as an example on which to build a measurement index, as compared with the Baldridge Award criteria covered in Chapter 1, is that

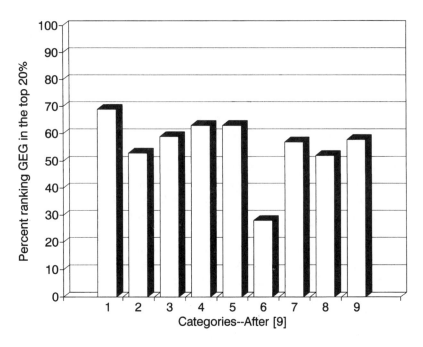

Figure 11.3 1989 GEG customer satisfaction survey (*After:* [9]).

Table 11.1
Classification of Satisfaction Measures

Measure	Service as an Innovator	The Product or Service Itself
1. Quality/Reliability		X
2. Timeliness	X	
3. Technology		X
4. Communications	X	
5. Responsiveness	X	
6. Cost competitiveness		X
7. Program/Contract management	X	
8. Quality of proposals	X	
9. Overall performance as a contractor	X	

Source: [9].

the nature of this division's business is more oriented toward innovation than the implementation of repetitive customer orders.

Skipping over product quality/reliability, which is subject to the same interpretation difficulties covered earlier, the remaining categories are clearly measures of value to the customer. As with earlier examples, measures of satisfaction with the supplier are more numerous than satisfaction with the product. Timeliness also parallels the firm's outcome criterion discussed earlier in Chapters 1 and 7.

11.1.5 Crafting the Evaluation Measurement

The various surveys discussed earlier use two basic types of survey measurements. The first type asks the respondent to rate the company against some yardstick, usually that of the competition. Thus, Motorola's "percentage—compared to other—customers" falls into this first category, as does the Baldridge Award's comparison to "percent of world-class companies." This is a desirable approach because it fixes in the respondent's mind exactly what is the range of measurement and allows for a continuous metric yielding more quantitative information for analysis.

The second type of scale used is an interval scale, typically from 1 to 5. An example might be "How did you like using our information service?" The corresponding scale might range from very highly satisfactory (5) through neutral (3) to very unsatisfactory (1). This scale is easier for the respondent to handle, involving only circling a number. Best results are found when the midpoint (3) is given a neutral rating with "best" at one end and "worst" at the other, or other similar terms, as in the example. Experience has shown that for many respondents, the interval scale may be construed as continuous. However, bunching at either end of the scale does sometimes occur, which may require more sophisticated statistical analysis. Also, a shift of 0.1 is 10% at the lowest end of the scale but only 2% of the top value, which also may not represent the customer's intentions. This type of scale tends to be more open to individual interpretation than the first type of scale described previously and, thus, typically has a wider standard deviation. When the number of customers being surveyed is kept small as a cost control measure, this can negatively impact the accuracy of results.

11.2 THE SURVEY INSTRUMENT

In the 1994 and 1995 studies, quantitative measures of customer satisfaction were used, based on those used by Motorola listed in Table 11.1 [9]. While it is better to mix the questions on the company and the service or product in the actual survey instrument, as is done in Table 11.1, it seems best to separate these categories for the purpose of explaining their characteristics.

11.2.1 Measuring Your Company as an Innovative Supplier

Each of the three classes of customers measures the effectiveness of your company's servicing of them in determining their satisfaction. The types of questions asked under each category will depend upon the nature of your business—yet, some or all of them, may be necessary for you to understand whether what you are doing is the right thing and therefore effective.

Timeliness of delivering new improvements is another measure of your customer's satisfaction with your company. In the examples above, lead time is identified as one measure: "How long does it take from notification of requirement until the needed result is in the customer's hands?" This is the "idea-to-customer time" of Chapter 7. A second issue is "performance to schedule," or similar measurement, which tracks what time was promised to the customer against what time was actually achieved.

This measurement, however, needs to be done from the customer's perception of your timeliness, not your own. An extreme example is that of a control system manufacturer.

The general manager had decided to bid for a waste water treatment plant with an innovative control system "off the drawing board." He considered the three-year delivery requested attainable. After three years, the development was a year late. However, since the control system was at the end of a long series of civil, mechanical, and electrical contractors, the site was not ready either. Ten months later, the company was notified that the site was ready, but the design still had three months to go. Site inspection showed that enough items still had not been done to delay start of installation two months more. Installation then started, and with the design finished, ended in less than two months. The customer then complemented the company on its timeliness, even though the internal time metric showed 14 months late on a 36-month project commitment!

While this is not a typical example, many customers for industrial products generate their own delays, such as, for example, in specifying and placing orders. Thus, what is important to be measured is the time metrics seen by the customer from when a "go ahead" is given the supplier.

Communications between the innovator and customer are important. Communications now go around the world in less than a second thanks to the technological developments of telecommunications satellites and fiber-optic cables. At the same time, they have become more impersonal, as any customer will attest after fruitlessly trying to reach you through your telephone answering machine or electronic mail (e-mail). As the AT&T slogan correctly says of customer communications: "Reach out and touch someone."

Thus, good communications is the start of your satisfying relationship with the customer. Do you listen, or just talk? For effectiveness, two-way communication is necessary. Lee Iacocca, the former CEO of Chrysler, used to say that he could find many courses to teach his people to speak, but none to teach them how to listen. The computer industry has addressed this problem through end users' groups where the customers may talk directly to management, with their peers in other companies, and with your firm's distributors and sales people listening in. Many industrial products companies, which traditionally use multiple distributors, have formed distributor councils for the purpose of having two-way communication. Compared with user groups, distributor's councils are usually much more frank and open, as subjects get discussed that neither the company nor the distributor would want end users to hear. If questionnaires are used, the comparable approach would be to ask, "Compared to other companies with whom you deal, how effective do you consider you are in getting your points understood by your supplier?"

Communications channels are also subject to distortion, noise, interference, and delay. It is human nature to pass along the good news quickly and accurately and to be afraid of the "shoot the messenger" syndrome when faced with the bad news. Questions on accuracy and timeliness thus should form the balance of measuring communications effectiveness. With user groups or distributors councils, a debriefing session after the meeting's end would serve the same function in measuring the meeting's communications effectiveness.

Responsiveness and complaint resolution are also types of communication but are tied to a specific difficulty that is stressful to the customer. Thus, the separate measurement of this category is likely to be helpful in determining where improvement may be needed in your innovation organization. With a lead user, sorting out your organizational problems at this point may lead to the greater satisfaction of subsequent customers.

Program and customer relationship management covers the satisfaction with the individual point of contact that the customer has with your organization. If your firm runs a project manager system, this is the project manager; otherwise, it may be the field salesperson or service department representative.

Commitment to customers is a more difficult and more subjective metric from the customer's viewpoint. An end customer may be quite specific and accurate about your being late but will hesitate to tell you that your commitment is being questioned. On the other hand, internal customers and distributors will be much more blunt. Regardless of difficulty, this dimension is also one that should be measured in characterizing customer satisfaction.

11.2.2 Measuring Your Product or Service

The metrics of your product or service are fewer by comparison. Does it differ from the competition in technology or features? Is it of high quality and reliability? Do you charge too much?

Technology and feature quality are both forms of what marketeers call *differentiation*. In recent deliberations, the IRIMER has split the technology question into two parts: customer rating of technical capability and customer rating of product technology benefits. These correspond to the division made earlier of customer rating of satisfaction with the individual firm as a supplier and consumer/end user satisfaction with the specific product.

Motorola's division dealing with the technologically sophisticated Department of Defense competes against others on the extent to which their technology is "state-of-the-art" [9]. Other classes of customers measure satisfaction in terms of what does the service or product do for me? Does it lower my costs? Does the computer system give me a leg up in getting new business? Again, the question is compared to what? If not to the competition, as is often the case with innovation, then how does it compare with other alternatives, such as the use of fewer people. The range of questions obviously needs to be tailored to the specifics of the product or service.

Defect quality and reliability of an innovative offering are two distinctive, but complementary, categories. As seen by the customer of an innovative service or product, defects are occasions when performance is not as expected. Percentage defects is a good measure if the customer is set up to measure them. Otherwise, defects per hour or per day may be more practical for the user.

Reliability is basically a reciprocal of defects per unit time and is most commonly measured as MTBF. For other users, particularly of services, "down time" or nonavailability is a more practical metric. Average down time is the sum of *mean time to receive attention* (MTTA) and *mean time to repair the defect* (MTTR). These may easily be transformed into percent availability or percent nonavailability.

Cost competitiveness is a third dimension by which customers measure product or service satisfaction. But the customer's cost is the supplier's price. For a commodity product such as coal, price differences are small between suppliers, and this is then a true measure. For many modern products, however, feature differences mask a true price comparison between competitors. The customer, however, may not value these feature differences equally and may have an impression that over-featured items are overpriced. Customers tend to be quite objective and quantitative about this measure, making it a useful metric.

11.2.3 Bias and Survey Reliability

As noted in many cases previously discussed, biases exist throughout the customer satisfaction survey process. A field sales force's reports on metrics tend to be biased toward optimism. Your own quality department may be biased toward pessimism. Distributors, who operate on the narrow margin between your price to them and what the end user will pay, often will give you a pessimistic report (your price is too high!) while being persuasive to the end user. And when querying technologists and innovators, as in the 1994 survey, there may be a bias toward what interests them most, which is technology.

How do you handle this tendency to biased answers? Cross checking is the basic tool to use in verifying the results from your satisfaction measurements. If there are independent consultants or industry rating services available, these will serve as a calibration of what is reported by surveys conducted internally. A comparison of the results recorded by your quality department and those reported by the customer may also highlight biases. Interviews with those answering surveys will bring out the finer distinctions not clear in the simplistic responses. Finally, higher levels of management should practice *management by walking about* (MBWA) to hear directly from the customer without intervening or subordinate units with their own slants to providing information.

11.2.4 Measuring Customer Satisfaction With Innovation

While the prior research base for selecting precursor or leading indicators is minimal, the discussion thus far indicates that all tasks that lead to greater understanding of the customer are those that contribute to increasing customer satisfaction. Thus, measuring your own organization's innovation chain is the area most likely to give you precursor or leading indicators of future satisfaction of your own customers.

The 1994 and 1995 studies attempted to find some more generalized answers to measuring customer satisfaction while accomplishing a broader survey of other issues in innovation management. Details of this research are covered in Chapter 14 and briefly summarized here. Customer satisfaction questions were aimed at determining the extent to which respondents measure customer satisfaction in their own firms. Over half of the respondents used a satisfaction index, a lead user, and/or market share as an indirect metric. However, none of the three use measurements showed statistically significant correlations with customer ratings of satisfaction. Thus, the type of measurement chosen to measure customer satisfaction seems not to bias the results.

The survey also sought self-reported assessments from individuals interested in R&D or product management of their views of how customers would rate their products and customer service using the categories listed in Table 11.1. The median values are shown in Figure 11.4 using the categories of Table 11.1 and Figure 11.3.

The comparison between Figures 11.3 and 11.4 is striking as they are closely correlated, despite being sampled five years apart. Particularly notable is that the lowest rating in both groups was customer satisfaction with cost competitiveness.

Only responsiveness, technology, and quality/reliability ratings were associated significantly with the overall rating, lending credence that measuring just these three leading indicators is sufficient to establish the dimensions of customer satisfaction.

Responsiveness is a measure of customer satisfaction with the innovative supplier rather than the product. Customer satisfaction with responsiveness is

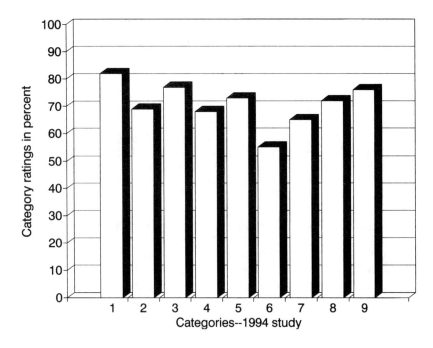

Figure 11.4 1994 customer satisfaction means.

correlated with that of communications. For some companies, the two questions may best be combined into a single rating of customer satisfaction with interpersonal relationships. Product quality and reliability and technology tend to be measures of customer satisfaction with the innovative product rather than the company as a supplier. The use of CE is associated with higher overall performance ratings but is a minor effect.

The absence of cost competitiveness in the overall performance regression sparked a parallel study of this factor that the author's experience foretold should have been included. Cost satisfaction is significantly associated with the use of market share as a measure of customer satisfaction, with responsiveness, using TQM in R&D, using QFD, and taking less time in the market development cycle and longer in the idea-to-customer cycle.

11.2.4.1 Selected Comments of Respondents on Customer Satisfaction [10]

This section gives some comments of respondents to the 1994 study that have been used in clarifying the earlier part of this chapter. The use of few and simple metrics for customer satisfaction is clearly not sufficient, and broader measures need to be used to fit the circumstances of your company.

Our end user is the consumer who views satisfaction in terms of the product. Our customer is increasingly the large chain stores, like K-Mart, who view satisfaction in terms of how the product handles and looks in packaging. No single measure fits both (consumer products).

Most important are timeliness and responsiveness. Communication and cost competitiveness are also important. Quality and reliability are more important in satisfying the bosses (petroleum).

Cannot connect to market share as a customer satisfaction metric as it has other factors not even peripherally related. Can buy into responsiveness, technology and quality/reliability, communications and timeliness measures as necessary, but not sufficient, components of an overall rating. Surprised at lack of correlation with the cost competitiveness rating. React positively to cost relating to time measurements, TQM in R&D, and shorter market development cycle, but can't make sense of a longer idea-to-customer time, which contradicts the other time measures (consumer durables).

Lack of correlation between cost competitiveness and overall performance satisfaction ratings, which is counterintuitive. Price is most important as a means of gaining market share in our commodity product industry, but responsiveness is a critical support. Need to split technology into rating of technical capability (which is what separates us from other producers since products are so alike) and rating of product capability. Time is less important since product life is long. Individual rewards are still related to cost competitiveness, but old rewards are not the future—change rewards to change behavior per Juran [7] (precision metal products).

Are we measuring a supermarket chain or the consumer? Expects companies will use at least two out of the three ways of measuring satisfaction. Cost competitiveness is only important to the high cost or marginal producer who has not handled technology well. Not surprised at correlation of overall rating with responsiveness, technology and quality/reliability. Timeliness may be a proxy for the cost of R&D (consumer foods).

We measure by lead user and market share. Responsiveness, technology and quality/reliability are a good representation of overall rating, as problems get reflected in these even if they are not the root cause. Surprised at cost findings—you can't walk away from all commodity business. Technology rating only needs splitting between company and product in certain areas, but not across all capabilities (chemical/metal industrial supplies).

Satisfaction index, market share and "teacher customer" (lead user) are useful ways to measure satisfaction. It is weird that none correlate with satisfaction ratings, particularly lead users since they get such special service. Responsiveness for us includes timeliness. These and quality are good components of an index, but surprised at high rating of technology as our customers care about it in only a few businesses. Splitting technology into company and product components would be artificial. Process is the key for us (electronic components).

11.3 LESSONS LEARNED ON MEASURING CUSTOMER SATISFACTION

This chapter has walked through the process of measuring customer satisfaction with the most useful factors to a broad group of companies.

- The customer must be identified not only as the end user but also as the downstream implementation chain and the distribution chain.
- Satisfaction must be defined in the two dimensions of conformance and value.
- Use a survey instrument in terms of desirable forms of metrics and in measuring the customer's satisfaction with your firm as well as the service or product.
- Measure overall customer satisfaction with three significant factors: technology, quality/reliability, and responsiveness.
- To increase customer satisfaction with your cost competitiveness, also measure market share and use TQM and QFD in R&D, which may lengthen idea-to-customer time as you do it right the first time.

References

[1] U.S. Department of Commerce, "Application Guidelines for Malcolm Baldridge National Quality Award," National Institute of Science and Technology, Gaithersburg, MD, 1991.

[2] U.S. National Research Council, *Information Technology in the Service Sector*, Washington, DC: National Academy Press, 1994.

[3] Gault, S. C., "Responding to Change," *Research Technology Management*, Vol. 37(3), May–June 1994, pp. 23–26.

[4] Curtis, C. C., and L. W. Ellis, "A Balanced Scorecard for New Product Development," *J. Cost Management*, to appear.

[5] Herstatt, C., and E. von Hippel, "From Experience: Developing New Product Concepts via the Lead User Method: A Case Study in a 'Low Tech' Field," *J. Product Innovation Management*, Vol. 9(3), Sept. 1992, pp. 213–221.

[6] Lutz, R. A., "Implementing Technological Change with Cross-Functional Teams," *Research Technology Management*, Vol. 37(2), Mar.–Apr. 1994, pp. 14–18.

[7] Juran, J. M., *Juran on Quality by Design: The New Steps for Planning Quality into Goods and Services*, New York: Free Press, 1992, pp. 9–13.

[8] Kaplan, R. S., and D. P. Norton, "Putting the Balanced Scorecard to Work," *Harvard Business Review*, Sept.–Oct. 1993, pp. 134–147.

[9] Motorola Corp., Presentation to the IEEE, Washington DC, Jan. 1990, Charts C-D 90, 0243A39 & 74.

[10] Ellis, L. W., and C. C. Curtis, "Measuring Customer Satisfaction," *Research Technology Management*, Vol. 38(5), Sept.–Oct. 1995, pp. 45–48.

Chapter 12

Improving Strategic Intent Results Through Other Evaluation Measurements

In addition to measuring the nonfinancial results of customer satisfaction and timeliness described in the previous two chapters, many companies employ still another group of nonfinancial measurements. These look at one or more of several available result measurements that help evaluate the accomplishment of the strategic intent of the company. Increasingly, as noted in Chapter 3, many firms use resulting market share as a measure of strategic intent results, while also using this as an indirect measurement of customer satisfaction. Three other measurement areas are covered in this chapter. New products or services has already been mentioned as an outcome and will be expanded upon. The process of benchmarking gives guidance to setting objectives for all forms of nonfinancial measurements that affect technology and innovation management. Finally, the rate of improvement of results is still another important measurement area, because the competition does not stand still and the interaction of growth and more common earnings measures is needed to measure and evaluate the creation of shareholder value.

12.1 NEW PRODUCTS AND SERVICES

New products or services, when measured as a percent of sales, provide one of the most comprehensive nonfinancial measures of innovation effectiveness [1]. If the customer were not satisfied with the product or service, or if it were not available in timely fashion, orders would not have been placed with the company. While the author was employed by ITT Corporation over three decades ago, strategic plans tracked this value for products introduced in the preceding three years. Even that long ago, it was an effective evaluation metric for R&D management action. Goodyear and Rubbermaid are among recent companies reporting use of this metric [2].

The 1994 and 1995 surveys of managers working in innovation and technology management gave some indications of the wide use of the new product-to-sales ratio metric. Of the executives answering the question "The approximate percent of your company's total sales volume attributable to new products is ____ percent," the median percentage reported was 25%, as shown in Figure 12.1.

If this seems a high percentage, in Rubbermaid the goal was 30% of sales from products that had been in the line less than five years, and this goal was exceeded [2, p. 26]. It should be noted that, because of the diverse industries surveyed, the length of time considered "new" was left open to the respondents' discretion. Depending on the industry, this might run from as little as one year for a toy manufacturer to many years for a capital-intensive industry.

The 1994 and 1995 studies were used to create models of the factors associated with the new product/sales percentage. There was, however, no similarity between the two studies, indicating a rather wide divergence of views among those responding in the two years. The two studies are described in detail in Chapter 14 and summarized briefly here.

A 1994 model with the percentage of new products to total sales as the dependent variable is summarized in Table 12.1.

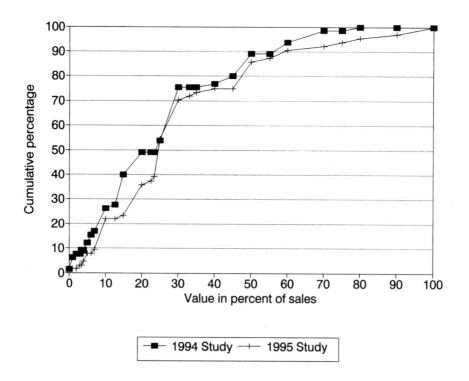

Figure 12.1 Percent reporting new products/sales.

Table 12.1

Factors Affecting New Product Sales

Positive Factors

- Approximate percent of your company's new product development product R&D investment budget on major new development.
- Approximate percent allocation to outcome benchmarking rather than process benchmarking (total 100%).
- Use of CE as measured by the percent of the R&D budget so spent.
- Does your company measure extent of customer satisfaction using market share as a measure?
- For how many years has your company been using time as a measure in any part of its new product development cycle?

Negative Factors

- Average life cycle of your company's products in years.
- To what extent does your company use value engineering?

Source: [3].

The percentage of major new projects was the primary positive result in 1994. Based on the timing of these factors, the decision to spend on major new development would appear to qualify as the cause of more new products, or a proxy for it. It is a substantial confirmation of a recent article advising to "go for the long shots" [4]. The use of outcome benchmarking was another positive result in 1994. Again because of timing, outcome benchmarking qualifies as a cause or proxy for new product percentage. Since the sum of outcome benchmarking and process benchmarking adds to 100%, this suggests moving benchmarking effort out of process benchmarking and on to outcome benchmarking if a greater new products percentage is your firm's goal.

A recent book on ABC and ABM recommends the contrary—greater use of process benchmarking [5]. This is not necessarily contradictory, as process benchmarking and ABC/ABM are designed to help on improving the quality, timeliness, and cost of current production rather than on improving innovation. There is a clear management tradeoff in these results between the interests of the innovation managers in new products and those of the production and finance managers as evidenced by use of ABC/ABM.

The remaining three positive factors involved with new products and services in the 1994 study seem to be the consequences of management direction rather than causes and effects of each other. The large group of companies that measure market share as an indirect indicator of customer satisfaction have a higher percentage of new products/services to sales. Each year that time has been measured in the innovation chain is associated with a higher percentage of new products/services to sales. Concurrent, or simultaneous engineering, which has a positive effect on the timeliness of innovation, also has a positive effect on the new product sales percentage. Management that is interested in customers, timeliness, and effective internal processes is also one that stresses innovation outcomes.

Financial factors were expected to affect new product sales, but this turned out not to be the case in the 1994 study. Cause and effect of financial factors is a debatable issue. Does the pursuit of new products cut into current income (a finding of the 1995 study)? Or should a higher new product sales percentage result in higher earnings? Or are higher earnings necessary to fund the innovation effort that results in higher new sales? Or is there a common higher strategic reason that cannot be measured externally? This latter case may be seen in the following example from the author's own experience.

In ITT's telecommunications transmission product line, the need to fund the innovation effort to stay competitive resulted in higher new product sales because of shorter product life cycles and, at the same time, in higher earnings because the company achieved lower product costs by its management efforts.

This was supported in the 1994 survey where one negative factor was the average product life cycle measured in years. While there is some logic in cutting down on new product introductions when the company has longer life products, the competitive risks involved need to be assessed by management. The other negative factor, use of value engineering, is also logical. If a firm's attention is on value engineering, or benchmarking noncompetitively, it is not likely to be so focused on increasing the percentage of new products.

In the 1995 study, the six most consistent associated factors with new products as a percent of sales are shown in Table 12.2.

The new product/sales percentage was generally associated with lower EBIT. On careful investigation, up to an EBIT of 3% in the 1995 responses, the new products/sales percentage was associated with higher EBIT; but above that point, increasing EBIT was associated with lower new product sales, and vice versa. Only if each additional percentage of new products to sales were able to be translated into

Table 12.2
Factors Affecting New Product Sales

Positive Factors

- Use of Quality Function Deployment;
- Company center of gravity close to the customer;
- External customer satisfaction rating with technology.

Negative Factors

- EBIT as a percent of sales;
- External customer satisfaction with overall performance as a contractor;
- Company age.

Source: [6].

more than a percent of annual growth rate would this be a rational tradeoff for most companies interested in shareholder value, according to the model introduced later in this chapter.

The other two negative factors are more intuitive. It would appear that young companies are focused on new products and older ones more on external customer satisfaction with performance.

In the 1992 study, the correlations of new products/services to sales were determined for a number of input, interaction, and internal process factors. Motivation and coordination of R&D and marketing were determined to be positively coordinated with new products/services, leading them in time, and with moderate coefficient values. While competence of staff and use of crossfunctional teams were also positively correlated with new products/services, the coefficient values were low, indicating less use in managing innovation. The following were determined to be negatively correlated with new products/services, but all with low coefficients: planning and management, generation of new ideas, knowledge of customer needs, financial project selection, conflict level and management, coordination and transfer downwards, coordination of R&D and engineering, and support to the rest of the organization.

12.1.1 Lessons Learned on New Products to Sales

The management implications of these studies are limited because they were each done with different, small, and judgementally selected groups whose interests were radically varied. Some limited conclusions are that new products and services result from the following factors.

- High percent of the company's new product development product R&D investment budget on major new development.
- Moving benchmarking effort on to outcome benchmarking and out of non-competitive and process benchmarking.
- Crossfunctional integration such as using CE, stage-gate tracking, and/or QFD.
- Measuring the extent of customer satisfaction using market share and satisfaction with technology as measures.
- Having the company's center of gravity close to the external customer.
- A motivated and competent staff, generating a substantial patent base.
- Avoiding an excessive focus on costs, quality, management interventions, and the distractions of too many ideas and customer needs.

12.2 USING BENCHMARKING FOR INNOVATION

As mentioned briefly in Chapter 1, the practices of benchmarking have barely begun to be applied to the elements of the innovation chain. Benchmarking is not by its nature a measurable output variable but rather is an input and internal process having its impact on outputs and outcomes. It is, however, included here as a non-financial measure of strategic intent because that is how it is usually considered by business strategists. For evaluation and measurement, however, the various forms of benchmarking need to be applied to any of the outcome-dependent variables. This section addresses benchmarking usage and the impact of benchmarking variables on three outcomes: financial performance; customer satisfaction, and new products and services.

12.2.1 Actual Benchmarking Usage

Benchmarking involves identifying and targeting the best practices adopted by sources outside the using organization. In a large multidivisional company, divisions may benchmark internally against other divisions within the company. The advantages of this practice are free information flow and more accurate cost estimates. The disadvantage is that the rest of your firm may not be up to the world-class standards of your own competitors.

Noncompetitive benchmarking has gained much favor in recent years. Companies may be selected for study that are clearly world class in their industries. Not being competitors, these companies may reveal information with little fear of anti-trust infractions. They may be, however, less open than other parts of your own company and still not as competent as your competitors.

Competitive benchmarking is harder to do than the other two methods because competitors are naturally secretive with their best practices and clearly more aware of anti-trust considerations. Also, what may be observed is what has been done and not what is on their drawing boards or computer-aided design screens.

Besides looking at the sources of benchmarks, companies also have the choice of obtaining benchmarks on outcomes to their organization or of internal processes within it. Table 12.3 shows usage data on all of these methods, that is, some to consistent use indicated by respondents by percent.

Mere use of any benchmarking practice, however, is no guarantee of its effectiveness. Thus, the R&D manager must also understand which of these practices has an effect on those outcomes desired by general management.

12.2.2 Impact of Benchmarking on Other Outcomes

In the analysis of the other major innovation outcomes not covered in this chapter, all but outcome benchmarking (mentioned above under new product sales) showed up as intervening variables. Three of these outcomes are discussed: financial performance, timeliness, and customer satisfaction.

Financial performance, as measured in a multiple regression analysis of earnings before interest and taxes as a percentage of sales, had noncompetitive and in-house benchmarking as significant factors. Since the effect of the former was

Table 12.3
Benchmarking Practices Used

Use	Percent
• Benchmarking from among competitors	73
• Benchmarking internally within the company	68
• Outcome benchmarking	50
• Benchmarking from among non-competitors	41
• Process benchmarking	31

Source: [3].

negative and that of the latter was positive, they were mutually offsetting, and with such a small net effect as to suggest no management action.

Timeliness, as measured in time from idea to customer, also had in-house benchmarking as a small but significant effect. Each 1% higher use of in-house benchmarking was associated with a trivial increase in idea-to-customer time.

Customer satisfaction, as measured by a multiple regression analysis of the external customer satisfaction rating of cost competitiveness, had use of competitive benchmarking as a minor negative effect. None of the benchmarking measurements were correlated significantly to satisfaction with overall performance as a contractor.

12.2.3 Benchmarking Lessons Learned

The few lessons learned on benchmarking for innovation are as follows.

- Outcome benchmarking has a positive effect on increased new products as a percent of sales.
- Noncompetitive and process benchmarking were negatively related to new products as a percent of sales.
- The remaining benchmarking metrics do not seem to rate highly as precursor or leading indicators. The high percentage use of these shown in Table 12.3 appears to be an unjustified expenditure of scarce effort. The R&D manager should keep this in mind in arguing against the diversion of technical staff for benchmarking instead of primary R&D tasks.

12.3 MEASURING IMPROVEMENT AND GROWTH

Rate of improvement, or rate of growth, is another measure of strategic intent results which can be applied to any other measured factor. For example, Motorola measures rate of improvement of quality [7]. Since continuous improvement is now often a strategic intent of many companies, measuring the rate of improvement is an appropriate non-financial metric.

The Baldridge Award for quality makes improvement part of their rating system: quality assurance of products and services via design and introduction of quality products and services, process quality control, *continuous improvement of processes* (emphasis added), quality assessment, documentation, business process and support service quality, and supplier quality [8].

Benchmarking is usually a top-down system either direct from upper management or put into effect by management endorsing the recommendations of those who have analyzed other companies. In contrast, best results from managing continuous improvement come from placing trust in those who are closer to the scene of action. It is rare that those in upper management have as much knowledge of the work being done and the possibilities of improving it as those who are tackling on-the-job problems daily.

Growth of financial returns as a measurement has a place in the theory of total return in finance but is seldom measured by current financial accounting practices. Total return leads to the concept of shareholder value creation [9,10]. This concept holds that the job of the manager is to maximize the value to the shareholders as the stockholders who are the residual bearers of risk. This value is the price of the common shares of stock in public companies and the sum of the net present values of present and future streams of income in private companies.

Without going into financial management in depth, a simplistic perpetual growth model comes from that field, assuming measurements in decimals, constant annual growth of returns, and no outside financing—the model falls apart if growth is not self-financed from total return [10]. In terms of formulas, this model is as follows, with words substituted by the author instead of the formula letters in the source [10]:

$$\text{Total return} = \text{current return} + \text{annual growth} \tag{12.1}$$

which can be restated in terms of shareholder value as

$$\text{Total Return} = \frac{\text{current annual payment}}{\text{shareholder value}} + \text{annual growth} \tag{12.2}$$

Rearranging terms in (12.2), this then becomes a formula for shareholder value, expressed as

$$\text{Shareholder value} = \frac{\text{current annual payment}}{\text{total return} - \text{annual growth}} \tag{12.3}$$

With no growth, this is simply the formula for the value of a perpetual annuity—with a 10% return; shareholder value is ten times the annual payment. But with the same return and a constant 5% annual growth of return, the shareholder value is twenty times the annual payment. This then is the principal theoretical reason for measuring growth of financial return as a nonfinancial indicator of shareholder value creation. In relating this metric to innovation, one source stated as follows.

> The increase in shareholder value realized from seemingly modest increases in real growth rates is surprisingly high, and herein lies the financial rationale for sustained investment in R&D [9].

It should be noted that technical innovation is not the only way for a company to grow. The company that most nearly has matched the above model is the largest U.S. retailer, Wal-Mart. It grew from a single store a quarter century ago by market development and capital investment financed out of total return until recently.

A look at Figure 2.8 shows a set of results of a more curvilinear nature when R&D intensity is used as a proxy for growth. The linear formula of (12.1) may be considered as an approximation of the flat rounded top of the curves in Figure 2.8. Thus, there is a general management tradeoff between current return and growth to which the R&D manager must adapt.

12.4 A PROPOSED R&D EFFECTIVENESS INDEX

An alternative to the shareholder value approach is to create an effectiveness index that combines growth through new products with current return. One such EI was recently proposed [11]. Its formula is

$$EI = \frac{\% \text{ New Product Revenues} * (\text{Net profit\%} + \text{R\&D\%})}{100 * \text{R\&D\%}} \tag{12.4}$$

This formula is an attempt to register the tradeoff between growth and current return similar to that in the shareholder value model above. It does this by seeking that an increase in new product revenue does not correspondingly reduce net profit, if EI is to increase. The originators defined an index greater than 1.0 as where the return from new products was greater than the investment in them [11]. In their survey they found only 39% of participants exceeded that target.

R&D managers will quickly realize that this formula expects results on a very short time frame, such as the current accounting year, as opposed to the investment nature of R&D that is this author's view as stated in Chapter 2.

Purists among this author's colleagues also criticize (12.4) because it mixes net profit (which is after federal income tax) with R&D (which is before tax). Operating profit (revenues minus cost of goods sold) or EBIT are both before tax and may be more realistic metrics.

As a multiplicative model, its values can rise to much higher values than any of its components. Composed of intensity ratios, it does not allow for the diseconomies of scale incumbent in high intensities, as shown in Figure 2.8. For example, 100% net profit leaves nothing for R&D and vice versa. In the 1995 study, details of which are in Chapter 14, this index was calculated from the responses providing the distribution shown in Figure 12.2.

EBIT was used instead of net profit, and this figure has the index multiplied by 100 for greater clarity. The median index is just below 0.6 (60), and only 20% of responses are over 1.0 (100). This latter figure is well below the 39% found by the originators' research [9]. With the above caveats, it is an interesting vehicle for assessing related factors as shown in Table 12.4.

A longer idea-to-customer time is associated with major new projects that tend to be more profitable. Customers favor technology, cost competitiveness, and organizational integration through QFD over a supplying company focused too heavily on management, responsiveness, or competitive position.

The failure of the majority of companies surveyed to have this effectiveness index meet the originators' criterion of 1.0 (100) raises cautions for those who would use it as a guide to R&D effort. Apparently, its short-term nature pulls it to

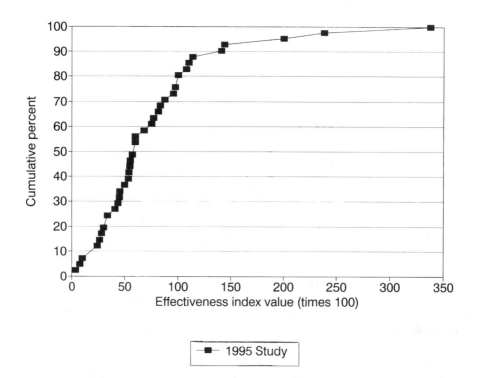

Figure 12.2 Percent versus EI.

Table 12.4
Factors Affecting the EI

Positive Factors

- Longer idea to customer time;
- Higher external customer satisfaction rating of technology;
- Higher external customer rating of cost competitiveness;
- Higher internal customer satisfaction rating with QFD's contribution to organizational integration.

Negative Factors

- Higher external customer satisfaction rating with responsiveness;
- Higher external customer satisfaction rating with management;
- Higher internal customer satisfaction rating with the company's competitive position;
- Each additional year of using QFD (minor effect).

Source: [6].

the current return end of formula (12.1) to the detriment of growth. A similar formula in ITT Corporation some years ago used three years' forecast net income rather than just that of the current year. Again, this emphasizes the tradeoff between the two components of total return that must be made by R&D managers.

Current research is attempting to replicate the 1995 study findings and to factor in growth more adequately by adding *compound annual growth rate* (CAGR) to the brackets in (12.4) [12]. From early responses, the 1996 EI percentage of responses over 1.0 is 37%, well the above 1995 results, and nearly as high as found by the original authors [11]. Adding in CAGR raises the percentage over 1.0 to 59.1%. This substantiates the need to modify the EI formula in a more long-term manner if the index is to serve as a reflection of the strategic intent of R&D spending by industrial firms. Still, the 40% of responses below 1.0 for the index even when growth is added is a caution for those R&D managers to defend more clearly their level of expenditures.

12.5 KEY LESSONS LEARNED ON MEASURING AND EVALUATING STRATEGIC INNOVATION

The lessons learned so far in this chapter have stressed suboptimizing separately each facet of strategic intent. What is needed is an overall view of how to blend these by managers of technology and innovation. Chapter 1 introduced the balanced scorecard as a method of achieving this optimization [13]. One example of the use of this technique follows.

Apple Computer, Inc., began the Macintosh PC development in 1981, after observing a prototype of a computer at the Xerox Palo Alto Research Center [14]. This computer originated the use of a mouse (pointing device) controlling through on-screen icons. First delivered in 1984, the Macintosh was a sharp break with earlier PCs using typed commands and drove the company to become the third-largest computer maker in 1995.

Apple Computer was one of the early users of the balanced scorecard [13, pp. 140–141]. For the financial metric, Apple chose shareholder value; for customer satisfaction, an index and market share; for internal processes, core competencies; and for innovation and improvement, employee attitudes.

These were stressed in the following order.

- Customer satisfaction used both an outside survey company and its internal surveys.
- Core competencies chose subjective measures: user-friendly interfaces, software architectures, and effective distribution.
- Employee attitudes were measured by full internal surveys each two years and by more frequent random employee interviews.
- Market share measured not only sales growth but also the ability to attract and retain software developers.
- Shareholder value was measured by common stock price.

  By 1996, Apple was a troubled company [14,15]. A new CEO joined in February 1996, when it appeared that the fiscal year ending September would show a substantial operating deficit and a large write-off as well. A review of the aforementioned metrics provides insight into where the firm had come in three years.
- Customer satisfaction had eroded on a relative basis as the main software competitor, Microsoft, had finally (with the Windows 95 release) achieved a comparably user-friendly human-machine interface.
- Core competencies not only had not kept a leading role in the human-machine interface, but only Apple, and NEC of Japan were hanging onto their proprietary operating systems, while all other competitors in the United States had shifted to the IBM file format, Intel microprocessors, and Microsoft DOS software.
- Employee attitudes may be inferred from the recent departure from Apple of one of the original software designers of the Macintosh [14].
- Market share in 1995 was third behind Compaq and IBM [16]. In preliminary first quarter of 1996 results, Apple was third behind Packard Bell and Compaq with 7.3%, but ahead of IBM with 6.1%. Both Apple and Packard Bell lost money during the quarter. More important, perhaps, was that Apple's 7.3% using its own operating system was appreciably a smaller opportunity for software developers than the over 80% using DOS.

- Shareholder value in mid-1996 was down, as the stock price was less than half of the 52-week high of $50.125 per share.

The cautionary lesson is as follows. When using the balanced scorecard, balance it also between retrospective outcome measures and enough prospective indicators to sense impending deterioration of outcomes.

The author recommends using the framework of shareholder value creation as the principal guide: total return = growth plus current return. Since the implementation chain in the company is largely focused on the latter, the R&D manager tasks are one source of internal growth, along with market development and capital investment. Measuring continuous improvement supplements benchmarking by placing the firm where competitors will probably be in time rather than where they were at the time of benchmarking. Measuring growth of financial results is an essential component for establishing shareholder value.

This leads to the first key lesson: Manage R&D for the strategic intent of growth and continuous improvement, subject to the limit that R&D costs should not exceed any consequent lowering of current return so that total return continues to rise.

To achieve growth and continuous improvement, the following key management actions should be taken.

First, increase the percentage of total sales based upon new products and services toward the median level of 25% shown in Figure 12.1. Do this by the following steps.

- Increase the percentage of the R&D budget spent on major new products;
- Benchmark on outcomes;
- Use CE, QFD, and stage-gate tracking to enhance crossfunctional organizational integration.

Second, measure the extent of customer satisfaction using market share, technology cost competitiveness, and your company's satisfaction with the results as metrics. Management should be encouraged by the positive effects of measuring market share on cost competitiveness satisfaction. Single-minded pursuit of increased market share is not the panacea presented by theory because all other things are definitely not equal in different types of industries.

Finally, market share is best measured by key accounts or served markets as a measurement of tangible benefits resulting from all earlier discussed metrics.

References

[1] Uttal, B., A. Kantrow, L. H. Linden, and B. S. Stock, "Building R&D Leadership and Credibility," *Research Technology Management*, Vol. 35(3), May–June 1992, pp. 15–24.

[2] Gault, S. C., "Responding to Change," *Research Technology Management*, Vol. 37(3), May–June 1994, pp. 23–26.

[3] Ellis, L. W., and C. C. Curtis, "Measuring Customer Satisfaction," *Research Technology Management*, Vol. 38(5), Sept.–Oct. 1995, pp. 45–48.

[4] Morris, P. A., E. O. Teisberg, and A. L. Kolbe, "When Choosing R&D Projects, Go with the Long Shots," *Research Technology Management*, Vol. 34(1), Jan.–Feb. 1991, pp. 35–39.

[5] Hronec, S., *Vital Signs*, New York: AMACOM, 1993.

[6] Curtis, C. C., and Ellis, L. W., "A Balanced Scorecard for New Product Development," *Journal of Cost Management*, Spring 1997, forthcoming.

[7] Motorola Corp., Presentation to the IEEE, Washington DC, Jan. 1990, Charts C-D 90, 0243A39 & 74.

[8] U.S. Department of Commerce, "Application Guidelines for Malcolm Baldridge National Quality Award," National Institute of Science and Technology, Gaithersburg, MD, 1991.

[9] Boer, F. P., "Linking R&D to Growth and Shareholder Value," *Research Technology Management*, Vol. 37(3), May–June 1994, pp. 16–22.

[10] Van Horne, J. C., *Fundamentals of Financial Management*, 7th ed., Englewood Cliffs, NJ: Prentice-Hall, 1989, pp. 97–98.

[11] McGrath, M. E., and M. N. Romeri, "From Experience: The R&D Effectiveness Index: A Metric for Product Development Performance," *J. Product Innovation Management*, Vol. 11, Nov. 1994, pp. 213–220.

[12] Curtis, C. C., and L. W. Ellis, research in progress, 1996.

[13] Kaplan, R. S., and D. P. Norton, "Putting the Balanced Scorecard to Work," *Harvard Business Review*, Sept.–Oct. 1993, pp. 134–147.

[14] Markoff, J., "Co-author of Macintosh Program Quits Apple," *New York Times*, June 6, 1996, p. D4.

[15] Fisher, L. M., "Apple Plans an Offering of 6% Notes," *New York Times*, June 5, 1996, p. D18.

[16] Zuckerman, L., "NEC and Packard Bell in Deal to Create the no. 4 PC Maker," *New York Times*, June 5, 1996, p. D1.

Chapter 13

Financial Frameworks in an Innovation Perspective

As much as those of us in the R&D management field are fascinated by the growth and management effectiveness possibilities of nonfinancial metrics, we still have to live in a commercial world that values much of its effectiveness in money. We must therefore return periodically to the use of financial metrics in order to satisfy our ultimate sources of money with which to innovate: The shareholders and our own higher levels of management who must interface with them.

This chapter first summarizes what we have learned about the financial impacts of the previous three chapters on internal processes, customer satisfaction, and other strategic evaluation measurements. Then, it looks at current research evaluating the use of financial selection techniques in innovation and what a model of earnings shows. Finally, it addresses again what to measure as outcome and precursor or leading indicators.

13.1 FINANCIAL EVALUATION OF R&D

From earlier chapters, it seems clear that evaluation of R&D processes is interwoven with financial and nonfinancial metrics and the views these have imposed on outside analysts and inside managers.

13.1.1 How Financial and Nonfinancial Innovation Metrics Relate

The three previous chapters have been dedicated to the issues raised when measuring nonfinancial factors. In the process, some interweaving has occurred with financial factors. These are among the questions asked in conducting the survey described as the 1994 and 1995 studies described in more detail in Chapter 14. A short recapitulation of these findings will help in understanding the surveys' findings when financial factors are addressed as the associated variables.

The relationship of customer satisfaction to financial measurements is ambivalent. Customer satisfaction with overall performance as a contractor, or with cost competitiveness, is not positively correlated with good financial results. Higher use of NPV in project selection, however, is negatively correlated with cost satisfaction. Thus, using financial techniques that identify which projects may cost too much money for a proper return, and thus be a candidate for pruning in order to meet the hurdle rate set by the selection process, may leave out some projects that satisfy desires of the customer.

Timeliness is of no advantage to a company if financial performance deteriorates as a consequence of deliberately speeding up development. In the 1993 study, a regression model of EBIT, including additional timeliness factors, supports the conjectured relationship (the shorter the time, the better the financial performance) at a statistically significant level. But companies would have to cut their cycles by half for a 1% financial improvement, a difficult feat for most firms. This finding was not replicated in the 1994 and 1995 studies, which showed no relationship between financial performance with idea-to-customer time, R&D cycle time, market development cycle time, or marketing time. A slight negative association was seen in 1995 between EBIT and the number of years of use of TQM in R&D, a tradeoff that management must consider.

Strategic evaluation nonfinancial metrics that had financial measurement interactions in the 1993 study involved only product life cycles. The average life cycle of a company's products in years has a time and financial performance tradeoff. A longer average product life was correlated with a higher EBIT ratio, an increase of up to 6% and longer R&D and idea-to-customer cycle times. Extending product life adds approximately six weeks per year of added life to both time through R&D and idea-to-customer time, a rather minimal time increase to achieve better financial results. This finding also was not replicated in the 1994 and 1995 studies.

Of the benchmarking methods studied in 1994, noncompetitive and in-house benchmarking have significant offsetting associations with financial performance, but with such a small combined negative effect as to suggest no management action. In the 1995 study, the negative association of noncompetitive benchmarking with financial performance was sufficiently greater to counsel against its use.

From this brief summary, it will be noted that some, but not all, of the nonfinancial metrics have financial associations. On the other hand, the 1994 and 1995 surveys found that financial metrics are now increasingly used as compared with their lack of acceptance by those large companies noted in the 1990 study.

13.1.2 Financial Project Selection and Evaluation

Usage of financial project selection techniques and other management accounting practices was found to be prevalent in a majority of companies surveyed in 1994. Some to consistent use was found of the practices measured in percent of responses, as shown in Table 13.1.

This finding may be explained by the large company bias of the 1992 IRI group versus a broader mix of company sizes in the 1994 study as well as the passage of time. There may also be a shift in time toward an increased use of financial selection procedures.

The impression one obtains from Table 13.1 is that there is little variation in the amount of use of the selected management accounting tools. In fact, there is a rather large variation in the results of the 1994 study. Option pricing is associated with the other five measures in Table 13.1. Except for this, target costing and contribution margin correlate only with each other. Payback, NPV, and IRR also correlate only with each other. The correlation of the last three is not surprising since they are mathematically related [2]. The actual correlation coefficients are shown in Chapter 14. In a model with option pricing as the dependent variable, however, target costing and IRR (the two lowest correlations) fall out of statistical significance. These results do not give a clear management direction as to what should be the preferred management accounting approach.

13.1.3 Management Accounting

A review of the applicable issues in management accounting was recently published [3]. This report covers the problems currently found in management accounting, most traceable to the dominance of financial accounting, and puts forth four

Table 13.1
Use of Selection and Management
Accounting Practices

New Product Development Project Selection Methods	Percent
Payback period	72
IRR	68
NPV	61
Target costing/pricing	69
Option pricing approaches	68
Contribution margin analysis	66

Source: [1].

proposals for reform: handle manufacturing development outside operating costs, allocate overheads to machines and materials as well as labor, handle all strategic investment costs alike to determine true product costs, and use option theory to value these R&D assets.

13.2   FINANCIAL ANALYSTS' VIEWS OF R&D

In the first of the 1990 sessions, four financial analysts addressed the meeting on the "Financial Environment for R&D Investment." These analysts addressed four different industry groups: aerospace, pharmaceuticals, cosmetics, and chemicals. Only the last two addressed the financial frameworks of R&D.

For the cosmetics industry, his analysis of the value of R&D is based on long-term trends in companies, ignoring short-term fluctuations [4]. Any reduction in R&D spending is viewed as a symptom of the disease of poor management. R&D payoffs should stay short: two years are normal, with three years maximum. Trends pushing R&D spending upward are regulation, globalization (although R&D dollars are spent increasingly overseas), alliances, point-of-sale packaging, and environmentalism.

In the chemical industry, shareholder value depends on long-term earnings growth rate, new products, and proprietary position, all of which R&D can influence. Short-term drops in R&D kill valuations—long-term R&D is a plus as long as earnings volatility is not high. Lowering R&D rarely does much for stock price. Consolidation of companies lies ahead to achieve critical mass, which increases R&D spending. Increases in value come from moves to specialties, longer patent lives, reduced regulation, and tax credits (both R&D and capital investment).

13.2.1   Commentary on the Financial Analysts' Views

In general, these analysts' views support the inclusion of their perceptions of longer term R&D growth as enhancing shareholder value. This is a welcome continuation of the view on which much of the R&D budget optimization literature is based [5]. Also added is a number of nonfinancial measures of new products and technical position.

As a consequence of this broad support for R&D by the financial analysis community, one would have expected the R&D executives present to have a broad-based acceptance of the use of financial frameworks for R&D in their decision making. This expectation was not borne out as covered in the following section on the R&D directors' panel discussion.

13.3   R&D EXECUTIVES' PANEL DISCUSSION

The panel that discussed financial frameworks for opened by reviewing principal advances in financial frameworks for R&D in the last decade [5,6]. There was a consensus of the attendees that the use of stock option methods was inappropriate despite the advantages of the financial option theory approach in communicating effectively to the Chief Executive Officer and Chief Financial Officer of the organization and in providing objective measures to support claims by the R&D department for funding against other contenders for funds in the firm. The comments of several of the attending executives for and against options are summarized in Table 13.2.

13.3.1 Views on Option Theory as a Financial Framework [7,9]

One viewpoint is that financial justification is needed for a central R&D lab. What are you going to do for the business in the future? How does the CEO know that R&D has the same view of the problem that he does? There are rapid rates of change and enormous uncertainty in some industries versus others. Option theory makes uncertainty irrelevant. We received recognition that the labs were supporting top-management objectives: "This is the right way to look at it," said our financially minded CEO (telecommunications utility). Which companies use option theory? Only this utility.

Another opinion is that options are a poor model due to lack of branch points. CEOs and CFOs love it, and it communicates. Systems are nonlinear, while people with whom you have to communicate are linear. Options are like the ante in poker, which is liked intuitively (chemical company).

Some believe that the analogy to poker is good: the ante is the price of being able to play. How long should you continue alternative possibilities? What are the cancellation costs? How much hedging should you do? Benefits need to be measured as how much certainty? It is adaptive decision making, as in signal processing. Option theory only translates it into financial language (automotive company).

Finally, options are a big trap (consumer products company).

The first broad observation was that there was surprisingly little support for letting financial frameworks impinge on the R&D managers' prerogatives of deciding their own priorities. This decoupling from the economic end of the business may have been a real manifestation of organizational dysfunction or perhaps only an indication that the topic attracted the most skeptical of attendees determined to be devil's advocates.

The second area of interest was that a clear line showed between activities of research and discovery, on the one hand, and that of product development, on the other. As for development projects closer to product introduction, a split in responses was evident, with most of them reluctantly having been led there by their

CEOs and CFOs. For a minority, there was grudging recognition that conformance to a financial mode of support of projects was inevitable in their organizations. The following section presents the comments of some executives in favor of a financial approach.

13.3.2 Views on Financial Frameworks [7,9]

Two examples of favorable views are as follows.

After discovery, we have been using for a few years, on a team basis, NPV in ratio to R&D budgets, done on a ten-year life basis, which is the R&D return identified in the literature [9] (chemical company).

We use the "reinforce history" approach.Our CEO is a lawyer and a historian. His finance is limited to cash flow payback of less than a year. He looks at funds going into a project from all sources, not just R & D.

The following five views are exemplary of negative responses.

The discontinuity between the past track record and future forecasts is why the high returns indicated by IRR are not accepted (chemical company).

Any measurement of the value of individual R&D projects needs to be prefaced with a clear understanding of the strategic business goals of the organization and an agreement with top management on business priorities. Different parts of the R&D process need different financial analyses. Discovery is hard to quantify. Product development lets you crunch the numbers. Decision-making levels are fourfold. (1) What business do you want to be in? (2) Then, what are the technical and commercial parameters to give success? This is a multifunctional decision. (3) Then, in which areas must you be expert to win? This is mostly a technical decision. (4) Then, the product development stage is the easy one. What has finance to do with the first three? These first three are a political process, not a financial one. The issue is strategic. You must have what the others have, plus an edge. No problem exists in selling central lab activity in the face of threats. The issue is not how good is your technology, but how good it is perceived to be (consumer products company).

We meet objectives however they were set, including nonfinancial, such as dates, subjective factors, views of others, and views of researchers. How do you measure the benefits side for financial analysis? There is a need for vision. This is a multifunctional debate and/or dialogue. It must link up with the strategic direction of the company (petrochemical company).

There is no creditability for high IRRs in my company. Our requests for R&D funds are related to the perception of the need and prospective results (building-products company).

High IRRs are not credible as they often occur because of high volumes of throughput, where a catalyst change, for example, looks good for R&D but has little overall effect in a capital intensive petroleum refinery.

For the majority, however, there was still an obvious reluctance to accept the dictates of finance over their own subjective instincts. Section 13.3.2 also provides the counter arguments made against the financial approach.

Little evidence was shown in 1990 of movement with time in the direction of greater use of financial frameworks. Whatever diffusion was taking place seemed to be at a glacial speed in the companies who attended the panel discussion. Because of the limited sample size, biased by the individual executive's judgmental decision to attend or not, it would be imprudent to extend this conclusion to a larger population of R&D managers.

Finally, there appeared a concept that the manner of gaining acceptance of the right of the R&D manager to select projects independently of higher financial review was to designate voluntarily a portion of the R&D department's resources (several mentioned twenty percent) to direct support of divisional needs, both as a means to convincing higher management of close coupling to the firm's needs, and of keeping the R&D department aware of the real world of the firm's operating managers. In summary, the R&D managers who attended showed themselves to be quite political, strongly resisting financially objective methods of influencing their decisions. The few who had converted appeared to have had some strong external factors applied such as top-management (CEO/CFO) commitment.

13.4 FINANCIAL RESULTS

In the 1994 and 1995 studies, financial results were measured by the ratio of EBIT to sales. This was the same metric used in the 1993 study discussed in Chapter 7 and shown in Figure 7.3. The three are not exactly comparable, however. First, the response samples were different, although from a similar range of companies. Statistically, one would not expect this to be a large effect. More important, however, is likely to be the evolution of measuring during the one-year period. That this is large may be seen by the rapid increase of measurement of idea-to-customer time discussed in Chapter 7. Third, the additional factors included in the 1994 and 1995 studies have probably masked the statistical significance of the weaker factors in the earlier survey.

13.4.1 An Earnings Model

Only government regulation shown in Figure 7.3 appears to be statistically significant in the 1995 (but not 1994) model, presumably for the reasons stated above. Thus, coming to strong conclusions from the 1994 and 1995 studies appears somewhat venturesome. First, however, the addition of external and internal customer satisfaction and benchmarking factors has clearly altered the model sufficiently to show that these nonfinancial measures need to be considered. Customer satisfaction again gives strong positive signals for management action when compared with financial metrics such as EBIT. The responsiveness satisfaction rating was positive in 1994 and negative in 1995, but the latter was offset in 1995 by positive ratings on overall performance and on communications.

Since internal satisfaction with QFD was introduced in the 1995 questionnaire, these new measures probably obscured the use metric. Use of QFD in 1994 and internal satisfaction with QFD's impact on improving internal integration in 1995 give support for QFD being the preferred quality method for innovation management. This contrasts with the negative effects of Taguchi methods in the 1994 study and TQM in R&D in the 1993 study. The small positive impact of IRR on EBIT in 1994 (but not in 1995) is a proxy for the other two correlated factors of payback and NPV and supports the value of financial discipline in project selection and evaluation. Economies of scale were found only in 1994, with higher sales volume associated with higher EBIT. Closer to the customer was associated with higher EBIT in 1994 and 1995, while an increase in the extent of the marketing/R&D interface in the early stages of product development was associated with lower EBIT in 1994, somewhat offsetting that closeness. A number of other metrics are covered in Chapter 14.

13.4.3   Is Speedy Innovation Really Financially Beneficial?

Following the 1993 study, an article was written asking "Speedy R&D: How Beneficial?" [10]. In addressing this issue in financial terms in the 1994 study, none of the cycle-time metrics (for example, R&D time, idea-to-customer time, and product life) and none of the timeliness metrics (stage-gate tracking and milestone measurement) were statistically correlated with EBIT in the regression model. In 1995, use milestones had a slight positive association, but otherwise the 1994 findings were confirmed. Thus, the benefits of speed in innovation seem to have eluded the "bottom line," which confirms that faster cycle times are an "acceleration trap" [11].

13.4.3.1   *Responses on Time and Financial Performance [10]*

Some comments of respondents are as follows.

- I can accept the notion that a fast new product development cycle is not the panacea it is made out to be (pharmaceutical industry).
- It certainly does seem to be counterintuitive, but the reality is that you have to have the right idea at the right time in order to be successful in the long term (consumer goods industry).
- This certainly challenges Smith and Reinertsen's [12] premise that acceleration is directly associated with improved financial results (consumer products industry).

- Intriguing. This raises questions about the assumption of project financial evaluation, that if a portfolio of projects has a positive net present value, it will add to financial performance. I do have a concern, though, that in your study industry differences may get homogenized in a large group (chemicals and energy industries).
- No surprise. There is a hit-and-run phenomenon at work here. Cycle time can speed up but create nightmares in terms of quality control problems—skipped steps and procedures (consumer products industry).
- I am not surprised that cycle time and financial performance are unrelated; in our industry (consumer goods), the major driver is what is invested in marketing and promotion.
- The acceleration trap makes great sense in the consumer products industry. The landscape is littered with products that were ahead of their time. Later entrants proved that the right products at the right time are the way to gain market dominance, equaling better financial results (consumer goods industry).
- Makes sense—at a certain point, if you reduce further, you have to add resources and costs that then have to be recovered and might not be (chemical industry).
- There is a corporate mentality that thinks time is free—to waste or to recover (chemical industry).
- This is an overlooked cost in industry. There is an assumption that time, like quality, is free (consumer products).
- Makes sense. Major new products take longer to create. If they also have high margins, getting them sooner to market may simply result in attracting competition even sooner, unless you have some countermeasures in place. Then you may be forced to compete on price. The acceleration trap exists (consumer products).

13.4.3 Product Extensions Versus Major New Projects

One of the findings of the 1993 study was that greater investment in product feature extensions was negatively correlated to EBIT. The greater the investment, the worse the financial performance. Because R&D budgets are usually set by higher management, to make additional investment in feature extensions of existing products (a policy of incrementalism) means shifting investment out of both major and minor new projects.

Having argued for a decade [5] that product enhancements and extensions should be profitable, since the technical risks are lower with a known product, and the commercial risks are also lower because the market is more clearly defined, it is humbling to be shown from this research that this does not hold true. In a current attempt to replicate the 1993 findings in the 1994 study with a different respondent group, the correlation of EBIT as a percent of sales was also found to be negative with product feature extensions (the higher the percentage of product extensions of the total R&D budget, the lower the EBIT ratio). However, limited modeling of the more recent data with additional questions in the survey instrument, showed that two factors, each independently, made the use of product extensions modestly profitable. The first of these was measuring, and thus presumably managing, the market development cycle of time from prototype to delivery to the customer. The second factor was the accounting practice of target costing or the practice of determining what the market requires in a product's functions and targeting the lowest cost that meets those requirements. When both of these factors were introduced into a limited EBIT model, a small increase in product extensions raised EBIT, demonstrating that discipline is needed in selecting project feature extensions to avoid the profit deterioration shown in the overall responses. It might be critical to reassess whether a company's investment among the project types is properly balanced toward higher profit major projects, despite the cycle-time increase.

13.4.4 Summary of the Earnings Regression Models

None of the other independent variables shown in Figure 7.3 appear to be statistically significant in the new model, presumably for the aforementioned reasons.Thus, coming to strong conclusions from the 1994 and 1995 studies appears somewhat venturesome. First, however, the addition of the positive customer satisfaction factors and the negative effect of noncompetitive benchmarking has clearly altered the model sufficiently to show that these particular nonfinancial measures need to be considered. In terms of management action, however, only improving the customer's rating of your firm's responsiveness and technology is a management imperative for financial improvement. QFD is preferred as a quality method for innovation, which also enhances customer satisfaction. The small positive impact of IRR and NPV on EBIT supports the value of financial discipline in project selection and evaluation. CE also shows a positive correlation with EBIT confirming earlier results.

13.4.5 Innovation and Shareholder Value Creation

In the last chapter, *shareholder value creation* (SVC) was defined in terms of profitability and growth [13]. How far has this research gone toward helping understand managing to improve SVC? The answer is "not sufficiently far, since we have not factored in growth." Even the effectiveness index noted in the last chapter only imperfectly addresses growth through the new products percentage of sales. To obtain growth more correctly, one must analyze longitudinally from the same base of companies, which these annual cross-sectional studies have not done. Ideally this would have been desirable, but the resources to do it have just not been available to this author.

What is clear, however, is that the nonfinancial factors analyzed so far are not the most important in enhancing EBIT as a ratio to sales (note that EBIT is not the same as the current return after interest and taxes of the SVC formulas of Chapter 12). Thus, the positive role of innovation in increasing new products and services as a percent of sales seems to require that the R&D manager should focus her or his efforts on growth rather than on current income. Taking what has been outlined here through the next step of relating innovation to growth to creating shareholder value is a task for future research.

13.4.6 Company Culture and Innovation

To date, the analysis has focused heavily on multiple regression methods. These require a designation by the analyst of a dependent variable (presumed effect) from among the factors studied. This is a reasonable method for the current research, since most of the selected dependent variables have been outcomes or overall metrics that occur later in time than the other independent variables (presumed causes). However, it does not give much guidance to the relative weight of the outcomes, particularly between financial and nonfinancial metrics. For this reason, the responses to the 1994 study were subjected to factor analysis, which makes no designation of the dependent variable among the responses. Instead, it seeks to create new factors that most strongly group the responses into associated clusters. Thus, the question for additional study may be phrased as follows. If we had no preconceived ideas about lagging and leading indicators, what would factor analysis say is the relative weight of financial and nonfinancial indicators? It should be noted that nothing constrains factor analysis to answering just this question, as the computer program for factor analysis selects what it finds as the strongest relationships. What turned up was that the clusters grouped around factors relating to company cultures.

The resulting groupings are shown in Table 13.2 and in more detail in Chapter 14. These have been given arbitrary new names reflecting what the author perceives might have been intended by responders as they replied to the questionnaire. After each new factor, the percent of total variation in the responses that it explains is indicated.

Among financial frameworks, EBIT had a correlation above 0.5 with the fifth new factor but failed to have a correlation greater than 0.5 against any other new factor. A positive correlation over 0.4 was found between EBIT and new factor 1, hinting at a higher profitability of this group of companies. Low correlations were found between EBIT and new factors 2, 3, and 4, indicating that such strategies neither promote nor detract from profitability. Financial methods in new project selection were seen in new factors 2 and 4, without an associated correlation with EBIT. A negative correlation over 0.3 was found between new factor 6 and EBIT, but also a similar positive correlation of that factor with new product percentage, perhaps indicating a tendency to force new products at the expense of

Table 13.2
Factor Analysis of the 1994 Study

Factor/Component

1. Regulated/Disciplined firms (17.2%);
2. Finance selection-driven/customer adverse firms (14.8%);
3. Large/Old-line firms (11.8%);
4. Technology-driven/individualistic firms (9.7%);
5. Long-lived/patented-products firms (9.0%);
6. Marketing-driven firms (6.9%).

Note: Cumulative percent variation explained by the first
six factors = 69.3%.
Source: [7,8].

profitability. For each of the groupings, the other key associated factors may be found in Chapter 14. One may conclude that the use of factor analysis has only partially answered the question of the balance between nonfinancial and financial metrics since it provides a grouping that is characterized more by company characteristics rather than offering a more general or universal answer.

13.5   FINANCIAL FRAMEWORKS LESSONS LEARNED

The message from looking at the financial scene in 1990 was twofold.

1. Financial frameworks are not enough to satisfy innovation managers, nor the more astute financial analysts.
2. A broader selection of nonfinancial measurements is required to judge R&D effectiveness adequately.
   a. Customer satisfaction tops the list;
   b. New products and services as a percent of sales is also near the top;
   c. A selection of internal process metrics such as QFD is needed to support the financial frameworks.

References

[1]   Ellis, L. W., and C. C., Curtis, "Measuring Customer Satisfaction," *Research Technology Management*, Vol. 38(5), Sept.–Oct. 1995, pp. 45–48.
[2]   Ellis, L. W., *The Financial Side of Industrial Research Management*, New York: Wiley, 1984, pp. 20–27.

[3] Ellis, L. W., and R. G. McDonald, "Reforming Management Accounting to Support Today's Technology," *Research Technology Management*, Vol. 33(2), Mar.–Apr. 1990, pp. 30–34.

[4] Salzman, J. L., Goldman, Sachs & Company, New York, Comments to the IRI, May 15, 1990.

[5] Ellis, L. W., "What We've Learned: Managing Financial Resources," *Research Technology Management*, Vol. 31(4), July–Aug. 1988, pp. 21–38.

[6] Mitchell, G. R., and W. F. Hamilton, "Managing R&D as a Strategic Option," *Research Technology Management*, Vol. 31(3), May–June 1988, pp. 15–22.

[7] Industrial Research Institute, *Minutes of ROR and SIS Meetings*; and tapes of the SIS meeting, Phoenix: Tape Productions, 1990.

[8] Ellis, L. W., "Financial Frameworks for Research and Development," West Haven, CT: University of New Haven, Faculty Working Paper, May 1991.

[9] Foster, R. N., L. H. Linden, R. I. Whitely, and A. Kantrow, *Improving the Return on Research and Development*, New York: Industrial Research Institute, 1984; summarized with the same title in *Research Management*, Vol. 28(1), 1985, pp. 12–17, and Vol. 28(2), 1985, pp. 13–22.

[10] Ellis, L. W., and C. C. Curtis, "Speedy R&D: How Beneficial?", *Research Technology Management*, Vol. 38(4), July–Aug. 1995, pp. 42–51.

[11] Von Braun, C.-F., "The Acceleration Trap," *Sloan Management Review*, Vol. 32 (1), 1990, pp. 49–58.

[12] Smith, P. G., and D. G. Reinertsen, *Developing Products in Half the Time*, Florence, KY: van Nostrand Reinhold, 1991.

[13] Boer, F. P., "Linking R&D to Growth and Shareholder Value," *Research Technology Management*, Vol. 37(3), May–June 1994, pp. 16–22.

Chapter 14

Methods of Quantitative Measurements

This chapter covers all quantitative research results that are only briefly summarized in the earlier chapters of the book. It is intended for use by R&D managers who desire additional guidance from survey research, by academic instructors who prefer a more quantitative type of instruction, and by researchers who wish to follow the paths of research in technology and information management.

14.1 METHODOLOGY

Although the R&D manager would like to have a comprehensive study of outcomes, outputs, interactions, internal processes, and inputs, the number of potentially independent variables has been found to be so large that the survey size required for validity would exceed the resources available to most investigators. Thus, more limited studies have been used.

Qualitative analysis involves the use of interviewing or other nonquantitative investigation. Most journal articles (other than academic) have little space in which to present much of the details of the methods used. The IRIMER committee has used interviews as a primary source of information to date. Under these conditions, the mention of a metric relies on the expert knowledge of both interviewee and interviewer to have considered thoughtfully what impact the metric may have had on the operation of the firm.

Quantitative analysis is used in other studies, most of which are only partial answers to the larger system problem. Most of these use the methods of statistical inference. The metrics mentioned are those found by the original source to be statistically significant at the confidence level used by the originating author, that is, usually that the result was different from random chance at or less than 5% or sometimes 10%. Since they and this book are addressing metrics, continuous measures may be compared by correlation, which measures only the association of two variables and their corresponding directional relationship. They also may be measured by regression, which may involve two or more independent variables and measures their quantitative relationship [1].

Correlation does not mean causation—to establish causal inference, any study must meet the following three conditions [1].

1. The variables are associated and move together in a specified direction.
2. The variables have a relationship that is not explained by another variable.
3. The assumed cause occurs before the assumed effect.

By segregating outcomes and outputs from interactions, internal processes, and inputs that come earlier in time, the third condition is met, as will be the first if a correlation is measurable. The second criterion, however, is not a measurable quantity, as the unpublished strategic direction of the firm most certainly explains the variables. However, measurable outcomes and outputs may be assumed to sufficiently closely reflect this underlying strategy that is not obtainable for measurement, so the second condition may also be assumed to be met.

Subjective scales are typically interval data and not continuous, usually measuring opinions on a 1-to-5- or 1-to-7-point scale. Experience has shown, however, that this interval data may be assumed to be continuous because of the respondents viewing the scales as quasi-linear in responding and, therefore, usable in bivariate and multivariate analysis [2]. Thus, subjective scales and continuous metrics, as used by others and proposed in this book, may be used to evaluate, by correlation analysis, the direction of the relationships of potential leading indicators upon outcomes and outputs.

Regression analysis also addresses the innovation manager's interest in the issue of how much effect the leading indicator candidate has on an outcome or output. For example, it would not be of much use if an input that is correlated with an outcome could not be managed so as to have a substantial impact on that outcome. To answer this point requires multivariate regression analysis, as it may be assumed that a number of the input, internal process, and interaction metrics are covariant. Clearly, this requires some substantial survey research, as will be seen in the studies reviewed in subsequent sections.

Regression analysis assumes that there is a dependent variable that has been selected from knowledge external to the mathematics. To place in perspective the financial and nonfinancial factors in responses to the questionnaire, factor analysis was used in the 1994 study, as reported briefly in Chapter 13, and in more detail here. Factor analysis makes no a priori assumptions of dependence and, thus, is of use in establishing the relative importance of the responses by clustering them around dominant groups of answers.

14.2 HOW THE 1990 THROUGH 1995 STUDIES WERE DONE

The six studies from 1990 to 1995 were named for the year in which their activity began, or took its principal form. This chapter outlines the research environment of each, comments on its general applicability for innovation managers, and indicates the principal publications from which further details may be obtained. The first four years' studies served to set the stage for the major longitudinal studies in 1994 and 1995 from which most of the findings presented in earlier chapters were derived.

The 1990 study was initiated by the Research-on-Research Committee of the IRI, which organized two sessions: one by financial analysts and the second by a panel from the R&D community at the 1990 Spring Annual Meeting of the Industrial Research Institute. In the first of these sessions, four financial analysts addressed the meeting on different industry groups: aerospace, pharmaceuticals, cosmetics, and chemicals. This was followed by a panel of practicing R&D executives and discussion from the floor (with the results summarized in Chapter 13). Publications include the recorded proceedings [3] and a faculty working paper [4].

The 1991 study began in a doctoral seminar in management in 1991 when Carey C. Curtis began research on cycle time. The findings were published in an article by another author (Table 7.2) [5] and jointly by the student and this author in a conference publication [6].

The 1992 study began at the formation of the IRIMER committee in 1992. The author elected to sample the potential of survey research in a pilot study among committee members. Results were sent to committee members, but not published elsewhere until this book.

The 1993 study was the dissertation research of Carey C. Curtis [7]. It involved surveying by mail some 600 companies nationally in a variety of technologically driven industries, revisiting and extending the 1991 study measurements. Three publications that resulted are in journal articles [8–10].

The 1994 study, funded in part by the Consortium for Advanced Manufacturing International, involved surveying by mail some 900 companies nationally in a variety of technologically driven industries. The purpose of the study was to accomplish two things, specifically, to validate by replication the existence of the acceleration trap and to add other new product development-related variables to extend factors studied in 1993 (financial performance, cycle time, public policy issues). These additional issues included customer satisfaction with R&D, management accounting practices (R&D project selection criteria and target costing), benchmarking practices, market development cycle time (Figure 4.2), reward systems, and quality practices. Of the total sample, about one-sixth came from individuals employed by large IRI companies, a like amount from companies in the Product Development and Management Association, and about two-thirds from companies listed with the large national CorpTech™ data base allowing the inclusion of small, medium, and privately held companies. Replies were received from one-third of those surveyed, yielding 128 quantitatively usable responses. Analysis was done by correlation and multivariate regression and by factor analysis. Reliability, as measured by Cronbach's alpha, was 0.66. This is an improvement over the 1993 study with all the prior questions and a similar response number. It appears due to the inclusion of 15 new questions, particularly those on external customer satisfaction and management accounting. Thus far, one paper has been accepted for publication [11].

The 1995 study, also funded in part by the Consortium for Advanced Manufacturing International, involved surveying by mail companies nationally in a variety of technologically driven industries. The purpose was further longitudinal study of this field in order to validate earlier studies and to extend the range of questions on QFD and overall technology strategy. Some 75 responses were received by mid-1995. The results are of general use in guiding innovation managers, especially those results that replicate findings between the 1995 and earlier studies. Reliability, as measured by Cronbach's alpha, was 0.56. The author attributes this decline from the 1994 study as due to a 40% smaller response number, plus the addition of 12 new questions on internal customer satisfaction and strategic technology planning.

14.3 MEASURING LEADING INDICATORS OF CUSTOMER SATISFACTION

Research in the 1994 study [11] attempted to find some more generalized answers to measuring customer satisfaction while accomplishing a broader survey of other issues in innovation management. This survey first addressed customer satisfaction through the questions listed in Table 14.1, which were aimed at determining the extent to which respondents measure customer satisfaction in their own firms.

When the self-reported overall performance rating was used as a dependent variable, however, none of the three use measurements showed statistically significant correlations with it.

Table 14.1
Customer Satisfaction Survey Questions on Use

- Does your company use some sort of customer satisfaction index? (Yes = 54%; No = 46%).
- Does your company measure the extent of customer satisfaction using market share as a measure? (Yes = 60%; No = 40%).
- To what extent does your company use a lead user to determine customer satisfaction levels? (1 to 5 scale). There were answers from 97% of the respondents. "Some" to "high" use was reported by 51%, and "no" or "little" use was reported by 36% of the respondents. The average score was just below "some use."

Source: [11].

The survey also sought self-reported assessments of their views of how customers would rate their products and customer service from individuals interested in innovation management. The rating questions used in the same survey were, "Over your portfolio of products, how would your customers rank you (1 to 5 scale) against your top five competitors for the following: (questions listed in Table 11.1)."

For clarity in the discussion of results of this survey, all of these 1 to 5 scales have been converted to 0 to 100 scales so that they may be more easily compared with questions that asked for percentages. The converted median values are shown in Figure 11.4 using the categories of Table 11.1 and Figure 11.3. The comparison between Figures 11.3 and 11.4 is striking as they are closely correlated ($r = 0.69$) despite being sampled five years apart. Particularly notable is that the lowest rating in both groups was customer satisfaction with cost competitiveness.

Using overall performance as a contractor as the dependent variable in multivariate regression analysis, five of the component questions proved not to be significant, namely, timeliness, communications, quality of proposals, cost competitiveness, and program/contract management. In the early responders, however, timeliness and communications were statistically significant. Do early responders have these two factors in their personal make-ups? The simplest precursor measurement of timeliness is how much your organization uses concurrent or simultaneous engineering instead of the conventional or serial form of marketing to R&D to operations [11].

The author is frankly puzzled by the lack of correlation of overall performance to cost competitiveness and the latter's low ratings in the 1994 study, which will be addressed further. He concedes, however, that the quality of proposals and program/contract management components may perhaps be too industry-specific for a more general survey.

When the self-reported overall performance as a contractor rating was used as a dependent variable in a multiple regression analysis, 69% of this rating was explained by 10 factors, at a probability of less than 5%. Only the three component questions listed in Table 14.2 were significantly correlated with the overall performance rating as a contractor.

A 1% improvement in each of the Table 14.2 components is associated with a 0.87% increase in overall rating. This lends credence to the idea that measuring just these three leading indicators is sufficient to establish the dimensions of customer satisfaction. One should recognize the potential bias of the respondents towards technology.

Responsiveness is a measure of customer satisfaction with the supplier rather than the product. A 2.5% higher customer satisfaction rating on responsiveness is associated with a 1% higher overall performance rating. Customer satisfaction with responsiveness is correlated with that of communications. As previously mentioned, however, communications was not significantly correlated with the overall performance rating for the full respondent sample. For some companies,

Table 14.2

Components Correlated with Overall Performance Rating

Variable	Coefficient	Standard Error	T-stat	Sig T p plain
Responsiveness	0.397	0.062	6.370	0.0000
Technology	0.276	0.057	4.890	0.0000
Quality/Reliability	0.195	0.069	2.828	0.0062

Note: These three customer satisfaction variables explained 49% of the variation in overall performance rating. Seven other noncustomer satisfaction variables explained another 20% of the variation.
Source: [11].

the two questions may best be combined into a single rating of customer satisfaction with interpersonal relationships.

Product quality and reliability and technology tend to be measures of customer satisfaction with the product rather than the company as a supplier. A 3.6% higher rating of customer satisfaction with technology is associated with a 1% higher rating on overall performance. A 5.1% higher satisfaction rating on quality and reliability is associated with a 1% higher rating on overall performance.

Intervening variables other than customer satisfaction variables showed up in the multiple regression analysis of satisfaction with overall performance as a contractor. While they explained an additional 20% of the variation of overall performance, their impact is less important than the customer satisfaction variables. These seven variables included three factors measuring time and one each measuring company center of gravity, rewards, CE, and portfolio mix.

The three time factors offset each other: higher use of stage gate tracking, longer market development cycle, and lower use of milestones are associated with a higher overall rating. This small net effect tends to reinforce the management approval discipline inherent in the stage-gate approach.

Rewards entered into the final overall performance regression with one question: the 40% of companies that use stock options as part of its R&D professional compensation package reported a 9.1% lower customer satisfaction with overall performance rating. This is a cautionary warning concerning rewarding shareholder value creation via stock options as against its negative impact on the customer.

A 4.7% higher share of product extensions is associated with a 1% higher overall performance rating. Since extensions were shown in Chapter 4 to be negatively associated with financial performance, this does not seem a worthwhile management action to enhance customer satisfaction. The greater use of CE and moving the center of gravity away from the customer are associated with slightly higher overall performance ratings, but not significantly higher to suggest management action. In summary, the intervening variables individually have small effects, despite the noted improvement from 49 to 69%.

14.3.1 Satisfaction With Cost Competitiveness

The absence of cost competitiveness in the overall performance regression sparked a parallel study of this factor that the author's experience said should have been included. This was done by making the rating of customer satisfaction with cost competitiveness the dependent variable in a separate multiple regression. In the 1994 study, 83% of the cost satisfaction rating is explained by a total of 13 independent variables if the acceptance probability is extended to 10%.

Customer satisfaction metrics provided two of these factors. The use of market share as a measure of customer satisfaction is associated with a 39% increase in the rating customer satisfaction with cost competitiveness. This is a strong effect, but both are likely to be derived from a common cause in managerial strategy rather than a cause and effect relationship. Each 3.6% higher customer satisfaction with responsiveness rating was associated with a 1% higher rating for customer satisfaction with cost competitiveness. This reinforces the finding reported in Table 14.1.

Customer satisfaction with cost competitiveness was associated with four timeliness factors. The strongest effect found was that each extra year using TQM in R&D was associated with 2.5% higher customer cost satisfaction rating. An additional 1.9 years of measuring time in R&D for any reason was required for a 1% higher such rating, a much less important effect. Both time measurements must have preceded the satisfaction measurement and, thus, may be considered causes. Cycle-time metrics produced two small offsetting effects. A shorter market development cycle or a longer idea-to-customer cycle were independently associated with a higher rating of customer satisfaction with cost competitiveness. Such small effects that are offsetting do not suggest any management attention.

Two quality factors were also offsetting, namely, higher use of QFD or lower use of Taguchi methods associated with a higher rating of customer cost satisfaction. This suggests that QFD is a better quality strategy for innovation management.

Five other factors were significantly correlated. Awarding stock options for R&D was associated with 48% lower customer cost satisfaction in the 40% of companies that used them. Higher use of NPV was related to a lower rating of customer satisfaction with cost competitiveness. Again, the picture is of a tradeoff between using financial frameworks or higher customer satisfaction with costs. Added years of patent life, higher use of group rewards, and higher use of competitive benchmarking were related to lower cost satisfaction.

This study led to the conclusions made in Section 10.3. Reviewing the secondary factors detailed in here adds the following additional lessons learned.

- Since the type of measurement chosen to measure customer satisfaction seems not to bias the results, select those with which your company is comfortable.
- Measure overall customer satisfaction, in addition to responsiveness, technology, and quality/reliability, by timeliness and communication, which were significant with the early replies.
- Consider carefully the tradeoff of potential negative impact on overall customer satisfaction and customer cost satisfaction of stock options being part of the R&D compensation package; consider rewarding R&D staff in ways other than stock options.
- For customer satisfaction with cost competitiveness, in addition to measuring market share and the number of years of using QFD and TQM in R&D, measure responsiveness.

14.4 MEASURING CYCLE TIMES

Cycle times measured in the 1994 and 1995 studies were idea-to-customer time, R&D cycle time, market development cycle time, and marketing cycle time.

14.4.1 Idea-to-Customer Time

In a 1994 model using idea-to-customer time as the dependent variable, 91% of this factor was explained by 10 independent variables. Six of these independent variables were newly asked questions in the 1994 survey, and only four were questions previously asked in the 1993 survey.

Customer satisfaction ratings provided five of these new factors. Overall performance as a contractor was not included among them. Two customer satisfaction ratings accelerated idea-to-customer time: Each 1% higher rating on technology was associated with 3.4 days less idea-to-customer time; each 1% higher rating on communications was associated with 4.3 fewer days. In these ratings, however, three offsetting negative satisfaction ratings were included. The use of a customer satisfaction index was associated with 184 days longer idea-to-customer time; each percent higher rating on cost competitiveness was associated with 3 more days; and each percent higher rating on program and contract management was associated with 6 more days. The pattern seems to indicate dual philosophies of innovation management: Speedy innovation involves satisfaction with high-technology and customer communication; formality in measuring satisfaction with innovation management and cost competitiveness go with slower idea-to-customer cycle times.

In-house benchmarking was the other new factor affecting idea-to-customer time. Each additional 1% increment of use of in-house benchmarking was associated with a 2.4-day longer idea-to-customer cycle time. Other forms of benchmarking were not correlated with idea-to-customer time. Does looking at your own company mean looking away from timeliness in serving the customer?

Other factors appearing in the idea-to-customer time regression included R&D time, use of Taguchi methods and TQM in R&D, and years of patent life. Each additional day of R&D time was associated with 1.5 days longer idea-to-customer time. Apparently the more the R&D group does, the more time has to be taken in other segments. Each additional 1% increment of use of Taguchi methods was associated with a 3.1-day longer idea-to-customer time; while each additional year that TQM was used in R&D was associated with a 30-day shorter cycle time. Each additional year of patent life was associated with a 13-day shorter cycle time. These factors had also been used in the 1993 survey questionnaire, but none of these latter three was in the comparable model of the 1993 survey, which was of limited reliability because of the then low usage of this metric. Also, none of the 1993 model's factors are in the 1994 idea-to-customer cycle time model, which is based on a much higher usage of this measurement, many additional factors, and a year's passage of time. Clearly also absent is any association of financial outcomes with idea-to-customer time.

14.4.2 R&D Time

R&D time begins when there has been an identification and definition of a new product or service to meet a customer need. The task of the R&D or team organization is usually considered complete when a prototype is handed over to the downstream organization together with all necessary information for manufacture if a product or software if a computer-based service.

Research and development cycle times were measured in the 1991, 1993, 1994, and 1995 studies by 31, 62, 74, and 82% of respondents, respectively. In the 1994 study, R&D cycle time was used as the dependent variable in a multiple regression model, with 128 responses. While this cycle is correlated with idea-to-customer time, of which it is a component, this overall metric was omitted to help identify which other independent factors would create a model and help explain what may drive the R&D time. Since only two factors entered the resulting model at the 5% probability level, the acceptance limit was expanded to 10%. Eleven independent variables were statistically significant at this level and explained 66% of the model variation with, however, only 44 of the 128 cases entering the model. Eight factors were from questions used in the 1993 study, and only three were from newly queried metrics. This replication between studies contrasts sharply with the previously presented findings on idea-to-customer time. This might possibly reflect the greater experience industry that has had with R&D time measurement.

Four 1993 factors, as shown in Figure 7.2, are also in the 1994 model. Sales volume is still a slowing factor, but now more significantly expressed as the logarithm of sales volume. Each ten times greater sales volume is associated with a 74-day longer R&D cycle time. This may reflect more the scale of projects attempted in larger companies rather than that they are more bureaucratic than smaller firms. Also, the 1994 study may have a wider range of company sizes than sampled in 1993. In either case, this finding highlights an area for innovation management attention to counteract this slowness with firm size.

The extent of QFD method use and percent of the R&D budget invested in CE projects were slowing factors in the 1993 study but appear as accelerating factors in the 1994 survey. Each 1% increase in the use of CE or QFD is independently associated with a 2.2- or 2.1-day shorter R&D cycle time, respectively. The amended sample distribution and the passage of a year of experience may account for this shift in sign. These impacts are also large enough to attract an innovation manager's actions. The extent of early R&D/marketing interface, however, is a slowing factor in the 1994 survey whereas it was an accelerating factor in the 1993 study. Each 1% increase in this interface is now associated with a 1.5-day longer R&D time. As in the 1993 study, QFD and R&D/marketing interface are offsetting each other while being applied to similar innovation management actions. This may be due to the differences in the group sampled or may reflect a shift toward preference for QFD as a more disciplined approach to R&D/marketing relations. Government regulation, product life, and investment in product extensions are three factors seen in Figure 7.2 that were not significant in the most recent model, presumably reflecting the different studies sampled.

Four other old factors that are not in the 1993 model shown in Figure 7.2 are significant in the 1994 model. Each one-year increment of time used in the product development cycle is associated with a 8.8-days shorter R&D time. This hints at an experience factor in measuring time in organizations. Each 1-day increment of time used in marketing is associated with a 1.2-days longer R&D time. This finding needs to be weighed with the results on QFD and marketing interface mentioned in the previous paragraph. Each additional year of patent age and each additional patent per million dollars of sales is independently associated with a 14- and 42-day slower R&D time, respectively.

Three new factors added in the 1994 study were found to be statistically significant. Each additional 1% use of milestones is associated with a 2.5-day longer R&D time. Each 1% increase in customer satisfaction ratings with technology and with product quality and reliability were separately associated with a 2.2-day decrease and a 5.3-day increase in R&D time, respectively. As in the idea-to-customer time model, financial outcomes are not statistically significant. As a recent article asks, "Is speedy R&D really beneficial?" [9]. It is not financially beneficial on findings to date.

A second model was created to try to bring more cases into the regression. This model has a lower explanatory factor (60% instead of 66%) but raised the number of cases to 63 from 44, so it is more representative of the 128 cases surveyed. Six factors dropped out of the regression equation: use of QFD, use of time for any purpose, use of CE, R&D/marketing interface, age of patents, and ratio of patents-to-sales. Five of the same factors are included. The lengthening of R&D

time for ten times sales is 68 days (in lieu of 74). Each 1-day increment of time used in marketing is associated with 0.6 (versus 1.2) days [R&D time. Each 1% use of milestones is associated with 1.9 (rather than 2.5) days of R&D time. Each 1% increase in customer satisfaction ratings with technology and with product quality and reliability were separately associated with a 2.7-day (against 2.2-day) decrease and a 6.3-day (rather than 5.3-day) increase in R&D time, respectively. These small shifts do not basically alter the earlier comments.

Three other new factors entered the second model equation. Each 1% increase in the use of value engineering is associated with a 1.9-day decrease in R&D time. This is logically related to the use of extensions as reducing R&D cycle time. Each 1% increase in the use of option pricing is associated with a 1.8-day increase in R&D time. Each 1% increase in the use of extra compensation to R&D staff based on overall company performance, as opposed to only that of the business unit, is related to a 1.9-day increase in R&D time. While all three are statistically significant, none has the kind of major impact that would suggest taking these actions just to alter R&D time. Since financial performance and the new sales percentage are related to major projects, the second model suggests innovation managers should consider rewarding on business unit performance and forego using value engineering and option pricing.

In summary, the most recent research results suggest the need that larger companies be increasingly watchful of their R&D cycle times, numbers and age of patents, and milestone management, lest these factors unnecessarily lengthen idea-to-customer times. QFD, CE, gaining experience with time metrics, and rewards based on the business unit have been shown to be useful strategies for shorter cycle times.

14.4.3 Market Development Cycle Time

In the pretesting of the 1994 study, one company added a fourth overall time measurement to the questionnaire: market development cycle time. This is composed of the time from the start of the prototype through manufacturability, production, testing, shipping to the customer, and the completion of customer service time on the first delivery.

A 1994 model was formed using market development cycle time as the dependent variable in a multiple regression analysis. Because it is correlated with idea-to-customer time, of which it is a component, this latter factor was omitted to highlight potential leading indicators. From 128 responses, using a probability level of 10%, six independent variables accounted for 63% of the variation in market development cycle time.

A shorter cycle time was associated with two factors. Each 1% increase in the share that product extensions have of the R&D budget, corresponds to a 1.3-day decrease in market development cycle time. This is a logical cause-and-effect relationship since the choice of extensions precedes the time cycle and less effort is required to learn to handle extensions than new products. Users of this route still have to deal with the negative profit impact mentioned in Chapter 4 and expanded upon in Chapter 10. Use of option pricing approaches, as broadly defined in the 1994 survey, rather than the narrow definition of Chapter 2, also has a time-shortening association: each 1% increase in the use of such approaches corresponds to a reduction of 1.4 days of market development cycle time, reflecting a greater management attention to the means of competition.

A longer cycle time was associated with four factors. Each additional 1-day increment in R&D time, as a precursor cause, was related to a 0.3-day increase in market development time. The effect of more R&D effort apparently spills over into more time to market. Each additional year of product life is associated with a trivial increase of 3 days in market development cycle time. Each added patent per million dollars of sales adds 21 days, and each ten times higher sales volume adds 42 days, both related to the effect of more R&D time mentioned earlier.

14.4.4   Marketing Cycle Time

The R&D cycle-time model mentioned earlier introduces conflicting results on the R&D/marketing interface. QFD and the R&D/marketing interface offset each other while applied to similar innovation management actions. The extent of an early R&D/marketing interface is a slowing factor in the 1994 survey, whereas it had an accelerating affect in the 1993 study. Each day of time used in marketing is associated with 1.2 days in R&D time in that overall model.

A marketing cycle time model from the 1994 study was created using this time segment as the dependent variable in a multiple regression analysis. While data on other time segments could also have been used in similar models, the author considered that the leading factors of marketing time were most important to innovation managers and omitted modeling at this point. The model explains 52% of marketing time at the 10% level, with seven factors as independent variables.

One slowing factor in the 1994 marketing time model is R&D time, paralleling the finding in the R&D time model: each day of marketing time is directly associated with 1.8 days in R&D, versus 1.2 days in that time's model. Although marketing occurs timewise ahead of R&D, it is more likely that both time segments are consequences of a common strategic intent regarding speediness rather than cause and effect of each other.

A second slowing factor was the use of CE. For low levels of use, each 1% increase in the use of CE was associated with a 7.3-day increase in marketing time when the square of use was introduced to offset that use's nonlinearity. This effect was canceled out by the square term at 63% use and a maximum of 226 days; above that point, increased use of CE was associated with less extended marketing time. By 100% use, marketing time was only delayed by 146 days. This may be the effect of introducing a new management technique to the firm.

Four accelerating factors of marketing time were statistically significant, namely, use of NPV in project selection, percent of new product sales, center of gravity closer to the customer, and specifying a reason for using time measurement in innovation. Each 1% increase in use of NPV in project selection was associated with a 1.4-days decrease in marketing time. Does the use of financial discipline in selection spur marketeers to speediness? Each 1% increase in new products or services in total sales is associated with 1.9 days of less marketing time. With each 1% increment that the firm is closer to the consumer is associated with 1.3 fewer days of marketing time. Neither QFD nor the R&D/marketing interface were significant in the marketing model, further raising doubts about the finding that these were offsetting in the R&D model. Any reason given for using time measurement in the company's new product development cycle is associated with 149 days less marketing time. The impression obtained from these accelerating factors is that a speed-to-market company strategy is most visible in speediness in the marketing department, which spills over into speed in R&D.

In addition to the lessons learned on time measurement covered in Section 6.6, consider also these secondary lessons learned from the details of the research.

- Speedy innovation involves satisfaction with high technology and customer communication.
- Formality in measuring satisfaction with innovation management and cost competitiveness go with slower idea-to-customer cycle times.
- Since financial performance and new sales percentage are related to major projects, R&D managers should consider rewarding on business unit performance and forego using value engineering and option pricing.
- Four accelerating factors of marketing time were use of NPV in project selection, percent of new product sales, center of gravity closer to the customer, and specifying a reason for using time measurement in innovation.

14.5 MEASURING NEW PRODUCTS AND SERVICES

The 1994 survey of managers working in innovation and technology management gave some indications of the wide use of the new product-to-sales ratio metric. 88% of the 128 executives responding answered the question, "The approximate percent of your company's total sales volume attributable to new products is ___%." The median percentage reported was 25%.

A multiple regression analysis was run with the percentage of new products to total sales as the dependent variable. 27% of the variation in this percentage was explained by the seven questions described in Table 9.1, at a confidence level of 5%.

The percentage of major new projects was the primary positive result: Each 2.6% increase in the major project percentage is associated with a 1% increase in the percentage of new product/service sales. The use of outcome benchmarking was another positive result. Each 5.1% increase in the use of outcome benchmarking was associated with a 1%$ increase in the percentage of new products/services to sales. The large group of companies that measure market share as an indirect indicator of customer satisfaction have a 9.6% higher percentage of new products/services to sales. Each additional year that time has been measured in the innovation chain is associated with a 0.57% increase in the percentage of new products/services to sales. Concurrent, or simultaneous engineering, which has a positive effect on the timeliness of innovation, also has a positive effect on the new product sales percentage. Each 4.9% increase of projects handled under CE is associated with an increase of 1% in new products and/or services to sales.

One negative factor was the average product life cycle measured in years. Shortening product life by 1.5 years was associated with an increased new product sales percentage of 1% (an additional 1.5 years of average life decreased new product sales by 1%). The other negative factor, use of value engineering, is also logical. If your attention is on value engineering, or using it to lower costs, it is not on increasing the percentage of new products. Each 5.5% increase in the use of value engineering is associated with a 1% drop in the new product percentage. Financial factors were expected to affect new product sales, but none of the financial measures investigated showed statistically significant correlations.

14.5.1   1995 New Products as a Percent of Sales Model

Three regression models were prepared for new products as a percent of sales (NEWSALES) with 30, 20, and 20 responses in the equations (20, 10, and 8, respectively, degrees of freedom).

All independent variables had substantial effects. Six factors appeared in all three models. QFD use was associated with 21, 22, and 19% increases in NEWSALES per step increase in the use of QFD. Center of gravity close to the customer was associated with 12, 8, and 10% increases in NEWSALES for each step increase. External customer rating of technology was associated with 12, 9, and 8% increases in NEWSALES for each higher step rating.

NEWSALES was associated with 0.9, 1.1, and 1.1% increases for each 1% decrease in EBIT. Some intimation of what is happening can be seen if EBIT squared is introduced into the formula. While not statistically significant, NEWSALES rises with increasing EBIT and falls with increasing EBIT squared. This results in an optimum level for the effect on NEWSALES of a low 3.18% of EBIT, before the decline of NEWSALES with EBIT begins. Only if each additional percent of NEWSALES were able to be translated to more than a percent of annual growth rate to offset this decline in EBIT would this be a rational tradeoff for most companies interested in shareholder value creation (based on the perpetual growth model).

Customer satisfaction with overall performance as a contractor was another negative factor with each higher step rating being associated with 23, 21, and 21% lower NEWSALES. This is not surprising since satisfaction measures are positively associated with EBIT. Each year of a company's age is associated with 0.15, 0.3, and 0.3% lower NEWSALES. Young companies create new products, and older ones hold onto customers they satisfy?

Other factors differ in the models. In the first model, which has the highest responses and degrees of freedom, each increment of more government regulation and each increment of lower customer satisfaction with reliability are each associated with a 5% increase in new product sales percent. With the smaller sample with lower degrees of freedom, there is a positive association of EBIT with patent numbers and a negative correlation with value engineering use and internal satisfaction with the financial results of using QFD. Sales volume was marginally not significant ($p = 0.06$) and the patent-to-sales ratio far away from being significant, so numbers of patents seem a proxy for economies of scale, not patent intensity. Companies interested in current return use value engineering and wish QFD did more for the bottom line rather than new products?

In Section 11.1.1, the positive and negative factors mentioned above were summarized for both the 1994 and 1995 studies. No additional lessons were learned from this section.

14.6 MEASURING MARKET SHARE

Market share is a traditional measurement of the marketing departments of companies. In Chapter 7, it was noted that some authors report the use of market share as an indirect measure of customer satisfaction [12]. This section addresses responses from firms that use this metric and how market share is associated with other measurements for some typical groups of industries.

The 1994 study included a question on market share. Some 57% of companies responded "yes" to the question, "Does your company measure the extent of customer satisfaction using market share as a measure?" For those companies measuring market share, their responses correlated with a number of other factors also being measured. Using a scale from 0 to 100, customer satisfaction with cost effectiveness is 1.9% higher, and use of milestones is 2.7% higher; product life is 70 days longer; and publicly held firms were slightly more likely to measure customer satisfaction this way.

14.6.1 How Market Share Affects Results

Market share's positive affect on financial results has a background in economic theory and strategic management literature. Research surveys, however, have shown rather mixed results that vary by industry.

Theory and strategic management precepts argue that increased market share leads to higher profits, all other things being equal [13]. However, since all other things are not equal, in 1993, Ford had higher earnings than General Motors on less sales. The theorists argue that, on an average basis in most industries, there are economies of scale, and higher market share equates to a greater amount of sales, and thus lower costs, and higher profits.

Industry market shares were analyzed in the 1993 study. The results are shown in Table 14.3. The depth of analysis was limited by the small sample size in each industry, although the total sample was reasonably large, with 131 responses.

The other factors correlated with telecommunications industry market share are as follows. Each additional year of product life correlates with an increased market share of 4.6%. Each 1% of major new products share of the R&D budget correlates with an increase of 1% in market share. And each additional patent per million dollars of sales correlates with an increased market share, but the numerical percentage is questionably high and probably an artifact of the limited sample.

Computer hardware was the second industry with enough responses for analysis. The computer hardware industry is a competitive, high-technology industry, accustomed to competing on time. In this industry, however, no relationship was found between market share and profitability. The other factors correlated with market share were as follows. Each 1% increase in interface with

Table 14.3
Industry Market Shares

Percent Share in Marketed Dominated	Percent[a] (No.[b])		Percent Market Share		
	Measuring		Minimum	Mean	Maximum
Personal care	4	(5)	4.0	22.2	70.0
Chemicals	7	(9)	9.0	27.7	52.5
Defense	10	(13)	0.5	16.9	90.0
Biotechnology	6	(7)	1.0	21.7	50.0
Consumer goods	12	(16)	1.0	30.0	95.0
Computer hardware	12	(16)	1.0	18.7	80.0
Telecommunications	16	(21)	0.5	17.7	40.0
Energy	5	(7)	20.0	27.9	45.0
Pharmaceutical	8	(11)	0.5	16.2	70.0
Other	9	(12)	0.0	31.8	80.0

[a]As a percent of total usable responses (131).
[b]Eighty companies gave information about dominant market share. The total for percent market share exceeds 80 because of companies reporting dominance in more than one industry.
Source: [8–10].

marketing (on a 0 to 100% scale) was associated with an 0.8% decrease in market share. A 20-day decrease in time through R&D was associated with a 1% increase in market share. A decrease of 1% in the share of the R&D budget devoted to major new projects is associated with a 1.3% higher market share. Each additional patent per million dollars of sales is associated with a 17% lower market share. As a less-deliberate industry than telecommunications, the factors cited reflect the timeliness characteristic of the computer hardware industry.

The remaining industry samples shown in Table 14.2 were too small to obtain a reasonable base for analysis in the 1993 study. Using this source's data base, the author paired four of them into two groups.

Biotechnology and pharmaceutical industries are similar in that they have high risks, usually high rewards, and a long time for development, as a consequence of extensive government regulation. The combined *biopharm* series is an average of the biotechnology and pharmaceutical industries with the source file modified to change missing values to zero in each. Although combined to get a larger sample, this is an unstable model. Each 1% increase in biopharm market share is accompanied by a 2% drop in EBIT as a percent of sales, going against the theoretical proposition. There is also a high drop with increased sales, suggesting small firms in this grouping are more profitable than larger firms. Market share increases both with the age of patents and with the patent-to-sales ratio. It also increases with company age. To summarize, this is not a robust model but guides management actions toward the technology-driven characteristics of both industries.

Consumer goods and personal care are both industries with a high marketing input, closely coupled to the consumer, and with a short time horizon. A *concare* series was created from an equal combination of personal care and consumer goods responses with the missing variables set equal to zero. In this series, the theoretical relationship between market share and profitability was absent. Perhaps this is not so surprising since the opportunities for establishing economies of scale are low in these industries.

The factors correlated with market share in this series included patents. Each additional year of patent life was associated with an increased market share of 10%. This was a suspiciously high value since the average patent life was 7.75 years. However, since the maximum patent life is 17 years, it is unlikely that most companies could add more than a few years of patent life to their portfolio.

Greater marketing interface in this consumer area increased market share by 0.9% for each 1% increase in interface (on a scale of 0 to 100%), but with a rather low statistical significance level. Increasing the share of major new products in the R&D budget decreased market share, but also with a rather low statistical significance. Both of these findings are consistent with a market-driven group of industries.

The principal lessons learned on the two industries large enough for clean analysis were:

- With increased market share in telecommunications, expect higher earnings, longer product life, more major new products, and more patents per million dollars of sales;
- With increased market share in computer hardware, expect no impact on earnings, shorter R&D cycle time, fewer major new projects, and fewer patents.

14.7 MEASURING BENCHMARKING

As mentioned briefly in Chapter 12, the practices of benchmarking have barely begun to be applied to the elements of the innovation chain. For measurement, however, the various forms of benchmarking need to be applied to any of the outcome-dependent variables. Table 14.4 shows usage data on benchmarking methods from 128 respondents.

14.7.1 Impact of Benchmarking on Other Outcomes

In the analysis of the other major innovation outcomes not covered in this chapter, all but outcome benchmarking (mentioned in Section 14.5) showed up as intervening variables. Three of these outcomes are discussed: financial performance, timeliness, and customer satisfaction.

Financial performance, as measured in a multiple regression analysis of EBIT as a percentage of sales in Chapter 10, had noncompetitive and in-house benchmarking as significant factors. Since the effect of the former was negative and that of the latter was positive, they were mutually offsetting, and with such a small net effect as to suggest no management action.

Timeliness, as measured in time from idea-to-customer in Chapter 8, also had in-house benchmarking as a significant effect. Each 1% increase in the use of

Table 14.4
Benchmarking Practices Used

- Benchmarking internally within the company (68% indicated some to consistent use, 30% indicated no or little use, and 2% did not indicate use).
- Benchmarking from among competitors (73% indicated some to consistent use, 24% indicated no or little use, and 3% did not indicate use).
- Benchmarking from among noncompetitors (41% indicated some to consistent use, 56% indicated no or little use, and 3% did not indicate use).
- Process or outcome benchmarking (mean [median]) allocations were 31% [23%] to process benchmarking, 50% [57%] to outcome benchmarking, 19% did not indicate use).

Source: [11].

in-house benchmarking was associated with a 1.2-day increase in idea-to-customer time, a clearly trivial effect.

The principal lessons learned on benchmarking were listed in Section 11.2.3. No additional lessons were learned in this present section.

14.8 MEASURING FINANCIAL RESULTS

Models were derived on management accounting tools and on EBIT as a percent of sales.

14.8.1 Management Accounting

The impression that one obtains from Table 14.5 is that there is little variation in the amount of use of the selected management accounting tools. In fact, there is a rather large variation in the results of the 1994 study.

Option pricing correlates statistically significantly with the other five measures in Table 14.5, but except for this, target costing and contribution margin correlate only with each other and payback, NPV, and IRR correlate only with each other. The correlation of the last three is not surprising, since they are mathematically related [1]. The actual correlation coefficients are shown in Table 14.6.

In a multiple regression model with option pricing as the dependent variable, however, only 25% of that variable is explained by the factors contribution

Table 14.5
Use of Management Accounting Practices

- New product development project selection methods include:
  - Payback period: Some to consistent use 72%, little or no use 28%;
  - Internal Rate of Return: Some to consistent use 68%, little or no use 32%;
  - NPV of Project Cash Flows: Some to consistent use 61%, little or no use 39%.
- Target costing/pricing is the practice of determining what the market requires in a product's functions and targeting the lowest cost that meets those requirements: Some to consistent use 69%, little or no use 31%.
- Option pricing approaches taking into account that greater risks of longer term projects may be associated with greater returns as well as the time value of money, for example, using a lower hurdle rate for longer term projects (Note: This is a broader definition than that used in Chapter 2): Some to consistent use 68%, little or no use 32%.
- Contribution margin analysis assessing a project on the basis of whether unit sales price exceeds unit variable costs (costs varying directly with volume): Some to consistent use 66%, little or no use 34%.

Source: [11].

Table 14.6
Correlation Matrix of Selection/Accounting Methods; Number of Cases = 83

	PAYBACK	NPV	IRR	Target Costing	Contrib. Margin	Option Pricing
PAYBACK	1.000					
NPV	0.413*	1.000				
IRR	0.548*	0.671*	1.000			
TARGET	0.073	0.068	0.176	1.000		
CM	0.048	0.105	0.130	0.311*	1.000	
OPTION	0.332*	0.349*	0.306*	0.258*	0.375*	1.000

* = $p < 0.01$. (Others $p > 0.05$.)
Source: [11].

margin, payback, and NPV, with target costing and IRR (the two lowest correlations) falling out of statistical significance. Each 10% increase in the individual use of contribution margin, payback, or NPV is associated with a 3.1, 2.2, or 1.9% increase in the use of option pricing, respectively. Thus, a 10% increase in the use of all three techniques is associated with only a 7.2% higher use of option pricing, indicating incomplete explanation of this model. These results do not give a clear management direction as to what should be the preferred management accounting approach.

14.8.2   1994 EBIT Model

In the 1994 study, financial results were measured by the ratio of EBIT to sales. This was the same metric used in the 1993 study discussed in Chapter 7 and shown in Figure 7.3. The two are not exactly comparable, however. First, the response samples were different, although from a similar range of companies. Statistically, one would not expect this to be a large effect. It is likely, however, that the evolution of measuring during the one-year period will be more important. That this is large may be seen by the rapid increase of measurement of idea-to-customer time discussed in Chapter 8. Third, the additional factors included in the 1994 study have probably masked the statistical significance of the weaker factors in the earlier survey.

Eleven factors now are statistically significantly correlated with EBIT when this is used as the dependent variable in a multiple regression analysis. This regression using 128 responses explains 40% of the variation in EBIT. Five of these factors come from the inclusion of customer satisfaction and benchmarking metrics in the 1994 survey.

Customer satisfaction again gives confusing signals when compared with financial metrics such as EBIT. The customer satisfaction rating with overall performance as a contractor has a negative effect on EBIT. However, the ratings for customer satisfaction with technology and responsiveness have offsetting positive effects. It appears that the overall performance and technology satisfaction ratings are so highly correlated that they cause this interaction. Eliminating both of these, while retaining the customer satisfaction rating with responsiveness, creates an equally statistically significant model explaining 39% of the variation, which was used in evaluating the remaining factors. In the resulting nine independent variable regression with EBIT as the dependent variable, a 13% higher rating on customer satisfaction with responsiveness is associated with a 1% greater EBIT.

A similar ambivalence occurs with benchmarking. A 12% greater use of noncompetitive benchmarking is associated with a 1% higher EBIT, and a 17% increased use of in-house benchmarking shows an offsetting negative effect of a 1% decreased EBIT. These findings, taken together with earlier findings of customer satisfaction models, do not give a clear indication of desirable management actions concerning the use of these two forms of benchmarking for their financial impact. The most that one can conclude is that looking outside the firm is of benefit in benchmarking.

From among the metrics used in the 1993 study, measures of quality also give confusing indications. In the 1993 study, the more years that TQM was used in R&D, the lower was the associated EBIT. There is no longer a significant correlation between these two factors in the 1994 study. In the 1993 study, use of QFD and Taguchi methods were not significantly correlated with EBIT; while in the 1994 study, they are correlated, but with opposing effects. Each 20% increase in the use of QFD is associated with a 1% increase in EBIT; while each 15% increase in the use of Taguchi methods is associated with a 1% decrease in EBIT. These effects are not large and give only slight support for QFD being the preferred quality method for innovation management.

The four other significant variables were also used in the 1993 study but not found to be statistically significant then. Economies of scale are now found with each ten times higher sales volume now associated with a 1.2% higher EBIT. Each 21% higher use of internal rate of return in project selection is associated with a 1% higher EBIT. Each 13% increment that the firm is closer to the customer is associated with a 1% higher EBIT. However, each 17% increment that the company increases the extent of the marketing/R&D interface in the early stages of product development is associated with a 1% lower EBIT. These last two results must be considered by innovation managers as somewhat offsetting each other, although the correlation between them is very low. In a current attempt to replicate the 1993 findings in the 1994 study with a different respondent group, the correlation of EBIT as a percent of sales was found also to be negative with product feature extensions (the higher the percentage of product extensions of the total R&D budget, the lower the EBIT ratio). However, limited modeling of the more recent data with additional questions in the survey instrument showed that two factors, each independently, made the use of product extensions modestly profitable. The first of these is measuring, and thus presumably managing, the market development cycle of time from prototype to delivery to the customer. The second factor is the accounting practice of target costing, or the practice of determining what the market requires in a product's functions and targeting the lowest cost that meets those requirements. When both of these factors were introduced into a limited EBIT model, each 12% increase in product extensions raised EBIT by 1%. While this is not a strong result, it demonstrates that discipline is needed in selecting project feature extensions to avoid the profit deterioration shown in the overall responses. It might be critical to reassess whether a company's investment among the project types is properly balanced toward higher profit major projects, despite the cycle-time increase.

14.8.3   1995 EBIT Model

A multiple regression model was prepared for EBIT based on the 1995 responses. This model explained 85% of the variance in EBIT by 9 factors with 23 of the responses appearing in the equation. Three of the responses came from external customer satisfaction metrics. Each increment (25%) of a higher satisfaction rating with overall performance as a contractor and with communications was associated with an increase in EBIT by 6.0 and 5.1%, respectively. This was offset by each positive increment in responsiveness being associated with 3.6% lower EBIT, while in 1994 it was associated with higher EBIT. The balance still is as in previous years, supporting steps to improve external customer satisfaction.

Internal customer satisfaction was measured for the first time in 1995. The one internal customer satisfaction rating appearing in the model was that each step (25%) of a higher satisfaction with QFD's contribution to improving internal integration (that is, better teamwork and improved decision making in the innovation process) was associated with a 3.4% higher EBIT. This continues the pattern seen previously supporting QFD's impact on profitability.

Three other positive factors were regulation, center of gravity, and a newly asked question in 1995 concerning longer cycle time in going through the strategic technology process. Each positive increment (25%) of government regulation was associated with 2.0% higher EBIT. This is the opposite of the finding of the 1993 study, possibly due to a company mix away from low-profit defense work or to high-profit regulated products such as pharmaceuticals. Each step the company's center of gravity is closer to the customer was associated with a 2.7% higher EBIT. This confirms the 1994 study with a slightly higher effect. Each additional year taken before going again through the strategic technology planning process was associated with 4.9% higher EBIT. It would appear that companies that have a stable technology evolution are more profitable than those in fast-changing environments that must update their plans in less than a year (some reported monthly).

The remaining two factors were negative. Each positive 1% increment of major new projects in the R&D budget was associated with a 0.2% decrease in EBIT. Each additional year of measuring time in the new product development cycle was associated with a 0.9% lower EBIT. These are shifts in sign from earlier years and may reflect a more difficult business environment due to interest rate and taxation increases in 1994.

14.8.4 Summary of the EBIT Regression Models

Only government regulation shown in Figure 7.5 appears to be statistically significant in the 1995 (but not 1994) model, presumably for the reasons previously stated. Thus, coming to strong conclusions from the 1994 and 1995 studies appears somewhat venturesome. First, however, the addition of external and internal customer satisfaction and benchmarking factors has clearly altered the model sufficiently to show that these nonfinancial measures need to be considered. In terms of management action, however, only improving the customer's rating of your firm is a management imperative for financial improvement. The responsiveness satisfaction rating was positive in 1994 and negative in 1995, but the latter was offset by positive ratings on overall performance and on communications. Use of QFD in 1994 and internal satisfaction with QFD in 1995 show a preference as a quality method for innovation as contrasted with the negative effects of Taguchi methods in the 1994 study and TQM in R&D in the 1993 study. The small positive impact of IRR on EBIT in 1994 (but not in 1995) is a proxy for the other two correlated factors of payback and NPV and supports the value of financial discipline in project selection and evaluation. Economies of scale were found only in 1994, with higher sales volume associated with higher EBIT. Closer to the customer is associated with higher EBIT in 1994 and 1995, while increase in the extent of the marketing/R&D interface in the early stages of product development was associated with lower EBIT in 1994, somewhat offsetting that closeness. These lessons learned are completely, but more briefly, summarized in Section 12.4.4.

14.9 1995 EFFECTIVENESS INDEX MODEL

An EI is a creation of reference [14]. Its formula is

$$EI = \frac{\% \text{ New Product Revenue} * (\text{Net profit\%} + \text{R\&D\%})}{100 * \text{R\&D\%}} \tag{14.1}$$

This formula is an attempt to register the tradeoff between growth and current return in the perpetual growth model of SVC. It does this by seeking that an increase in new product revenue does not correspondingly reduce net profit if EI is to increase. It does not, however, match the additive model of SVC. As a multiplicative model, its values can rise to much higher values than any of its components. Being of intensity ratios, it does not allow for the diseconomies of scale incumbent on high intensities, for example, 100% net profit leaves nothing for R&D, and so on.

With these caveats, it still is an interesting dependent variable for analysis of underlying associated independent variables other than those from which it is constructed. Four factors are positively associated. Longer idea-to-customer cycle time is associated with a 0.06 higher EI for each additional day. Speedy R&D is not beneficial.

An increased external customer satisfaction rating of technology and cost competitiveness by one step is associated with an increase of EI by 24 and 17, respectively. An increase by one step in the internal customer satisfaction rating with QFD's contribution to organizational integration is associated with an EI increase of 41.

These customer satisfaction ratings are offset by three negative ratings. Each one-step increase in the external rating with responsiveness or with management is associated with a decrease in EI of 28 or 12, respectively. Each one-step increase in the internal customer satisfaction rating with the company's competitive position is associated with a decrease of EI by 46. And each additional year of using QFD has a minor lowering effect on EI of 2.3. The factors above are listed without quantitative values in Table 12.4. This can be summarized as: Satisfaction with technology, cost, and organizational integration are offset in the EI if the company's focus is too heavily on management, responsiveness, or competitive position.

14.10   FACTOR ANALYSIS

The analysis to date has focused heavily on multiple regression methods. These require a designation by the analyst of a dependent variable (presumed effect) from among the factors studied. This is a reasonable method for the current research since most of the chosen dependent variables are outcomes or overall metrics that occur later in time than the other independent variables (presumed causes). However, it does not give much guidance to the relative weight of the outcomes, particularly between financial and nonfinancial metrics. For this reason, the responses were subjected to factor analysis, which makes no designation of which is the dependent variable among the responses. Instead, it seeks to create new factors that most strongly group the responses into associated clusters. Thus, the question for additional study may be phrased as follows. If we had no preconceived ideas about lagging and leading indicators, what would factor analysis say is the relative weight of financial and nonfinancial indicators? It should be noted that nothing constrains factor analysis to answering just this question, as the computer program for factor analysis selects what it finds as the strongest relationships.

The resulting new factors are shown in Table 14.7.

Table 14.7
Factor Analysis of the 1994 study ($n = 128$)

Factor/Component	Component Loading
1. Regulated/Disciplined Firms (17.2%)	
Share of R&D budget devoted to product extensions	−0.85
Extent to which government regulation restricts R&D	0.77
Years using TQM in the new product area	0.75
Use of Taguchi methods	0.70
Use of value engineering	0.70
Responsiveness ranking by customers	0.65
Program/contract management ranking by customers	0.62
Use of noncompetitive benchmarking	0.62
Use of option pricing of greater risks of longer projects	0.62
Use of stage-gate tracking	0.61
Use of in-house benchmarking	0.59
Communications ranking by customers	0.57
Use of Quality Function Deployment in new product design	0.56
Percent of R&D budget on major new development	0.53
2. Finance Selection-Driven/Customer Adverse Firms (14.8%)	
Quality of proposals ranking by customers	−0.81
Use of IRR in new product development project selection	0.73
Use of payback period in new project selection	0.71
Timeliness ranking by customers	−0.66
Product quality/reliability ranking by customers	−0.60
Use of in-house benchmarking	0.60
Program/contract management ranking by customers	−0.56
Use of milestones	0.55
Use of stock options for R&D staff compensation	−0.54
Overall performance as a contractor ranking by customers	−0.51
3. Large/Old-Line Firms (11.8%)	
Logarithm of sales volume	0.84
Company age in years	0.79
R&D cycle time	0.66
Idea-to-customer cycle time	0.59
Firm's center of gravity closer to customer	0.57
Publicly held company	0.55
Percent of R&D budget on major new development	−0.54

Table 14.7 (Continued)

Factor/Component	Component Loading
4. Technology-Driven/Individualistic Firms (9.7%)	
Compensation over and above base salary to individuals	0.90
Use of NPV of cash flows in new project selection	0.77
Number of active patents per million dollars of sales	−0.76
Technology ranking by customers	0.58
5. Long-Lived/Patented-Products Firms (9.0%)	
Average life cycle of products	0.66
Use of a target pricing/costing strategy	0.63
Measuring customer satisfaction by market share	0.62
Earnings before interest and taxes as a percent of sales	0.56
Communications ranking by customers	−0.53
6. Marketing-Driven Firms (6.9%)	
Extent to which there is marketing/R&D interface and involvement in the early stages of new product development	0.72
Use of Quality Function Deployment in new product design	0.57
Overall performance as a contractor ranking by customers	−0.55

Note: Cumulative percent variation explained by the first six factors = 69.3%.
Source: [11].

These have been given arbitrary new names reflecting what the author perceives might have been intended by responders as they replied to the questionnaire. After each new factor the percent of total variation in the responses that it explains is indicated. The loading (expressed as a correlation coefficient) of old factors correlated more than 0.5 against the new factor is indicated after each old factor. Just the first six new factors explain 69.3% of the total variation. As may be seen from Table 14.7, the factor analysis program has chosen to form clusters around what might be called groupings of companies with like strategic intents.

Among financial frameworks, EBIT had a correlation above 0.5 with the fifth new factor but failed to have a correlation greater than 0.5 against any other new factor. A positive correlation over 0.4 was found between EBIT and new factor 1, hinting at higher profitability of this group of companies. Low correlations were found between EBIT and new factors 2, 3, and 4, indicating that such strategies neither promote nor detract from profitability. Financial methods in new project selection were seen in new factors 2 and 4, without an associated correlation with

EBIT. A negative correlation over 0.3 was found between new factor 6 and EBIT, but also a similar positive correlation of that factor with new product percentage. This may indicate a tendency to forcing new products at the expense of profitability, which is often the case with newer firms.

The first cluster identified by factor analysis has been named "regulated/disciplined" reflecting its constituent elements. The variation in the total accounted for by this group is 17.2%. The third highest component was that of government regulation, while the remaining components suggest a rather disciplined innovation management approach. Cause and effect are not clear—regulation may impose discipline, or disciplined managements may choose to enter regulated fields. This group shows negative correlation only with product extensions while showing a lesser positive correlation with major new product development, further supporting a "go with the long shots approach" [15]. Positive correlations with three quality management approaches, three customer satisfaction rankings, two benchmarking methods, two metrics of time, and two metrics of pricing methods round out the disciplined management image. While the leading indicators suggested by this grouping are clear, an extension to other than regulated industries may not be applicable.

The second largest cluster accounts for 14.8% of the variation in factor analysis. It has been titled by the author as "finance selection-driven/customer adverse." The positively correlated financial project selectors of IRR and payback are supplemented by positive correlations of the new factor with use of milestones, longer idea-to-customer time, and greater use of in-house benchmarking. Not far below the 0.5 loading limit is customer satisfaction with cost competitiveness, further supporting the "finance-driven" title.

Most notable in the second new factor is the negative correlation of five of the customer satisfaction ratings. Three other customer satisfaction ratings did not make the 0.5 correlation cutoff, but also have negative correlations, leading to the "customer adverse" subtitle. This is the clearest support thus far to the tradeoff between financial frameworks and customer satisfaction, with the former predominant in this cluster. The lack of correlation with EBIT, however, does not rule out this as a viable strategy, although scarcely a role model for most companies who value their customers more highly.

The third new factor accounts for 11.8% of the analysis variation and has been titled by the author as representing "large, old-line companies." This strategic intent is positively correlated with sales volume, company age, and being publicly held as befitting a large firm. The cycle times through R&D and from idea to customer are also positively correlated, echoing a warning made earlier in Chapter 8 that these large companies need to beware of this deliberate speed. Also positively correlated is the center of gravity of the company nearer the customer. These factors give the impression of companies that have survived to a position of some dominance in their industries to the extent that their customers have become somewhat dependent on them. This makes a good role model when there are barriers to entry in the industry, but one must not be overcomplacent and remember that this was once the position in which buggy-whip manufacturers found themselves at the time when the auto came on the scene.

The fourth new factor accounting for 9.7% of the analysis variation has been called by the author as "technology-driven/individualistic." It is the one new factor correlated positively with customer satisfaction with technology. Its highest positive correlation was, however, with compensation to individuals rather than groups. The remaining positive correlation is to the use of NPV in project selection. This suggests attention more to cash flows as the dominant financial discipline than to traditional cost accounting methods. The negative correlation with patents per million dollars of sales may possibly reflect some newness of the technology. This seems a good role model for the newer and smaller company that stresses technology and individual rewards. It is, however, limited in its applicability to larger company status where teamwork is becoming the norm.

The fifth new factor accounts for 9% of the variation in the factor analysis and is called "long-lived/patented-products." The product life cycles are long in this group, and the patent age is also positively correlated but just below the 0.5 level. Profitability as measured by EBIT, use of target pricing/costing methods, and measuring customer satisfaction by market share are also positively correlated with this new factor. Customer satisfaction with communications is negatively correlated with the cluster, again continuing the pattern of higher profitability being offset by lesser customer satisfaction. The profitability, long life, and patent protection speak of barriers to entry; but this may not be a role model for innovative management.

The sixth factor with 6.9% of the variation appears to show a marketing-driven environment with positive correlations of the new factor to marketing/R&D interface and use of QFD. A companion component is the low customer ranking of overall performance as a contractor.

One may conclude that the use of factor analysis has only partially answered the question of the balance between nonfinancial and financial metrics since it provides a grouping characterized more by company characteristics rather than offering a more general or universal answer.

14.11 SUMMARIZING FINDINGS

The findings that add to the lessons learned in the earlier chapters can be stated as follows.

- Since the type of measurement chosen to measure customer satisfaction seems not to bias the results, select those with which your company is comfortable.

- Measure overall customer satisfaction also by timeliness and communication, which were significant with the early replies.
- Carefully consider the tradeoff of potential negative impact on overall customer satisfaction and customer cost satisfaction of stock options being part of the R&D compensation package—consider rewarding R&D staff other ways than stock options.
- For customer satisfaction with cost competitiveness, also measure responsiveness.
- Speedy innovation involves satisfaction with high-technology and customer communication.
- Formality in measuring satisfaction with innovation management and cost competitiveness go with slower idea-to-customer cycle times.
- Since financial performance and new sales percentage are related to major projects, R&D managers should consider rewarding on business unit performance and forego using value engineering and option pricing.
- Four accelerating factors of marketing time were use of NPV in project selection, percent of new product sales, center of gravity closer to the customer, and specifying a reason for using time measurement in innovation.
- With increased market share in telecommunications, expect higher earnings, longer product life, more major new products, and more patents per million dollars of sales.
- With increased market share in computer hardware, expect no impact on earnings, shorter R&D cycle time, fewer major new projects, and fewer patents.
- Satisfaction with technology, cost, and organizational integration are offset in the EI if the company's focus is too heavily set on management, responsiveness, or competitive position.

References

[1] Nachmias, D., and C. Nachmias, *Research Methods in the Social Sciences*, 3rd ed., New York: St. Martin's Press, 1987, pp. 108–109.

[2] Zikmund, W. G., *Business Research Methods*, 2nd ed., Chicago: Dryden Press, 1988.

[3] Industrial Research Institute, "Minutes of ROR and SIS Meetings;" and tapes of the SIS meeting, Phoenix: Tape Productions., 1990.

[4] Ellis, L. W., "Financial Frameworks for Research and Development," Faculty working paper, University of New Haven, New Haven, CT, May 1991.

[5] Wolff, M. F., "Working Faster," *Research Technology Management*, Vol. 35(6), 1992, pp. 10–12.

[6] Ellis, L. W. and C. C. Curtis, "Practices in Concurrent Engineering," *Managing in a Global Environment: 1992 International Engineering Management Conference*, IEEE Catalog No. 92CH3222-7, Piscataway, NJ: IEEE, 1992, pp. 115–118.

[7] Curtis, C. C., New Product Development Cycle Time: Investigation of Cycle Time and Accounting Measures, Determinants of Cycle Time and the Impact of Cycle Time on Financial Performance," Sc.D. diss., University of New Haven, New Haven, CT, 1993.

[8] Curtis, C. C., "Nonfinancial Performance Measures in New Product Development," *J. Cost Management*, Vol. 8(3), 1994, pp. 18–26.

[9] Ellis, L. W., and C. C. Curtis, "Speedy R&D: How Beneficial?" *Research Technology Management*, Vol. 38(4), July–Aug. 1995, pp. 42–51.

[10] Curtis, C. C., and L. W. Ellis, "A Balanced Scorecard for New Product Development," *J. Cost Management*, Spring 1997, to appear.

[11] Ellis, L. W., and C. C. Curtis, "Measuring Customer Satisfaction," *Research Technology Management*, Vol. 38(5), Sept.–Oct. 1995, pp. 45–48.

[12] Kaplan, R. S., and D. P. Norton, "Putting the Balanced Scorecard to Work, *Harvard Business Review*, Vol. 71(5), Sept.–Oct. 1993, pp. 134–147.

[13] Thompson, A. A., and A. J. Strickland, *Strategy and Policy*, revised ed., Plano, TX: Business Publications, 1981.

[14] McGrath, M. E., and M. N. Romeri, "From Experience: The R&D Effectiveness Index: A Metric for Product Development Performance," *J. Product Innovation Management*, Vol. 11, Nov. 1994, pp. 213–220.

[15] Morris, P.A., E. O. Teisberg, and A. L. Kolbe, "When Choosing R&D Projects, Go with the Long Shots," *Research Technology Management*, Vol. 34(1), Jan.–Feb. 1991, pp. 35–39.

Chapter 15

What Is the Best Set of Leading Indicators?

While the preceding chapters have given a smorgasbord of evaluation metrics from which R&D managers may choose, many also wish to have a shorter and more manageable list of leading or precursor indicators. A first selection of such a list, based on the limited research base available to the end of 1995, is derived from the following considerations.

- Select those measurements that have been found important by earlier studies. Two measures of importance have been given earlier: number of studies supporting the metric and views of participants in the interviews.
- Select those measurements that have been shown to have more than a minor correlation with outcomes of interest to general management.
- Select a set of metrics balanced as to their value as precursors of each of the four major outcomes: customer satisfaction, timeliness, new products and/or services, and financial results.
- Select those metrics that more nearly match your company's strategic intent, as shown in the results of factor analysis.

15.1 INNOVATION OUTCOME EVALUATION AND MEASUREMENT

The 1994 and 1995 [1,2] studies have generally validated the need to evaluate and measure innovation by four principal outcomes: customer satisfaction, timeliness, nonfinancial strategic results, and financial results. The research base now established allows reducing the number of metrics suggested earlier to those few that have been shown to be the most effective in innovation management over a broad variety of firms. Industry, company culture, and stage of development differences are high and may be more important to your company than a more general list. Such a reduced general list does not mean that the other measures previously discussed are not appropriate to some industries or in some circumstances. However, fewer metrics may ease the cost of measurements and focus the company on what is most important.

15.1.1 Reengineering the R&D Process

Implicit in selecting these metrics is the realization that after introducing new metrics, the R&D manager will be faced with the task with which this book began: "Doing a lot more with a lot less" [3]. The task generally is named "re-engineering," but in reality has three components: restructuring, reorganizing, and rethinking. Each in turn has associated evaluation metrics.

Restructuring involves leaving the R&D organization as it was, but just using fewer people. In Chapter 9, it was stated that the flatness of the organization was a good measurement. With today's more educated staff and empowered work places, fewer supervisors are needed. Word processors lower the need for clerical and secretarial support. All of this will lead to a higher ratio of productive staff to indirect people. A derivative financial metric is the "lowest possible overhead rate" [4, p. 46].

Reorganizing involves changing the R&D organization to minimize interactions among sections. For example, when computers were specialized and costly, it made sense to have a specialized software group. Now with personal computers and engineering work stations so inexpensive and computer software knowledge so diffused, distributing the software group to R&D units makes sense. The same can be said for advanced development groups in some industries, leading to the decline of central laboratories. How should this be evaluated? This is still a very subjective area, but some measure of the wholeness of the task needs to be selected. How many times does the section have to interface with others? How many times is it waiting on others? These questions carry on into rethinking addressed next.

Rethinking the R&D process is the next logical step. Why reorganize within R&D without reorganizing the whole innovation process? Here we are back to the issues discussed in Chapter 6. As shown in Figure 6.2, a median of 65 percent of responders in the three-year period had adopted CE as the rethinking process. Measuring this percentage then becomes the desirable metric. It must be recognized so that 100% is not the goal because some activities must necessarily be serial, as indicated in Figure 1.1. However, an actual measurement below the median is an occasion for reflection. With these thoughts on reengineering, one must next ask, "How does the R&D manager address the highest rated outcomes of interest to general management?" These are customer satisfaction, timeliness, nonfinancial strategic metrics, and financial measurements.

15.1.2 Customer Satisfaction

The simplest two measures of customer satisfaction are to create an index and to measure market share (which is covered in a subsequent section as a strategic intent metric) as a proxy for customer satisfaction. The components of a satisfaction index should be those most appropriate to your company's industry from among the leading indicators discussed in a later section. It should include at least one measure of satisfaction with your company and at least one measure of satisfaction with your product or service. An index should measure at the consumer or end user level and, if appropriate to your industry, at the more direct customer level in the distribution chain. For internal purposes, measuring satisfaction with your firm's own implementation organization is also desirable.

15.1.3 Timeliness

Two measures of timeliness stand out from the results of the studies reported: cycle-time measures and measures of compliance with date commitments. A third time measure, staff hours, is also needed as an essential component of financial cost data. Idea-to-customer time was shown in Figure 7.4 as the least measured cycle time in the 1991 study [5,6] and by the 1995 study [2] as the most measured. It is the most inclusive measure and should be used by all companies. Its use implies that all of the functional component cycle times are also measured.

The choice of a measure of meeting committed dates is less clear. Stage-gate tracking appears as a factor raising customer satisfaction, while milestones lower it and lengthen R&D cycle time. This tends to favor the stage-gate metric. While discipline in meeting dates is essential, managers should ask themselves whether the stage-gate method is not overly mechanistic in its application, and that in the future of empowered teams may not be so compatible.

Once you are into measuring time, keep at it. Either the number of years measuring time at all or the years of using TQM in R&D shows as an accelerating factor in idea-to-customer time and R&D cycle time as an enhancement of cost competitiveness and increases new products as a percent of sales.

15.1.4 Nonfinancial Strategic Metrics

Nonfinancial strategic intent results are best measured by several rather different factors: percent of sales in new products and services, market share, outcome benchmarking, growth and continuous improvement.

New products and/or services as a percent of sales is an integrative measure of the effectiveness of innovation management. It is used by 88% of responders to the 1994 study [1] and should be a metric in all companies. Market share should not be measured only in the pursuit of financial results as the industry examples of

Chapter 12 have shown. It needs to be among the firm's metrics as a measure of customer satisfaction as noted previously. It is best measured by served markets or by key accounts as an integrative measure of other outcomes. If only two metrics are to be used, these two are the obvious choices.

Three other measurements may be added to measure strategic intent nonfinancially. Outcome benchmarking, as it is positively associated with new products, was shown to be more suitable for innovation management than the process benchmarking preferred in implementation operations. Growth and continuous improvement are also strategic intent metrics worth pursuing—growth as part of shareholder value, and continuous improvement to position the firm where the competition will be in the future.

15.1.5 Financial Metrics

The financial results of innovation need to be measured. The 1993, 1994, and 1995 studies [5–9] have used EBIT in a ratio to sales to measure results free of the financial structure of the firm, and this is still a recommended metric. The return on sales was found to be a less satisfactory metric than EBIT in the 1993 study [7–9]. SVC was identified earlier as a better metric, but growth also needs to be measured in order to infer SVC by its proxy of total return.

15.2 THE BEST SET OF INNOVATION PRECURSORS

Based on the 1993, 1994, and 1995 studies [5–9], a list of evaluation metrics for general use can be formulated. The factors and considerations for inclusion on the list are derived from the outlined principles and the extent of research data available to end-1995. The author's expanded composite list of best overall innovation precursor metrics follows.

1. Measure upstream relations with the customer by conducting the following measures.
   a. Measure customer satisfaction with responsiveness as the most frequently effective leading indicator of customer satisfaction with overall performance as a contractor, and with cost competitiveness;
   b. Measure knowledge of customer needs and generation of new ideas by interval scale formality surveys, as leading indicators of new products and services.
2. Measure crossfunctional participation by the percent of the R&D budget spent on development projects using CE as a leading indicator of timeliness, new products/services as a percent of sales, and a metric of rethinking the reengineering of the R&D process.
3. Measure upstream relations with marketing using the following.

    a. Use QFD as the most effective method of establishing formality in the R&D/marketing interface and as a leading indicator of EBIT, R&D cycle time and cost competitiveness satisfaction;

    b. Use a formality scale measurement of coordination with marketing as a leading indicator of timeliness.

4. Measure downstream relations with implementation chain departments by a formality scale measurement of downstream coordination, design standards, and technology transfer as a leading indicator of customer satisfaction.

5. Measure management of internal processes and inputs by measuring the following.

    a. Measure the proportion of projects under any one of the financial selection disciplines as a leading indicator of financial results, percent of new products and/or services, and of speed through marketing leading to overall timeliness;

    b. Measure the percent of the total R&D investment in major new projects as a leading indicator of percent of new products and services [10];

    c. Measure customer satisfaction with your technical capability as a leading indicator of speed in R&D leading to overall timeliness;

    d. Measure the proper results orientation of the reward system by internal survey as a leading indicator of outcome oriented R&D output leading in turn to financial results;

    e. Measure the flatness of the internal organization by the average number of direct reports and the lowest possible overhead rate as indicators of managerial effectiveness in restructuring.

Even this revised list from research results needs to be considered further in terms of how individual companies need to be managed for effectiveness when managing the innovation management process. The chapters of this book have attempted to put this process all together in managing time, the financial boundary with innovation, its other external boundaries including customer satisfaction, and internal processes within R&D. These then led to revisiting this list in terms of a "balanced scorecard" for innovation management, as was started in Chapter 1 [11].

15.3 AFTERTHOUGHTS

The reader who has come this far must still realize that what has been presented here is just a beginning. Each new issue of management journals brings new insights into measuring innovation effectiveness. Measures that once produced useful results quickly become so commonplace that they no longer lead—in fact, the lack of using them sometimes becomes a hindrance. The rate of change in metrics for managing innovation is now more rapid than ever—one has only to look back at Figure 7.4 to realize this rapid rate of change.

Several areas of prospective change stand out. The first of these is shareholder value. In Chapter 2, the financial view was offered that total return equals current return plus growth. Innovation for profit enhancement was not found in the research reported, because while the costs were down, so were the benefits. This leads naturally to the view that the R&D manager is responsible for growth and cost reductions but rarely for the decline in benefits that may be due to competition and the acceleration trap. Thus, we may expect in the future to see innovation more clearly measured by growth metrics, such as new products/services as a percent of sales, plus cost reductions achieved as a percent of sales, and SVC reconciled as innovation gains minus benefit losses.

Investment analysis also reflects on the value of a portfolio as opposed to a single investment. Optimization of the portfolio requires balancing forecast returns with forecast risks. Little research or concept development has taken place to date on how to integrate risks with R&D management as it has so far with investment management.

Technology assets create a barrier to the entry of other firms into the company's business. Much of the research to date has been done on patent protection. Yet other barriers to entry exist in intellectual property such as copyrights, particularly of computer software, and trade secrets. Valuation of the total value of technology is a leading indicator of the potential for the creation of future SVC.

On the measurement of the integration of the innovation chain with the rest of the departments of the business, the author has fallen back on the use of formality scales in the absence of better metrics. One can confidently expect improved measurements in this area.

Finally, the practice of the management processes that support innovation is an area of continued evolution in both academic research and innovative companies. In this area, dozens of new potential metrics are proposed each year, and some of these will supplant those covered in this book.

Until this evolution appears and has been tested, however, the weight of what has been seen to date favors focusing R&D management on new product growth for future profits rather than on the ephemeral search for improved current profitability with which so many other investigators seem currently infatuated.

References

[1]   Ellis, L. W., and C. C. Curtis, "Measuring Customer Satisfaction," *Research Technology Management*, Vol. 38(5), Sept.–Oct. 1995, pp. 45–48.

[2]   Curtis, C. C., and L. W., Ellis, "A Balanced Scorecard for New Product Development," *Journal of Cost Management*, Spring 1997, forthcoming.

[3] Tipping, J. W., "Doing a Lot More with a Lot Less," *Research Technology Management,* Vol. 36(5), Sept.–Oct. 1993, pp. 13–14.

[4] Ellis, L. W., *The Financial Side of Industrial Research Management,* New York: Wiley, 1984.

[5] Wolff, M. F., "Working Faster," *Research Technology Management,* Vol. 35(6), Nov.–Dec. 1992, pp. 10–12.

[6] Ellis, L. W., and C. C., Curtis," Practices in Concurrent Engineering," *Managing a Global Environment: 1992 International Engineering Management Conference,* Piscataway, NJ: IEEE Catalog No. 92CH 32227-7, 1992, pp. 115–118.

[7] Curtis, C. C., *New Product Development Cycle Time: Investigation of Cycle Time and Accounting Measures, Determinants of Cycle Time and the Impact of Cycle Time on Financial Performance,* Sc. Diss., University of New Haven, 1993.

[8] Curtis, C. C., "Nonfinancial Performance Measures in New Product Development," *Journal of Cost Management,* Vol. 8(3), Fall 1994, pp. 18–26.

[9] Ellis, L. W., and C. C., Curtis, "Speedy R&D: How Beneficial?" *Research Technology Management,* Vol. 38(5), Sept.–Oct. 1995, pp. 45–48.

[10] Morris, P. A., E. O. Teisberg, and A. L. Kolbe, "When Choosing R&D Projects, Go with the Long Shots," *Research Technology Management,* Vol. 34(1), Jan.–Feb. 1991, pp. 35–39.

[11] Kaplan, R. S., and D. P. Norton, "Putting the Balanced Scorecard to Work," *Harvard Business Review,* Vol. 71(5), Sept.–Oct. 1993, pp. 134–147.

Glossary

ABC	Activity-based costing.
ABM	Activity-based management.
AIA	Anything-Invented-Anywhere (Contrast with NIH).
Alcoa	Aluminum Company of America.
AT&T	American Telephone and Telegraph Corporation.
CE	Concurrent engineering.
CEO	Chief executive officer of a company, often the chairman.
CFO	Chief Financial Officer of a company.
CFPB	Cash-flow payback.
COO	Chief operating officer of a company, often the president.
CTO	Chief technical officer of a company.
DFA	Design for assembly.
DFM	Design for manufacture.
EBIT	Earnings before interest and taxes, expressed as a percent of sales.
EI	Effectiveness index.
Firmware	Software that is imbedded in the read-only memory (ROM) of a semiconductor device. This software is normally not easily changed and is set in place at the time of manufacture.
Formality scale	An interval scale used to measure the degree of coordination between two parts of a company—the lowest level representing almost no coordination and the highest level representing joint participation in all decisions.
GEG	Code for one division of Motorola Corp.
Hardware	The tangible manifestation of a product.
IBM	International Business Machines.
IEEE	Institute of Electrical and Electronics Engineers.
IRI	Industrial Research Institute.
IRIMER	IRI Research-on-Research Subcommittee 92-3, Measurement of the Effectiveness of R&D on Company Productivity.

IR&D	Industrial research and development, a specifically defined term by the U.S. Defense Department as to how much of a company's R&D may be allowable as an overhead rate in contracts.
IRR	Internal rate of return.
IT	Information technology.
ITC	Idea-to-customer-time.
ITT	ITT Corporation, formerly International Telephone and Telegraph Corp.
MBWA	Management by walking about.
MTBF	Mean time between failures.
MTTA	Mean time to receive attention.
MTTR	Mean time to repair.
NIH	Not invented here, a term often used to describe an attitude of innovators that rejects using what has been developed by outsiders.
NPV	Net present value of cash flows (net of inflows and outflows).
NSF	U.S. National Science Foundation.
OSHA	U.S. Occupational Safety and Health Administration, Washington, DC.
PLC	Public limited company, a term used in the United Kingdom, equivalent to Inc. in the United States, for those companies publicly traded on a stock exchange.
PV	Present value of cash flows (either in or out).
QFD	Quality function deployment—a structured method of coordinating marketing and R&D for quality in products.
R&D	Research and development.
RAM	Random access memory for software.
ROI	Return on investment equal to net income divided by total company assets.
ROM	Read-only memory for software.
ROR	Research-on-Research Committee of the IRI.
S-Curve	Saturation curve of a technology.
SEC	U.S. Securities and Exchange Commission.
Software	The manifestation of a service that is imbedded in the memory of a computer processing unit used to provide the service in the form of a stored program or list of instructions to be used in providing the service. These instructions may usually be modified as necessary, except when part of firmware. A hardware product may use software or firmware.
SVC	Shareholder value creation.
SWOT	Strengths, weaknesses, opportunities, threats—an acronym for a process of strategic analysis.
Taguchi	A Japanese author of methods for improving quality processes.

TFP   Total factor productivity is an index that measures the ratio of output (net sales) to inputs of labor, capital, research and development, and material.

TQM   Total quality management—a structured method for obtaining increased quality in products from marketing through R&D through manufacturing.

TRD   Time through research and development (R&D cycle time).

10Ks   The mandatory financial returns filed annually with the SEC by public companies.

About the Author

Dr. Lynn W. Ellis is a scholar-in-residence and retired professor of management at the University of New Haven (Connecticut) and president of Lynn W. Ellis Associates, a consulting firm for telecommunications, technology management, and strategic planning. He was formerly vice president of engineering at Bristol Babcock, Inc., and before that director of research at ITT. A Fellow of the Institute of Electrical and Electronic Engineers and of the American Association for the Advancement of Science, Ellis has a B.E.E. degree from Cornell University, an M.Sc. degree from Stevens Institute of Technology, and a Doctor of Professional Studies in Management degree from Pace University.

Index

ABC. *See* Activity-based costing
ABM. *See* Activity-based management
Acceleration trap, 35, 111–12, 135–36, 207
Accounting
    management, 223–24
    1994 study, 207
Activity-based costing, 27–28, 30, 32–33, 179
Activity-based management, 27–28, 179
Ad hoc committee, 74
AIA. *See* Anything invented anywhere
Alcoa. *See* Aluminum Corporation of America
Alliances
    evaluation of, 56–57
    management of, 52–53
    in technical planning, 65
Allied Signal, 119
Aluminum Corporation of America, 76, 120
Anything invented anywhere, 55
Apple Computer, Inc., 111, 188
Applied research time, 120
Applied time, 129
AT&T Bell Laboratories, 84

Balanced scorecard proposal, 15–16, 239
Baldridge Award. *See* Malcolm Baldridge
        National Quality Award
Banking industry, 154
Basiltown Electronics Company, 129
Benchmarking, 8–9, 115, 179, 181–83, 197
    EBIT, 225
    as effectiveness measure, 238

financial evaluation, 192
    idea-to-customer time, 212–13
    measurement of, 222–23
    product development, 218
Benefit-to-cost ratio, 22, 109
Bias, and survey reliability, 172–73
Biotechnology industry, 221
BOC Group, PLC, 54
Bottom-up management, 74, 106
Boundaryless organization, 3
Boundary spanning, 57–58
Brown and Svenson innovation model, 17
Budget optimization, 25, 38–41
Budget rationing, 41

CAGR. *See* Compound annual growth rate
Calendar days, 104, 112
Causation, 206
CE. *See* Concurrent engineering
Centralization, 75
Certainty, in R&D measurement, 29–30
Change, control of, 136, 157
Chemical industry, 121, 194
Chi Data Services Bureau, 29
Chrysler Corporation, 3, 54, 57, 64,
        92–93, 115–16, 144, 157
Closed system innovation model, 17–18
Commercial development, new product,
        75, 92
Commitment, to customers, 171
Common stock, 25

Communications, customer and innovator, 170–71
Company size, 148
Competence, staff, 149, 181
Competition, assessment of, 50–51
Complaint resolution, 171
Compound annual growth rate, 187
Computer industry
    communication with customers, 171
    market share, 46–47, 220
Concentration principle, 130–31
Concept development, 62–63
Concept finalization, 120
Concept generation, 65
Concept-to-production launch time, 104
Concorde, Chrysler, 93
Concurrent engineering, 3, 74–75, 78
    arguments for/against, 90
    background, 89–92
    at Chrysler Corporation, 116
    crossfunctional teams, 144
    internal R&D processes, 151
    management of, 92–94
    manufacturing cycle, 134–35
    marketing cycle, 216
    new product sales, 179–80
    other factors, 94–97
    quality function deployment, 214
    and throughput maximization, 97
    time for, 117
    use of, 94
    work hours, 108
Conflict level management, 146, 181
Consortium for Advanced Manufacturing International, 207–8
Consumer goods industry, 221
Contribution, innovation, 131
Contribution margin, 193
Control
    of change, 136, 157
    in management, 65
Coordination, of executives, 146, 181
Core competency development, 62–63, 66, 69, 131–32
Correlation, 206
Cosmetics industry, 194
Cost
    cyle time, 108–9
    product, 69
    R&D, 4
Cost competitiveness, 68, 172, 174–75, 209, 211–12

Cost reduction of operations, 109
"Creeping elegance," 128
Cronbach's alpha, 208
Crossfunctional team, 3, 8, 69, 116
    background, 91–92
    CE correlation, 94–97
    CE management, 92–94
    at Honda, 143
    as innovation precursor, 238
    as input metric, 143–44
    internal R&D processes, 151
    new product sales, 181
    reasons for, 89–90
    throughput maximization, 97
Culture, company, and innovation, 201–2
Curtis, Carey C., 207
Customer, defined, 164–65
Customer needs, knowledge of, 45, 148, 181, 238
Customer satisfaction, evaluation of, 163
    associated with QFD, 78–79
    benchmarking effect, 183
    crafting evaluation, 169
    defining customer, 164–65
    defining satisfaction, 166–67
    EBIT, 224–25
    financial evaluation, 192, 197–98
    idea-to-customer time, 212–13
    for innovation, 173–75
    innovation outcome measurement, 237–38
    internal factors, 226
    leading indicators, 208–12
    lead user, 165–66
    Malcolm Baldridge award, 9
    market share, 46
    metrics, 67–68, 115
    Motorola's criteria, 167–69
    1994 study, 207
    for product/service, 171–72
    reliability of, 172–73
    for supply innovation, 170–71
    R&D time, 214
    survey instrument
Customer service time, 123
Cycle-time measurement.
        See Time measurement

DARPA. *See* Defense Advanced Research Projects Agency
Decentralization, 74–75
Decision making, 132–33
Deere & Company, 3–4, 93–94

Defect quality, 172
Defense, Department of, 15
Defense Advanced Research
        Projects Agency, 91
Defense Initiative on Concurrent
        Engineering, 91
Delay, in product development, 136
Design cycle, 120–21
Design finalization, 121
Design for assembly, 86, 149
Design for manufacturability, 86, 149
Design review, 145
Design standards, 149
Development cycle, 65–66, 121, 132
DFA. *See* Design for assembly
DFM. *See* Design for manufacturability
DICE. *See* Defense Initiative on
        Concurrent Engineering
Differentiation, 171, 173
Diminishing return, 38
Directed applied research, 66
Directors, R&D, 7–8
Distribution chain, 164–65
Dodge Intrepid, 93
Dodge Viper, 92–93, 116, 144, 157
Downstream interface, 239
Downstream output measurements
        direct R&D outputs, 80–83
        implementation process, 85–86
        technology transfer, 83–85
Downstream units, implementation
        chain, 165
Down time, 172
Drucker, Peter F., 127
Dump and run syndrome, 119
DuPont, 153–54

Eagle Vision, 93
Earnings model, 197–98
EBIT, 78–79, 109, 112, 145, 180, 185–86, 192,
        197–98, 200–201, 218–19, 230, 238
        1994 model, 224–26
        1995 model, 226–27
        regression model summary, 227
ECN. *See* Engineering change notice
Economic Recovery Act of 1981, 13
Education, as input metric, 144–45
Effectiveness index, 66, 185–87, 227–28
Effectiveness initiative, 5–7
EI. *See* Effectiveness index
Elf Aquitaine, 47
Empowerment, 3, 32

End user, 164, 171
Engineering change notice, 85, 134
Entrepreneurship, 12
Environment, external, 49–50
Escort, 93
Europe, R&D policy, 14
Evaluation. *See* Customer satisfaction,
        evaluation of; Financial evaluation;
        Internal R&D processes; Process
        management, evaluation of;
        Research and development,
        evaluation of
Expenditures, R&D, 4
Exploration stage, 65–66
External factors
        financial evaluation, 109–10
        outcome measurement, 104–5

Factor analysis, 201, 228–32
Feature quality, 171
Finance selection-driven/customer
        adverse cluster, 231
Financial culture types, 26–28
Financial evaluation
        analysts' views, 194
        company culture, 201–2
        cyle time, 109–12
        earnings model, 197–98, 200
        financial frameworks, 196–97
        innovation outcome, 238
        management accounting, 193–94
        new product sales, 180
        nonfinancial metrics, 191–92
        option theory, 195–96
        product extensions, 199–200
        project selection, 193
        results measurement, 223–27
        shareholder value creation, 200–201
        speedy innovation, 198–99
Financial frameworks, 196–97
        EBIT correlation, 230
Financial performance
        benchmarking, 182–83, 222
        1993 study, 207
Financial project control, 36
Financial project selection, 23–24, 147–48,
        181, 192–93, 232
Financial return, growth of, 184
Firmware development, 121
First-to-market, 111
Ford, 3, 46, 93, 116
France, 47–48

Funds, sources of, 14–15
Fuzzy front end, 119

Gantt, Henry, 128
Gantt chart, 106, 128
Gault, Stanley, 156
General Dynamics, 62
General Electric, 3, 143
General Motors, 46, 93
Goal clarity, 67
Goodyear, 3, 54, 57, 177
Government, federal, 13–14
Government laboratories, 55
Groups, temporary, 74
Growth, measurement of, 183–85, 238

Harley Davidson, 3
Harvester division, Deere & Company, 93–94
Hewlett Packard Company, 135
Honda, 142–43
"House of quality," 76–77
Human resource management
  cultural change, 157
  innovation effort, 157–58
  leadership, 156
  motivation, 152–56
  quality, performance, and planning, 158

Iacocca, Lee, 170
IBM. *See* International Business Machines
    Corporation
Idea generation, 45, 147–48, 181
Idea-to-customer time, 104–5, 108, 114–15,
    134, 186, 211–13, 222–23, 228
Implementation process, 85–86
Implementation chain, 4
Improvement, measurement of, 183–85, 238
Indicators, leading, 5
  customer satisfaction, 237
  financial metrics, 238
  nonfinancial metrics, 237–38
  reengineering R&D process, 236
  timeliness, 237
Industrial Research Institute, 5, 153, 207
Industry characteristics, in commercial
    knowledge, 50
Information technology, 3
Innovation
  benchmarking, 181–83
  company culture, 201–2
  contribution measurement, 131
  customer satisfaction, 68, 115, 173–75, 237
  as effectiveness measure, 5–7, 177–81
  group organization, 74

improving upstream process, 133
inputs to, 147–50
internal organization, 157–58
key lessons in, 187–89
manufacturing time, 134–35
precursors to, 238–39
process model, 16–18
product development time, 135–36,
    198–99, 228
shareholder value creation, 200–201
success measures, 8
See also Product development
Innovation chain, 4
Innovation outcome measurement
  by customer satisfaction, 237
  by financial metrics, 238
  by nonfinancial metrics, 237–38
  by timeliness, 237
Input metrics
  guidelines, 147
  internal organization, 141–45
  other, 145–46
Insurance industry, 154
Integrated engineering, 3–4
Integrated Product Development Team, 91
Integration mechanisms, 73–74
Interaction metrics
  guidelines, 147
  internal organization, 141–45
  other, 145–46
Interaction processes
  downstream, 80–86
  upstream, 73–80
Intermediate financial culture, 28
Internal factors, 104–5, 109–10
  company organization, 141–45
  outcome measurement, 104–105
Internal R&D processes
  cultural change management, 157
  importance ranking, 151
  innovation effort, 157–58
  innovation precursor, 239
  leadership, 156
  motivation/reward systems, 152–56
  quality, performance, and planning, 158
Internal rate of return, 23, 31, 34–35, 109,
    193, 200, 224
International Business Machines
    Corporation, 111
Intrapreneurial organization, 12
Introduction process, 4
IRI. *See* Industrial Research Institute

IRIMER. *See* Subcommittee on the
Measurement of Effectiveness
in R&D
IRR. *See* Internal rate of return
IT. *See* Information technology
ITT Corporation, 16, 75, 180, 187

Japan, 14
Joint ventures, 55

Knowledge, commercial
competitive assessment, 50–51
environmental assessment, 49–50
industry scenarios, 50
vision, 48–49
Knowledge, external sources of, 47–48
Knowledge, technological, 51–52
acquisition of, 56–57, 66
alliances with others, 52–53
self-sufficient, 52
sources of, 53–56

Lagging indicator, 5
Large, old-line company cluster, 231
Leadership, 64, 156
Leading indicator. *See* Indicators, leading
Lead time, 170
Lead user, 165–66
Long-lived/patented project cluster, 232

Macintosh PC, 188
Malcolm Baldrige National Quality Award,
9–10, 143, 144–45, 169, 184
Management
concurrent engineering, 92–94
evaluation, 158
layers, 3
new product sales, 181
Management, senior
leadership of, 64
and product development, 136
Management accounting, 193–94, 223–24
Management by walking about, 173
Manufacturability, 121–22
Manufacturing cycle, 134–35
Market development cycle, 114, 117–18,
210–11, 215–16
Marketing
as input metric, 144
managing change in, 157
See also Research and Development/
marketing interface
Marketing cycle, 118–20, 216–217

Market share, 45
customer satisfaction with, 179, 189, 211
by industry, 220
measurement of, 219–22
in R&D evaluation, 45–47, 237
MBWA. *See* Management by walking about
MCC. *See* Microelectronics and Computer
Technology Corporation
Mean time between failures, 69, 172
Mean time to receive attention, 172
Mean time to repair the defect, 172
Measurement characteristics, R&D, 28–29
certainty and urgency, 29–30
empowered organizations, 32
medium-term risky projects, 30–31
optimum budgets/shareholder value, 38–41
project selection/evaluation integration,
33–38
short-term certain projects, 30
uncertainty, 31–32
Medium-term project, 30–31
Metallurgical industry, 121
Metrics
balanced scorecard proposal, 15–16
innovation process model, 16–18
lessons learned from, 18–19
methodology, 18
time frames, 16
time measurement, 124
Microelectronics and Computer Technology
Corporation, 55
Milestone measurement, 106, 112, 128, 210
Minnesota Mining and Manufacturing,
153, 154
Mitsubishi Electric Corporation, 68–69
Morale, 64
Motivation
benchmarking, 8–9
entrepreneurship/intrapreneurial, 12
importance of, 151–56
industrial measurement of, 5–7
Malcolm Baldrige award, 9–10
new product sales, 181
problems for R&D directors, 7–8
product development research, 12–13
product/technological life cycle, 12
strategy, structure, and uncertainty,
10–11
Motorola, 85, 143, 172, 183
customer satisfaction criteria, 167–69
MTBF. *See* Mean time between failures

MTTA. *See* Mean time to receive attention
MTTR. *See* Mean time to repair the defect

National Science Foundation, 15
Neles-Jamesbury, 134
Neon, 93, 116
Net present value, 22–23, 25, 29, 31, 35, 41,
    109, 119–20, 192–93, 198, 200,
    211, 217, 224, 227, 232
New products. *See* Product development;
    Product, new
NIH. *See* Not invented here
1990 through 1995 studies, 207–8
Nonfinancial strategic metrics, 237–38
Not invented here, 52, 55
NPV. *See* Net present value
NSF. *See* National Science Foundation
Nyquist sampling interval, 123

Omicron ElectroMechanical Corporation, 33
Open systems model for innovation, 16–17
Opportunity creation, 62–63, 66–69
Option pricing, 193, 223
Option theory, 24–25, 195–96
Organization, internal
    boundary spanning, 57
    input metrics, 141–45
Organization theory, 91
Outcome measurement, 66, 104–5
Output measurement, 106–8
Overall time, 104, 113–18

Parallel task interdependence, 91
Partnering, 55–57
Patents, 80, 82, 153–54, 221, 232
Payback, 193
Performance, evaluation of, 158
Performance, overall, 209–10
Performance-to-commitment time, 128
Personal care industry, 221
Pharmaceutical industry, 221
Pi Chart Instrument Division, 41
Planning
    evaluation of, 158
    new product sales, 181
    technical, 65
Platform team, 3
Pooled/reciprocal task interdependence, 91
Post-evaluation
    financial, 37–38
    in project selection, 25–26
Precursor indicator, 5
Present value, 80
Price-to-earnings ratio, 40

Process, as function of time, 62–70
Process design, 121
Process management, evaluation of
    benchmarking, 8–9
    entrepreneurship, 12
    government policy, 13–14
    industrial measurement, 5–7
    intrapreneurial organization, 12
    introduction to, 3–5
    Malcolm Baldridge Award, 9–10
    metrics approach, 15–19
    motivation for, 5–13
    problems for directors, 7–8
    product development, 12–13
    R&D funds, 14–15
    strategy, structure and uncertainty,
        10–11
Process model, R&D, 61–62
Process savings, 109
Product, measurement of, 171–72
Product, new, 4
    measurement of, 217–19, 237
    versus product extensions, 199–200
    See also Product development
Product development, 69, 75, 91–92, 121
    cycle time, 113
    delays in, 136
    in effectiveness index, 185–87
    as effectiveness measure, 177–81
    management research, 12–13
    speed in, 135–36
    See also Innovation
Product extension, 69–70, 130–31, 199–200,
    210, 215
Product improvement, 62–63
Production time, 122–23
Productivity, R&D, 23–24
Product life cycle, 12, 30, 33, 192, 218
Product planning committee, 75
Product-to-sales ratio, 178, 217
Profitability, and market share, 46–47
Project cancellation, 120
Project selection
    financial, 23–24, 147–48, 181, 192–93, 232
    project evaluation, 33–38
    R&D return improvement, 22–23
    using option theory, 24–25
Project team, 64
Prototype time, 121–22, 134
Psi Radio Limited, 34, 76, 134, 146
Public policy, 207
PV. *See* Present value

QFD. *See* Quality function deployment
Quality
  evaluation of, 158, 173
  measurement of, 225
  product, 69, 172–74, 210
Quality function deployment, 73, 97, 108,
      133, 145, 174, 186, 198, 200, 208,
      211, 214, 216–17, 219, 225,
      227–28, 239
  defined, 76–77
  use of, 77–78
  versus other metrics, 78–80
Quantitative analysis, defined, 205
Quantitative measurements
  benchmarking, 222–23
  customer satisfaction, 208–12
  effectiveness index, 227–28
  factor analysis, 228–32
  financial results, 223–27
  idea-to-customer time, 212–13
  market development cycle, 215–16
  marketing cycle, 216–17
  market share, 219–22
  methodology, 205–6
  new products/services, 217–19
  R&D time, 213–15
  six studies, 1990–1995, 207–8

R&D. *See* Research and development
Rayonier Company, 146
Redo loop, 115, 122
Reengineering, 3, 236
Regression analysis, 201, 206, 214, 217–19,
      223, 226–27
Regulated/disciplined cluster, 231
Reinventing corporation, 3
Reliability
  product, 69, 172–74, 210
  survey, 172–73
Reorganizing R&D process, 236
Research and development, evaluation of
  market share, 45–47
  methods
    budget optimization, 25
    financial post-evaluation, 25–26
    option theory, 24–25
    traditional, 22–24
  metrics, 65
  process model, 61–62
  project selection, 33–38
  time scale, 62–70

Research and development cycle time,
      114–17, 119
Research and development/marketing
      interface, 74–76, 119–20, 133
  marketing cycle time, 216–17
  new product sales, 181
  R&D time, 214
Research and development time, 213–16
Research consortia, 55–56
Response time, to competitors, 67
Responsiveness, to customers,
      171, 173, 175, 209
Restructuring R&D process, 236
Result indicator, 5
Rethinking R&D process, 236
Return, R&D
  improvement of, 22–23
  project selection, 24, 31
Return on investment, 6, 109
Return on sales, 25, 40–41
Reward systems, 80, 152–56
Risk
  in decision making, 132
  in R&D measurement, 30–31, 35–36
ROI. *See* Return on investment
ROS. *See* Return on sales
Rubbermaid, 156, 177, 178

Sales volume, 213
Sampling interval, 123
Satisfaction, defined, 166–67
  See also Customer satisfaction,
      evaluation of
Saturn, 93
Self-sufficiency, technological, 52
Serial task interdependence, 91
Service, measurement of, 171–72
Service creation, 4
Service industries, 154, 163
Services, new, 177–81, 217–19
Shareholder value, 40–41, 194
Shareholder value creation, 25, 200–201, 227
Shipping time, 123
Short-term project, 30
Simultaneous engineering, 3–4
Software development, 121
Speedy R&D, 34–35
Stage-gate tracking, 106, 112, 145, 210, 237
Standard deviation, 36
Stock options, 211
Strategy, and innovation, 10

Strengths, weaknesses, opportunities,
   threats, 48–49
Structure, and innovation, 10–11
Subcommittee on the Measurement
   of Effectiveness in R&D, 5–6, 62,
   80, 83, 107, 109, 171, 205
   innovation model, 17
Subjective scale, 206
Suppliers, 54
Supply chain. *See* Implementation chain
Support, to organization, 145–46, 181
SVC. *See* Shareholder value creation
SWOT. *See* Strengths, weaknesses,
   opportunities, threats

Taguchi analysis, 79, 198, 213, 225
Target costing, 193
Task forces, 74–75
Task interdependence, 91
Tau Controls Company, 31
Teams
   change management, 157
   integrated engineering, 4
   platform, 3
   process time cycle, 64
   project, 64
   reward systems, 155
   See also Crossfunctional team
Tech Clubs, 93
Technological life cycle, 12
Technology
   customer satisfaction with, 210
   as differentiation, 171, 173
Technology acquisistion organization, 56–57
Technology-driven/individualistic cluster, 232
Technology transfer
   to business units, 8
   downward, 83–85
Telecommunications industry
   market share, 46, 220
   reward systems in, 154
Testing time, 123
TFP. *See* Total factor productivity
Throughput, 97, 109
Time cycle, R&D, 33–34, 62–63
   core competence/product development, 69
   exploration through development, 65–66
   opportunity creation, 66–69
   product extension/improvement, 69–70
   unchanging R&D processes, 64–65
Timeliness
   benchmarking, 183, 222
   customer satisfaction, 170, 175, 210

financial evaluation, 192
   innovation outcome measurement, 237
Time management
   applied/unapplied time, 129
   building core competencies, 131–32
   concentration principle, 130–31
   consolidating time, 130
   decision making, 132–33
   diagnosing time use, 127–29
   innovation acceleration, 133–36
   innovation measurement, 131
   pruning time wasters, 129–30
Time measurement, 16, 103
   cost relationship, 108–9
   cycle-time reduction, 112
   financial evaluation, 109–12
   idea-to-customer time, 212–13
   market development cycle, 215–16
   marketing cycle, 216–17
   metrics, 85–86
   outcome measurement, 104–5
   output measurement, 106–8
   R&D time, 213–15
Time to market, 8, 104
   applied research segment, 120
   concurrent engineering time, 117
   customer service segment, 123
   design to concept finalization, 120
   design to design finalization, 121
   development time, 121
   idea-to-customer time, 114–15, 212–13
   key metrics, 124
   market development cycle, 117–18
   marketing segment, 118
   measurement schedule, 123
   measuring overall time, 112–18
   measuring time segments, 118–24
   process design, 121
   production segment, 122–23
   prototype to manufacturability, 121–22
   R&D cycle time, 115–17
   redo loops, 122
   shipping segment, 123
   testing segment, 123
Time wasters, 129–30
Top-down management, 74, 184
Total factor productivity, 21–22
Total quality management, 8, 78, 91, 96,
   119, 145, 174, 192, 198, 211,
   225, 227, 237
TQM. *See* Total quality management
Training, as input metric, 144–45

Trust, in alliances, 53

Unapplied time, 129
Uncertainty, 11, 31–32
Universities, as knowledge source, 54–55
Upsilon Radio Company, 36
Upstream interfaces
    in innovation precursor, 133, 238
    integration mechanisms, 73–74
    quality function deployment, 76–80
    R&D/marketing interface, 74–76

Urgency, in R&D measurement, 29–30
Utilities industry, 154

Value engineering, 95
Vision, 48–49, 56, 58

Walls, internal and external, 3
Wal-Mart, 185

Yield, R&D, 23–24